# ARCHAEOLOGY
# HOTSPOT
# EGYPT

# Archaeology Hotspots: Unearthing the Past for Armchair Archaeologists

Series Editor: Paul G. Bahn, independent archaeologist and author of *The Archaeology of Hollywood* (pgbahn@anlabyrd.karoo.co.uk)

**Archaeology Hotspots** are countries and regions with particularly deep pasts, stretching from the depths of prehistory to more recent layers of recorded history. Written by archaeological experts for everyday readers, the books in the series offer engaging explorations of one particular country or region as seen through an archaeological lens. Each individual title provides a chronological overview of the area in question, covers the most interesting and significant archaeological finds in that area, and profiles the major personalities involved in those discoveries, both past and present. The authors cover controversies and scandals, current digs and recent insights, contextualizing the material remains of the past within a broad view of the area's present existence. The result is an illuminating look at the history, culture, national heritage, and current events of specific countries and regions—specific hotspots of archaeology.

*Archaeology Hotspot Egypt: Unearthing the Past for Armchair Archaeologists*, by Julian Heath (2015)

*Archaeology Hotspot Great Britain: Unearthing the Past for Armchair Archaeologists*, by Donald Henson (2015)

# A R C H A E O L O G Y
# H O T S P O T
# E G Y P T

## Unearthing the Past
## for Armchair Archaeologists

### Julian Heath

ROWMAN & LITTLEFIELD
Lanham • Boulder • New York • London

Published by Rowman & Littlefield
A wholly owned subsidiary of The Rowman & Littlefield Publishing Group, Inc.
4501 Forbes Boulevard, Suite 200, Lanham, Maryland 20706
www.rowman.com

Unit A, Whitacre Mews, 26-34 Stannary Street, London SE11 4AB, United Kingdom

British Library Cataloguing in Publication Information Available

Library of Congress Cataloging-in-Publication Data Available

ISBN 978-0-7591-2401-1 (cloth : alk. paper)
ISBN 978-0-7591-2402-8 (electronic)
ISBN 978-0-8108-9498-3 (pbk : alk. paper)

♾TM The paper used in this publication meets the minimum requirements of
American National Standard for Information Sciences—Permanence of Paper
for Printed Library Materials, ANSI/NISO Z39.48-1992.

Printed in the United States of America

For Mum and Dad (*again*),
and Jim—my Blood Brother.

# CONTENTS

# ACKNOWLEDGMENTS

First, I must say a special thank you to Joyce Tyldesley for providing me with the unexpected but welcome opportunity to write this book, and for helping out with various Egyptological queries. Several people also generously provided images for the book, and I must therefore thank Steven Snape, Campbell Price, Lenka and Andy Peacock, Pierre Vermeersch, Bill Manley, Bjørn Christian Tørrisen, Ricardo Liberato, Didier Descovens, Philip Pikart, Richard Seaman, Przemyslaw Idzkiewicz, and Berthold Werner. Finally, I must thank Leanne Silverman, Andrea O. Kendrick, and Alden Perkins at Rowman & Littlefield, and my editor, Paul Bahn, all of whom helped this book through to completion.

# CHRONOLOGY OF ANCIENT EGYPT*

**Paleolithic Period (700/500,000–7000 BP\*\*)**
Lower Paleolithic c.700/500,000–200,000
Middle Paleolithic c.200,000–35,000
Upper Paleolithic c.35,000–21,000
Late Paleolithic c.21,000–10,000
Epipaleolithic c.10,000–7000

**Saharan Neolithic Period (8800–4700 BC)**
Early Neolithic c.8800–6800
Middle Neolithic c.6600–5100
Late Neolithic c.5100–4700
**Early Dynastic Period (3000–2686 BC)**
*First Dynasty* c.3000–2890
*Second Dynasty* 2890–2686
**Old Kingdom (2686–2160 BC)**

*Third Dynasty* 2686–2613
*Fourth Dynasty* 2613–2494
*Fifth Dynasty* 2494–2345
*Sixth Dynasty* 2345–2181
*Seventh and Eighth Dynasties* 2181–2160

**Predynastic Period (5300–3000 BC)**
*Lower Egypt*
Neolithic c.5300–4000
Maadi Cultural Complex c.4000–3200

*Upper Egypt*
Badarian Period c.4400–4000
Amratian/Naqada I c.4000–3500
Gerzean/Naqada II c.3500–3200
Naqada III/Dynasty 0 c.3200–3000

**First Intermediate Period (2160–2055 BC)**
*Ninth and Tenth Dynasties* 2160–2055 (based at Herakleopolis)
*Eleventh Dynasty* 2125–2055 (based at Thebes)

---

* All dates before 664 BC are approximate
** BP stands for "Before Present."

## Middle Kingdom (2055–1650 BC)

*Eleventh Dynasty (all Egypt)* 2055–1985

*Twelfth Dynasty* 1985–1733

*Thirteenth Dynasty* 1733–after 1650

*Fourteenth Dynasty* 1733–1650 (minor rulers probably contemporary with the Thirteenth or Fifteenth Dynasty)

## New Kingdom (1550–1069 BC)

*Eighteenth Dynasty* 1550–1295

## Ramesside Period (1295–1069 BC)

*Nineteenth Dynasty* (1295–1186)

*Twentieth Dynasty* (1186–1069)

## Late Period (664–332 BC)

*Twenty-Sixth Dynasty* (664–525)

*Twenty-Seventh Dynasty* (525–404)

*Twenty-Eighth Dynasty* (404–399)

*Twenty-Ninth Dynasty* (399–380)

*Thirtieth Dynasty* (380–343)

*Second Persian Period* (343–332)

## Second Intermediate Period (1650–1550 BC)

*Fifteenth Dynasty* 1650–1580

*Sixteenth Dynasty* 1650–1580 (Thebes-based rulers)

*Seventeenth Dynasty* 1580–1550

## Third Intermediate Period (1069–664 BC)

*Twenty-First Dynasty* 1069–945

*Twenty-Second Dynasty* 945–715

*Twenty-Third Dynasty* 818–715

(Kings in various centers, contemporary with the later Twenty-Second, Twenty-Fourth, and Twenty-Fifth Dynasties)

*Twenty-Fourth Dynasty* (727–715)

*Twenty-Fifth Dynasty* (747–656)

## Ptolemaic Period (332–30 BC)

## Roman Period (30 BC–AD 395)

# **①**

# INTRODUCING ANCIENT EGYPT

In the long course of human history, many great civilizations have come and gone, but the most remarkable is arguably the one that emerged in Egypt some five thousand years ago at the end of the fourth millennium BC. Ancient Egyptian civilization subsequently endured for some three thousand years and its people left as their legacy an abundant collection of stunning monuments and artifacts, which continues to expand as new discoveries are frequently made by archaeologists who continue to work in Egypt despite its ongoing political troubles.

In this introduction, after first examining the geographical setting of ancient Egyptian civilization—which had a considerable bearing on its emergence and subsequent longevity—we are going to look briefly at the chronological story of ancient Egypt. Although ancient Egypt is often defined by the spectacular archaeology of the pharaohs this story actually begins in the prehistoric period many thousands of years before their magnificent tombs, temples, and artworks ever saw the light of day. The first "Egyptians" lived during the Paleolithic or "Old Stone Age" and followed a mobile hunter-gatherer lifestyle that was eventually replaced as agriculture appeared in the Nile Valley during the Neolithic or ("New Stone Age"). The Neolithic marks a hugely significant time in ancient Egypt (as does its appearance elsewhere in the prehistoric world), as the settled agricultural economy of Egypt's first farmers ultimately gave rise to the unification of Egypt into a single state, which was ruled over by a succession of ruling families or dynasties at the head of which sat the king or pharaoh. The latter stages of the Neolithic are thus referred to as the Predynastic Period and the time of the pharaohs that followed is known as the Dynastic Period, which eventually came to an end under the heel of the mighty Roman Empire (see the timeline, "Chronology of Ancient Egypt," for a detailed breakdown of the various periods of Egyptian prehistory/history as archaeologists and historians generally define them).

In chapter two, we are going to delve more deeply into the remarkable archaeological heritage of Egypt and examine famous discoveries such as the tombs of Tutankhamen and the sons of Rameses the Great, the "sky boats" of King Khufu, the superb painted stone bust of Queen Nefertiti, and the Rosetta Stone, which unlocked the secrets of ancient Egypt. However, as well as looking at famous finds such as these, we will also examine lesser-known but nonetheless interesting discoveries including the mysterious prehistoric art found in Upper Egypt, disturbing burials from the Paleolithic, a grim war grave from Egypt's Middle Kingdom, and haunting portraits of the dead from the Roman Period.

Chapter three is concerned with Egyptology's famous figures; here we will encounter such people as the renowned French scholar François Champollion, who "cracked the code" of ancient Egypt, and the larger-than-life Italian adventurer the "Great Belzoni." In this chapter, we will also meet English and American scholars such as Flinders Petrie and George Reisner, two men who did much in regard to the foundation of modern Egyptology, and Howard Carter and Lord Carnarvon, the men responsible for the world's greatest archaeological discovery—the tomb of Tutankhamen.

As with other academic disciplines, Egyptology is not without controversies that continue to generate much heated scholarly debate (e.g., was Tutankhamen murdered?), and these will be examined in chapter four along with some of the more scandalous goings-on in the world of Egyptology.

Chapter five will look at a hugely serious problem that is plaguing the archaeological heritage of Egypt and other countries—the antiquities market. As we will see, irreversible damage is being caused to this heritage mainly by unscrupulous dealers in the Western world who trade in illegal antiquities, with this trade worth millions, if not billions, of dollars per year.

Chapters six and seven give us more cause for optimism. In the former, the important contributions that earlier and more recent Egyptologists have made to the field of archaeology and our knowledge of the past in general will be examined. The latter is concerned with some of the major archaeological projects that are currently taking place in Egypt: projects such as

Mark Lehner's investigation of the town of the pyramid builders at Giza, and Kent Weeks' excavation and restoration of the hugely impressive KV5 tomb in the Valley of the Kings.

The book concludes with an epilogue that provides some useful suggestions for those readers who have hopefully been inspired by this book to explore the story of ancient Egypt in greater detail. It also provides some pointers for readers who want to get up close and personal with the ancient Egyptians by actually working on an archaeological dig in Egypt, which, although not easily done, is an experience that is highly recommended.

## THE GEOGRAPHY OF ANCIENT EGYPT

Egypt is located in northeast Africa at the northern end of the River Nile, which rises in the Ethiopian Highlands over 4,000 miles to the southeast.[1] Its geographical position is rather unusual, as its northern border is in the eastern Mediterranean facing Europe, its southern and western borders are in Africa, and its eastern border is situated on the coast of the Red Sea, across which lies western Asia.

The importance of the Nile cannot be underestimated, as without its life-giving waters ancient Egyptian civilization could not have developed in this eastern corner of the vast Sahara Desert. Without the fertile alluvium that was left by the annual Nile flood, farming would never have been possible

The River Nile seen from the east bank at Luxor (ancient Thebes). The Valley of the Kings lies in the desert cliffs to the right.

in the Nile Valley,[2] and undoubtedly "the civilization of Egypt and its spectacular achievements were based throughout its history on the prosperity of a mainly agrarian economy."[3] Indeed, this was realized a long time ago by the famous Greek historian Herodotus (c.490–420 BC), who says in his *Histories*: "It is clear to any intelligent observer, that the Egypt to which the Greeks sail nowadays is, as it were, the gift of the river, and has come only recently into the possession of its inhabitants."[4]

The annual flood or "inundation" was not a uniform event from year to year, and sometimes the flood waters were too high, or too low, leading to the destruction of great swathes of agricultural land, or a dearth of fertile land for the planting of crops and the grazing of livestock. The Nilometer (Nile flood gauge) reveals that there were several low floods between 930 and 1350 AD, and Medieval Arab scholars have left us records covering some 1,300 years, which tell us that during this time, there were alternating episodes of low and high inundations. Such floods caused famines, droughts, plagues, civil unrest, and even cannibalism, although whether people in ancient Egypt resorted to such desperate measures as a result of the low or high floods that took place is not known. However, some of the evidence left by the ancient Egyptians themselves make it clear that at various times throughout their history, they faced very hard times as a result of disastrous Nile floods. This is graphically illustrated in the reliefs that cover the walls of the causeway at the Fifth Dynasty pyramid complex of King Unas at Saqqara. Here, there are depictions of people who are close to the point of starvation; their rib cages are clearly visible and they are seated on the ground, seemingly weak from hunger. It is possible that these reliefs provide evidence that the Old Kingdom declined as a result of a prolonged drought, which was caused by a series of low inundations. Near the village of el-Mo'alla in Upper Egypt, an inscription still survives in the First Intermediate Period tomb of the provincial governor or warlord Ankhtifi. It records how Ankhtifi stopped his people from "dying on the sandbank of hell" and this perhaps indicates that there was also a low inundation and subsequent famine during this time.

Since the completion of the Aswan High Dam in 1971, Egypt no longer faces the possibility of such catastrophic inundations, as the annual Nile flood has been stopped by a new system of locks, irrigation canals, and drainage ditches, in turn giving rise to thousands of acres of new agricultural land in the Nile Valley. However, for many ordinary Egyptians, life is far from easy and poverty remains a huge problem. The completion of the Aswan Dam has also given rise to an unforeseen and serious problem: Egypt's water table is now permanently high. As a result, many of the buildings of ancient Egypt (particularly the mud-brick ones) are now threatened with serious damage and, in some cases, destruction.

The most common crops grown by ancient Egyptian farmers included emmer wheat and barley, used to make bread and cakes, as well as a coarse but wholesome beer, often flavored by the addition of spices, honey, or dates. These staples were supplemented by pulses and vegetables such as chickpeas, lentils, and fava beans, and vegetables including lettuces, cucumbers, leeks, onions, garlic, and radishes. Farmers also grew fruits including melons, dates, figs, and pomegranates along with cumin, dill, and other herbs. Meat also played its part in the ancient Egyptian diet, with goats, sheep, pigs, and cattle seen in the villages, although for many people, meat was probably something of a luxury (beef in particular was a prestigious meat reserved for the elite). Red and white wine cultivated from grapes was another luxury product generally reserved for royalty and the upper classes, and wine made from dates and pomegranates was also known. Tomb scenes showing drunken guests at feasts, or in one case, being carried away because they were too drunk to stand,[5] reveal that the Egyptians were not exactly great believers in sobriety. Wine jar labels and seals found at archaeological sites in Egypt show that the Delta and the oases of the Western Desert were both important wine-making regions. Various species of birds both wild and domestic (e.g., pigeons, ducks, and geese) and fish such as tilapia and perch were also caught in abundance in the Nile.

Two of the most significant plant crops in ancient Egypt were papyrus and flax. The papyrus plant was put to a variety of uses, such as making baskets, and boats and skiffs for fishing and hunting. However, it is for its transformation into papyri that the plant is best known, as the scribes who wrote their hieroglyphs on these paper-like sheets have opened a window onto ancient Egyptian society. Many types of clothing were made from flax, as well as sails and ropes, which were obviously very important in a riverine civilization.

The Nile Valley proper comes to an end near Cairo, where the Nile splits into two branches known as the Damietta and Rosetta (several more existed in antiquity but these had dried up by the Islamic Medieval Period). The Damietta and Rosetta flow out into a triangular or fan-shaped area of fertile land that terminates at the Mediterranean coast. The ancient Greeks referred to this northern part of Egypt as the Delta (the name by which it is still commonly known) because they thought that it resembled the letter *delta* of their alphabet (Δ). The ancient Egyptians recognized the distinct geographical dichotomy of the Valley and the Delta and labeled them Upper Egypt and Lower Egypt, respectively.

The southern border of ancient Egypt was located at the first Nile cataract—one of a series of six rocky rapids lying between Aswan and Khartoum in the Sudan. It was here in the narrow strip of fertile land, which the cataracts interrupt, that the ancient kingdom of Nubia (Kush) was founded. The Egyptians were active in Nubia at least as early as the late Predynastic Period, and the Early Dynastic Period rock inscriptions and reliefs found at the second cataract are probably related to incursions made by the early Egyptian state. In the Predynastic and Early Dynastic periods, Lower Nubia was home to the indigenous "A-Group culture" who traded with the Egyptians, and who were given their unimaginative moniker by the famous American Egyptologist George Reisner. The Egyptians basically viewed Lower Nubia as an extension of their own country: during the Old Kingdom and the succeeding Middle Kingdom, they built a series of fortresses between the second and third cataracts. During the Second Intermediate Period, Egypt became a divided and weaker country as the Hyksos people from Palestine rose to power in Lower Egypt. Subsequently, the Egyptians lost control of Nubia and power passed into the hands of the indigenous Kushite culture whose capital was at Kerma in Upper Nubia, which made at least one attempt at the invasion of Egypt.

The Egyptians regained control, with Thutmose I pushing deep into Upper Nubia between the fourth and fifth cataracts and creating a vast area under Egyptian control. The Egyptians, though, once again lost control of Nubia at the beginning of the Third Intermediate Period. The Kushite elite of the Napata region subsequently emerged as the rulers of Nubia, incorporating the whole of Egypt into their new kingdom and compromising the Twenty-Fifth Dynasty in the Late Period.

Nubia contained several sources of gold and good-quality building stone that stimulated Egyptian interest in the area. It was also a trading conduit for various exotic products coming from sub-Saharan Africa, including spices, ivory, ebony, baboons, and even occasionally pygmies (who, we might suspect, were not treated particularly well), which were prized by the Egyptian elite.

The Nile Valley and Delta effectively split the eastern corner of the Sahara Desert in two, forming the Western and Eastern Deserts, with the Sinai region representing an extension of the latter across the Gulf of Suez. The Western Desert, which is also known as the Libyan Desert, is the larger of the two and covers about two-thirds of Egypt. A chain of oases can be found running parallel to the Nile in the Western Desert, with the most notable being Dakhla, Kharga, Bahariya, Farafra, and the remote Siwa Oasis, some four hundred miles west of Cairo. A considerable amount of important archaeological evidence from various periods has been found at these oases, and Alexander the Great is also reputed to have visited the oracle of Amun (one of the chief gods of the Egyptian pantheon) at Siwa in 332 BC, in order to legitimize his claim as the rightful pharaoh of Egypt. Some scholars have claimed that the famous Macedonian warrior king was also buried at Siwa, rather than Alexandria, but most feel that this is very unlikely.

The largest oasis in the Western Desert is found in the Faiyum region (about thirty-seven miles southwest of Cairo), a fertile depression covering an area of around eight thousand square miles. In prehistoric times there was an enormous salt-water lake occupying most of the Faiyum but this has now dwindled to form the much smaller, freshwater Lake Moeris. Evidence of Neolithic farming communities dating from c.7000–4000 BC has been found in the Faiyum along with settlements and other archaeological remains from the Ptolemaic and Roman Periods.

The Western and Eastern Deserts also contained an abundant and diverse range of raw materials used for the magnificent monuments and countless dazzling artifacts that played such an essential part in reinforcing the power of the pharaoh and the ancient Egyptian state. Of obvious importance were the many different types of building stone that could be found in both deserts, such as granite, sandstone, gneiss, fine limestone, quartzite, travertine ("Egyptian alabaster"), and graywacke, or *bekhen*-stone as the Egyptians called it. This latter type of stone was used to produce some of the finest ancient statues the world has ever seen. As well as quarrying various types of stone in the Eastern Desert the Egyptians also mined gold, copper, tin, iron, lead, galena (used to make eye paint), and precious stones such as turquoise, emerald, and amethyst.[6] Copper was the first metal to be mined in Egypt and the earliest simple copper artifacts (e.g., beads from necklaces) date to the Predynastic "Badarian" Period. Although bronze (which is an alloy of copper and tin) objects appear in Early Dynastic times, it was not until after the Middle Kingdom that it became more commonly used, although copper continued to be important throughout the Pharaonic Period. A wide variety of objects for use in both religious and secular activities were made from both copper and bronze, including altars, statuettes, amulets, cymbals, jars, basins, dishes, and various tools and weapons. Gold—as in many other societies—was valued highly by the Egyptians as a prestigious metal and as early as the Predynastic Period, jewelry was being made from native gold sources. However, it was in the Pharaonic Period that gold really came into its own, being used by kings and the higher echelons of Egyptian society to make numerous beautiful artifacts that were often of a ritual or religious nature. Egyptian gold also found its way into the hands of foreign rulers in neighboring countries, as revealed by a letter written to Amenhotep III by a king of Mittani in Mesopotamia, who argues for a larger gold consignment to be sent to him because "gold occurs in Egypt like the sand on the roads."[7] Many stunning objects made from silver have also been recovered from ancient Egyptian sites, with the standout example being the hawk-headed solid silver coffin of the Libyan king Sheshonq IIa, who was buried in one of the richly furnished Twenty-First through Twenty-Second Dynasty tombs discovered at Tanis in the northeastern Delta.

Many impressive ancient Egyptian quarries and mines, and their associated settlements, can still be seen in many parts of the Western and Eastern Deserts, providing us with an enduring testament to the skill and back-breaking work that went into the exploitation of the many raw materials found in their unforgiving landscapes. It also seems that for the people who lived and worked at some of these quarries and mines, an untimely death was a real possibility. During the reign of Rameses IV, for example, a workforce of around nine thousand men was sent to the important quarry at the Wadi Hammamat to obtain graywacke (gold was also mined here) and nearly 10 percent of this workforce subsequently lost their lives as a result.[8]

## THE EARLIEST EGYPTIANS: FROM HUNTER-GATHERERS TO THE FIRST FARMERS

The Pharaonic civilization of ancient Egypt is rightly renowned for its many stunning cultural achievements, but it was preceded by a much lengthier prehistoric period. Several different cultures lived during this time, and for most of Egyptian prehistory, people followed a largely mobile hunter-gatherer lifestyle. These hunter-gatherers, or "foragers" (as they are alternatively called), lived in temporary or seasonal camps, moving around in small bands, as they hunted, fished, and gathered the edible plant foods that were available at this time. Ancient Egypt's first hunter-gatherers were early members of the human species who dropped their distinctive "Acheulean" stone hand axes at various sites along the margins of the Nile Valley, and in the Western Desert, during the Lower Paleolithic or Old Stone Age. Archaeologists have trouble pinning down definite dates for these ancient stone tools, but the earliest examples probably date back at least five hundred thousand years ago. Although, as yet, we do not know who Egypt's earliest toolmakers were, it seems likely that they belonged to the species known as *Homo erectus* who first emerged around two million years ago in east Africa, from whence they migrated into many other parts of the Old World. The Nile Valley would have provided these migrating *Homo erectus* groups with a useful migratory corridor, and would also have been a resource-rich environment for those groups that stayed in Egypt.

## THE MIDDLE PALEOLITHIC

During the earlier stages of the Middle Paleolithic in Egypt, the Acheulean hand axe tradition disappeared and a more diverse range of stone tools began to be made using the "Levallois technique," which was named after the suburb of Paris where it was first recognized by archaeologists in the nineteenth century. It is interesting to note that in Europe and western Asia, the Middle Paleolithic is associated with the famous Neanderthals, but these mysterious ancient members of the human species do not appear to have been present in Egypt. However, several Neanderthal burials have been discovered in Israel (e.g., at Kebara Cave, Mount Carmel, and Amud Cave in the Wadi Amud), and given that Neanderthals could have easily reached Egypt along the Levantine coast, then perhaps we should not totally rule out the possibility that one day, such burials will come to light in Egypt too.[9]

*Middle Paleolithic bifacial (worked on two sides) hand axe from the Valley of the Kings. These artifacts may have been multifunctional tools used for a variety of tasks. Photo, taken 25 December 2010, courtesy of Didier Descouens*

Egyptian Neanderthals or not, Middle Paleolithic stone tools have been found at various sites in the Nile Valley and Nubia, although the best-preserved evidence has come from the Western Desert and the sites of Bir Sahara East and Bir Tarwafi, which were excavated by Professor Fred Wendorf of Southern Methodist University. A series of workshops and living sites were discovered at these two sites, which originally lay next to lakes surrounded by savannah-type grasslands that formed during wet intervals between 175,000 and 70,000 BP. The people at Bir Sahara and Bir Tarwafi caught fish in the lakes and hunted various animals including antelope, gazelle, and hare in the grasslands, but they would have had to be more wary of the larger mammals such as rhinoceros and giant buffalo that also lived around the lakes.

Anatomically modern humans appear to have originated in southern Africa around 120,000 BP, and although the date of their arrival in Egypt is not known, the burial of a boy or girl who died about fifty-five thousand years ago was discovered at Taramsa Hill in Upper Egypt. We will look in more detail at this important burial in the next chapter, along with other fascinating Paleolithic burials that have been discovered in Egypt.

## THE UPPER AND LATE PALEOLITHIC

Sites dating to the Upper Paleolithic in Egypt are rare, and our knowledge of this period is thus rather limited. However, it is evident that the Levallois technique disappeared during the Upper Paleolithic, and instead, people began to produce different types of stone tools such as blades and burins (pointed tools used to pierce and engrave various materials such as bone, leather, and ivory).

The Late Paleolithic in Egypt provides us with a contrasting picture to the rather impoverished one of the Upper Paleolithic, as the archaeological record from this period is considerably richer, with many sites found in Upper Egypt (and Nubia). Late Paleolithic sites are not found in Middle and Upper Egypt, but this is probably because they are hidden under layers of alluvium deposited by later Nile floods. There is considerable variation to be seen in Late Paleolithic stone tools and a number of different stone tool industries from this time have been identified by archaeologists, such as the Fakhurian and the Ballanan-Silsilian.

Evidence found at Late Paleolithic sites shows that its hunter-gatherer communities ate a lot of fish, with genera such as catfish and Tilapia caught in huge quantities, probably in the pools that were left behind after the waters of the Nile flood had receded. Although fish seem to have provided the major source of protein, people also hunted animals such as hartebeest, wild cattle, and gazelle. These animals may well have been hunted with early bows, as some of the very small flint bladelets or "microliths" found at Late Paleolithic sites are likely to have been hafted as projectile points into either arrow or spear shafts (or both). It also appears likely that the diet of Egypt's Late Paleolithic communities was supplemented by edible plants such as club rush, chamomile, and nut-grass tubers.

## THE NILE VALLEY EPIPALEOLITHIC (FINAL PALEOLITHIC)

The Epipaleolithic marks the time of the last hunter-gatherers in Egypt, although evidence of their lives is rather limited, probably because many of their sites are buried under mud left by the Nile floods. As a result, only two Final Paleolithic cultures have been identified in Egypt—the Elkabian in Upper Egypt, and the Qarunian in the Faiyum region.

The Qarunian people lived on the higher ground overlooking the proto-Lake Moeris (which was not fully formed until about 7000 BC) and its shallow waters provided them with easy pickings. Thus it is no surprise that fish formed a major part of their diet. Hunting and food gathering were still practiced, though, and there appears to be no evidence suggesting that they were domesticating crops and animals. Included among the animals they hunted were gazelle, hartebeest, and hippopotamus.

The Elkabian sites were originally located on a beach near a channel of the Nile that has long since dried up, and it is evident that they caught many fish not only from this channel, but from the Nile itself, which points toward the use of boats at this early date. Some of the grinding stones found at their sites were probably not used to process wild plant foods, as some still contain traces of pigment, indicating perhaps that Elkabian people decorated their bodies. Dorcas gazelle, aurochs, and Barbary sheep were also hunted by the Elkabians and it is likely that they followed game into the desert, which at this time was less arid.

## THE SAHARAN NEOLITHIC

The earliest Neolithic sites in Egypt are found in the Western Desert and belong to the first of three Neolithic periods identified by archaeologists for this eastern part of the Sahara: Early (c.8800–6800 BC), Middle (c.6500–5100 BC), and Late (c.5100–4700 BC). Rather than being full-fledged farmers like the Neolithic communities of the Levant (from whence the Neolithic lifestyle spread), who lived in permanent villages that were based around domesticated crops and animals, the Early Neolithic people of the Western Desert were semi-nomadic pastoralists who herded wild cattle and lived in seasonal camps around the playa basins. Thousands of small, short-stay campsites consisting of hearths and scatters of stone artifacts have been found in the desert and were probably left by these pastoralists when they were moving their herds to the grasslands that sprang up after the summer rains (since about 3000 BC the Sahara Desert has been virtually rainless). Pottery (which shows similarities to contemporary pottery used further in the northern Sudan) was used, although it was rare and the many ostrich shells that are found at Early Neolithic sites were probably used more commonly for holding water, milk, and blood (the scarcity of cattle bones found at sites suggests that people were generally not using cattle for meat). Grinding stones on which people processed wild grass seeds, Ziziphus fruits, and wild sorghum are also found on many Early Neolithic sites along with wells featuring side basins for watering cattle. People also hunted wild animals, with hare and gazelle appearing to be their favorite prey.

Sites dating to the Middle and Late Saharan Neolithic are much more numerous and contain more wells and evidence of dwellings, among which are the remains of what are apparently the earliest wattle and daub houses. As well as cattle, domesticated sheep and goats probably introduced from the Levant also appear for the first time in Egypt, but wild animals and plant foods still formed the bulk of people's diets. Smaller temporary settlements are still common during these periods, but some are actually quite substantial, such as Site 270 at Dakhla Oasis, where there are the remains of some two hundred round and rectangular stone huts.[10] It is probable that these larger settlements were lived in all year round. New "bifacial" (worked on both sides) stone tools appear in the Middle Neolithic, and around 4900 BC, a new type of pottery abruptly replaced the "Sahara-Sudanese" and "Khartoum" wares, perhaps indicating the appearance of a new people in the Western Desert. By 4400 BC, the climate of the desert, which had become increasingly arid, became so inhospitable that it was only at the oases that settlement was possible.

## THE NILE VALLEY NEOLITHIC

The earliest Neolithic sites in (or close to) the Nile Valley are found in the Faiyum and date to c.5500–4500 BC. Although the people of the Neolithic

"Faiyum A culture" used both domesticated cereals (emmer wheat and six-row barley) and animals (sheep/goats, cattle, and pigs), they did not live in permanent villages and their sites appear to be more like the temporary campsites of earlier hunter-gatherers. Many Faiyumian sites also contain large storage pits or granaries in which grain was stored, probably by the community as a whole (one example excavated by archaeologists still contained a wooden sickle with hafted flint blades that had been used to harvest cereals). It is likely that these pits were used to stockpile grain for the drier periods when wild resources became scarcer. The people of the Faiyum A culture also made crude and simple pots, some of which were coated with a red slip. Seashells from both Mediterranean and Red Sea species are also found at their sites, indicating the existence of a long-distance trade and exchange network.

The earliest evidence we have for fully sedimentary farming life in or near the Nile Valley comes from Merimda Beni Salama, located on the western edge of the Delta about thirty-seven miles northwest of Cairo. This important site was inhabited between c.5000 and 4100 BC and covers an area of around eighteen thousand square meters, with the average depth of the settlement debris—which relates to the three main phases of settlement at the site—measuring up to two and one-half meters deep. In the first two phases of settlement, people lived in insubstantial shelters and then simple oval dwellings made from wood and wicker work; by the final phase, people were living in a large and well-planned village containing oval houses made from straw-tempered mud, which had sunken floors and roofs made from branches and reeds. From its earliest phase, the site of Merimda Beni Salama "represents a fully developed Neolithic economy [with] evidence of ceramics, as well as farming and the herding of domesticated species."[11] Nonetheless, hunting and fishing also continued alongside agriculture at this settlement.

## THE BADARIAN CULTURE

The first farmers in Upper Egypt belonged to the "Badarian culture," whose communities mainly lived in small settlements in an area covering some thirty miles along the east bank of the Nile between Matmar and Qua, although Badarian artifacts have also been found farther south and to the east of the Nile. The Badarian culture ranges in date from c.5000 to 4000 BC, and while several settlements have been excavated, it is their cemeteries that are more abundant. People were buried in simple pits, usually positioned on their left side, with their faces looking to the west. The bodies were often placed on mats and although grave goods (e.g., stone cosmetic palettes and beads) are usually limited, the dead were often accompanied by the distinctive black-topped "rippled bowls" that are such a characteristic feature of the Badarian culture. Some examples of these pots have extremely thin walls, and somewhat remarkably, none of the subsequent potters of ancient Egypt were able to produce pots with walls that were as fine.

Like their northern counterparts at Merimda Beni Salama, people of the Badarian culture herded domesticated sheep, cattle, and goats and cultivated wheat and barley; lentils and tubers have also been discovered at their settlements. It is apparent that fish from the Nile formed a significant part of their diet, and they do not appear to have been particularly big hunters. Although the archaeological evidence suggests that Badarian settlements were rather small-scale in nature, it nevertheless remains possible that larger settlements closer to the Nile Valley were destroyed by later Nile floods or lie hidden under their alluvial mud. It may be that the origins of the Badarian culture lie in the Levant, but in this respect, most scholars tend to look toward the Late Neolithic of the Western Desert.

## THE NAQADA PERIOD

The earliest roots of ancient Egyptian civilization can be found in the Neolithic cultures of the earlier Predynastic Period,[12] but it is in the later Naqada culture that many of its major traits can be seen in their embryonic form. The Naqada culture takes its name from the major site of Naqada in Upper Egypt, where a vast cemetery area containing more than three thousand graves was excavated by Sir Flinders Petrie and his colleague James Quibell in 1895.

The remains of a Predynastic walled town founded at least as early as c.3600 BC was also discovered at Naqada, indicating that its community was exploiting (and benefiting from) the gold found at Wadi Hammamat across the Nile in the Eastern Desert. Naqada continued to be occupied into Dynastic times and was known as Nubt, the "town/city of gold."

Petrie initially labeled the largest cemetery at Naqada the "Great New Race Cemetery" as he believed that the pottery found in the graves (numbering over two thousand), which was different from that he had recovered from Dynastic graves, was brought to Egypt by invaders after the collapse of the Old Kingdom.[13] However, Petrie later realized that the graves he had uncovered were from the Predynastic Period, and he subsequently devised an ingenious dating system for the pottery found in the graves, in the process identifying three major periods: the Amratian, Gerzean, and Semainean. Petrie's dating system has since been revised, and his three periods renamed Naqada, I, II,[14] and III, respectively, but "they have never been fundamentally questioned, and today they still constitute the loom upon which Egyptian prehistory is woven."[15]

There is not space here to examine the abundant archaeology of the Naqada Period in detail but as early as the Amratian/Naqada I Period, there are hints to be found amongst this archaeology of a prehistoric society undergoing significant change. For example, at Hierakonpolis, there are large rectangular tombs in which magnificent stone mace heads were found. It is likely that these unusual tombs mark the burial places of powerful individuals who went to the afterlife with objects that symbolized this power, and that were perhaps also used in warfare. White-painted decoration also appears on some of the red pottery ware of the Amratian, with animal and vegetal motifs, and simple depictions of hunters as well as victorious warriors conquering their enemies, revealing "the beginnings of an iconography that would eventually lie at the core of pharaonic civilization."[16]

In the Gerzean/Naqada II Period, there was an increase in the number of larger and more elaborate tombs, and Cemetery T at Naqada and the well-known "Painted Tomb" (Tomb 100) at Hierakonpolis are noteworthy in this respect. At Cemetery T, which was set apart from the other Naqada burials, there were large tombs lined with mud-brick. One of these contained many carved stone vessels and jewelry made from exotic materials such as gold and lapis lazuli. Tomb 100 was one of five tombs that were similar to the larger examples found at Naqada and its excavators discovered a remarkable decorative scene painted on its walls that included several boats and warrior figures. Boats were clearly important during the Naqada II Period and were probably used to import the exotic materials with which an elite marked themselves out in both life and death, and also to facilitate the expansion of the Naqada II culture northward and southward.

During the Naqada II Period, there was also a great leap forward in stonework techniques and many different types of stone were used to make beautiful items such as cosmetic palettes, stone vessels, and pear-shaped mace heads, the latter a characteristic feature of the later iconography of the all-conquering pharaoh. These artisans were the forerunners of the master masons and artisans of the Pharaonic Period who often achieved levels of greatness in their work. Remarkably delicate and beautiful ripple-flaked flint knives are also a characteristic of the Naqada II Period, and we would be hard pressed to find finer examples of the art of the prehistoric flint knapper anywhere in the world.

## THE BUTO-MA'ADI CULTURE

Twentieth-century excavations in Lower Egypt have revealed the existence of a separate Predynastic culture in the north of the country, contemporary with the Naqada I–II Periods. This is known as the "Buto-Ma'adi culture" (or simply the Maadian culture) and takes its name from the settlements of Buto and Ma'adi, which are located in the northwestern Delta just south of Cairo, respectively. Like their southern counterparts of the Naqada culture, the people of the Buto-Ma'adi culture lived a settled farming lifestyle.

At Ma'adi (which was occupied between c.3900 and 3500 BC), people used pottery made locally and imported pottery and other artifacts from Upper Egypt (e.g., stone cosmetic palettes and mace heads), and some of the cultural material found at the site is strikingly different from that found at Naqada sites. For example, some people at Ma'adi lived in oval houses with entrance passageways that were actually dug out of the living rock. These semi-subterranean dwellings contained hearths and storage jars half buried in the ground, indicating that they were intended for permanent use. Interestingly, these unusual houses are very similar to those found at contemporary settlements of the Beersheba culture in southern Palestine. Further evidence of contact with this region (or perhaps further evidence of emigration from here?) is seen with the imported Beersheba storage vessels and other artifacts found at Ma'adi, such as copper chisels and pins, and finely made Palestinian-style flint tools. Buto-Ma'adi and Naqada culture artifacts have been found on Palestinian sites and these may have come from Ma'adi, as Egyptologists have suggested that it functioned as a trading depot. The donkey remains also found at Ma'adi perhaps indicate how trade goods were transported in and out of this depot.

For some unknown reason, Ma'adi was abruptly abandoned during the middle of the corresponding Naqada II Period in Upper Egypt, which marks the earliest phase at Buto, when its inhabitants lived in simple wattle and daub houses (large, mud-brick houses superseded these in Early Dynastic times). In the earlier Predynastic levels at Buto, there was the same locally made pottery that was used at Ma'adi. Gradually, however, Naqada pottery became more common at the site at the expense of local pottery, which eventually disappeared altogether. This suggests that the Buto-Ma'adi culture was assimilated into the Upper Egyptian Naqada culture rather than being suddenly replaced by it.

## NAQADA III/DYNASTY 0: THE UNIFICATION OF EGYPT

The Naqada III Period marks the final stage of the Predynastic Period, and replaced Petrie's Semainean Period after his dating system was revised by the German Egyptologist Werner Kaiser. In the latter stages of Naqada III, kings preceding those of the First Dynasty were buried at Abydos in Upper Egypt, near the royal cemetery of their immediate successors, and this has given rise to some Egyptologists talking of a Dynasty "0." Tomb U-j (c.3150 BC) at Abydos, which was probably the burial place of a King "Scorpion," was excavated by a German team in 1988. They found many fine artifacts in its twelve subterranean chambers, including 400 jars (which may once have contained wine) imported from Palestine, and 150 small wooden and bone labels inscribed with what are probably the earliest known hieroglyphs in Egypt (including the Scorpion glyph).

It was during Naqada III/Dynasty 0 that all of Egypt—from the Delta to the First Cataract—was unified into a single and powerful state. Exactly how this state emerged from the independent, Neolithic farming villages of late Predynastic Egypt is not totally clear. It is probable, though, that warfare had some part to play in this momentous event, and it may have had a major rather than a minor role in the Egyptian late Predynastic stage. Although it has to be admitted that hard proof of late Predynastic warfare is hard to find, evidence pointing in this direction can be seen on decorated ceremonial artifacts found in the late nineteenth century by James Quibell and Frederick Green at the important site of Hierakonpolis. We will look at these important artifacts in more detail in the following chapter.

Unlike their earlier counterparts, some Egyptologists are now wary of seeing the warfare-related imagery found on these artifacts as proof that a Lower Egyptian kingdom was conquered by a more powerful one (traditionally seen as being led by King Narmer) from Upper Egypt, and argue that they may not actually represent real historical events. Nevertheless, this imagery is intriguing, and perhaps more than hints that armed conflict had an important part to play in the early stages of state formation in ancient Egypt. As has been pointed out, even if there are no signs of actual destruction at sites dating to Naqada III in the Delta, warfare could still have been the driving force behind the consolidation of the early state and its subsequent expansion into Lower Nubia and southern Palestine in the First Dynasty.[17]

Interestingly, the process of the unification of late Predynastic Egypt has been envisaged as being analogous to a game of Monopoly.[18] The players of the "game" were the ambitious individuals who had risen to become the rulers of their communities by amassing wealth in the form of various commodities, with the eventual winner (i.e., the king of both Upper and Lower Egypt) being the leader who was able accumulate the most wealth, which would put him in an unassailably powerful position.[19]

An interesting suggestion in light of this game-playing theory is that the powerful Upper Egyptian polity who came out on top in the Predynastic power struggle did so by seizing control of the lucrative northern trade routes with southwest Asia.[20] The identity of the ruler that unified Egypt will remain a matter of debate, but there can be little doubt that Naqada, Heirakonpolis, and Abydos were significant power bases in late Predynastic Egypt.

## THE EARLY DYNASTIC PERIOD

If the Egyptian historian Manetho (who lived around 300 BC) is to be believed, the Dynastic Period and the unification of Egypt began with the legendary King Menes, who some scholars believe is probably the same person as King Aha, who was buried in Tomb B19/15 at the Umm el-Qa´ab Early Dynastic cemetery, Abydos.[21] However, it is now more widely believed that Menes should be identified with King Narmer and that Aha was actually his son. Whatever the truth, it is likely that the thirty-three young men whose remains were found in the subsidiary burials close to Aha's "mastaba" tomb[22] were sacrificed to accompany the king in the afterlife.

There were two main capitals during the First Dynasty: Abydos and Memphis, although Heirakonpolis and the Delta site of Tell el-Fara´in also appear to have been important settlement areas. Large cemeteries with richly furnished burials were built throughout Egypt during the First Dynasty, with the finest belonging to the reign of King Den, and two tombs associated with King Den at Abydos contain the earliest examples of stairways from Egyptian tombs. The high officials of the First Dynasty were buried in very impressive tombs at North Saqqara near Cairo, some of which still had traces of paint on their niched facades as well as surviving wooden floors when they were excavated. These large tombs were also richly furnished with numerous grave goods, including a wide variety of stone vessels, many objects made from copper, and jewelry made from gold, turquoise, and amethyst.

At the beginning of the Second Dynasty, the royal necropolis moved to Saqqara, where the names of the first three kings of the dynasty (Hetep-sekhemwy, Raneb, and Nynetjer) were found on seal impressions recovered from two enormous underground galleries (both over one hundred meters long) close to the famous Step Pyramid of King Djoser. The tombs and funerary enclosures of two late kings of the Second Dynasty—Peribsen and Khasekhemwy[23]—have been found at Abydos, however. Khasekhem-wy's tomb is the more impressive of the two and consists of one long gallery measuring approximately seventy meters long and approximately forty meters wide. It was divided internally into fifty-eight rooms and a central burial chamber, and a huge quantity of grave goods was recovered from the former, including pots that, somewhat remarkably, were still filled with fruit and grain. Some Egyptologists have suggested that during or after Peribsen's reign there was conflict between Upper and Lower Egypt, and that this was finally resolved either through military or diplomatic means by Khasekhemwy.

As in the First Dynasty, high officials of the state continued to be buried at North Saqqara, while those of a lesser status were probably buried at Helwan on the east bank of the Nile, where over ten thousand graves dating from Naqada III to the early Old Kingdom are located. James Quibell and Walter Emery also found early Second Dynasty burials, which contained corpses wrapped in resin-soaked bandages, foreshadowing the mummies of later periods that have become so synonymous with ancient Egyptian civilization.

## THE OLD KINGDOM

The Old Kingdom marks one of the most significant periods in the history of ancient Egypt. During this time, Egypt entered a long and stable period of economic prosperity and political stability, with the foundations for this settled state of affairs having been laid in the Early Dynastic Period. The Old Kingdom soon grew into a centrally organized state ruled by the king, who was believed to be a semi-divine being endowed with supernatural powers, and there were also significant advances in religious ideas during the Old Kingdom, which are reflected in the breathtaking monuments and artworks of this time.

One of the most notable of these achievements was the building of King Djoser's magnificent Step Pyramid at Saqqara in the Third Dynasty. Designed by the famous architect Imhotep, who became deified in later times, it began life as a traditional large mastaba tomb but was subsequently modified to form a six-stepped pyramid that rises some sixty-two meters above the ground. Essentially, the Step Pyramid comprises six mastaba-type structures on top of each other, which progressively decrease in size toward the top. Some 2,400 years later, the Egyptian historian Manetho credited Imhotep as "the inventor of the art of building with hewn stone."

It was during the reign of King Sneferu that the form of the royal tomb changed from a step pyramid to a true pyramid, and he was responsible for building two—if not three—pyramids: the "North" or "Red" Pyramid, the curious "Bent" or "Rhomboidal" Pyramid, and the Meidum Pyramid.[24] The Bent Pyramid takes its name from the fact that there is a striking change of angle, from 54°27' in its lower courses to 43°22' in the upper ones. The Red Pyramid is still a very impressive monument, not that much smaller than the Great Pyramid at Giza, and is probably the place where King Sneferu was actually buried.

Egyptian pyramid building undoubtedly reached its apogee with the Great Pyramid at Giza, which is the largest of the three pyramids built on the Giza Plateau just outside Cairo.[25] This magnificent religious monument has to be seen to be believed, and was built for Sneferu's son Khufu as his

*King Djoser's Third Dynasty Step Pyramid at Saqqara. The world's oldest monumental stone building.*
© Rutherford Press Limited

*The awe-inspiring Old Kingdom pyramids at Giza, near Cairo. From left to right: the Pyramid of Menkaure, the Pyramid of Khafre, and the Great Pyramid of Khufu, one of the Seven Wonders of the ancient world. Photo courtesy of Ricardo Liberato*

resting place for all eternity. It stands around 138 meters high (it was originally around 147 meters high but has lost its golden capstone) and astonishingly, it has been estimated that around 2.3 million limestone blocks were used in its construction, each of which weighed on average two and one-half tons. The second pyramid at Giza was built for Khufu's son, Khafre, and his pyramid actually appears taller than his father's, but this is because it is built at a slightly higher elevation on the plateau. Nevertheless, it is still a hugely impressive monument (originally around 136 meters in height) and also retains some of its original covering of fine limestone blocks near its apex. It is also worth noting that many Egyptologists agree that Khafre built one of ancient Egypt's most famous monuments at Giza—the Great Sphinx statue. The third pyramid at Giza was built for Menkaure, Khafre's son, and although very much smaller in height than its counterparts, it is still an imposing monument that stands around some seventy meters tall.

Egyptologists continue to debate what the pyramid form actually symbolizes but it could be possible that their sloping sides were meant to represent the rays of the sun, allowing the king to ascend a "stairway" to the heavens, where he could be united with the great sun-god Ra, who was particularly important during the Old Kingdom. Alternatively, the pyramids may have symbolized the primeval mound, which the ancient Egyptians believed rose from the primordial waters during the time of creation.

Medieval European tradition held that the Great Pyramid at Giza was actually a giant granary built by the biblical Joseph, which allowed the pharaoh to store the grain that would be needed in lean years. Another tradition holds that Hebrew slaves built the pyramids, with some modern Jewish and Egyptian communities still believing this to be true. Some modern authors of the quasi-historical variety have argued (very unconvincingly) that the Giza pyramids were built as astronomical recording devices by an ancient society that predated the Old Kingdom by many thousands of years. Even less convincing is the ridiculous idea that the pyramids were built by extraterrestrials or "ancient astronauts," a theory that was most famously promoted by Erich von Daniken in his book *Chariots of the Gods*, and which is unfortunately still believed by some deluded people today.

The Old Kingdom was not just the "Age of the Pyramids," as it is often known, but also a time when Egyptian artisans reached new (and sometimes unequaled) heights, with many stunning statues and relief carvings made for the temples and causeways that were an integral part of the royal pyramid complexes. Of course, today we use the label "art" to describe such things, but they had a functional rather than aesthetic purpose in ancient Egypt, expressing ideas about such things as kingship and the afterlife. However, that is not to say that the ancient Egyptians did not admire the great achievements of the many extremely talented artisans who formed an integral part of their society.

During the long reign of Pepy II, the Old Kingdom went into serious decline, and by the time of Pepy's death, this great period in Egypt's history was effectively over. Scholars are not exactly sure as to why the Old Kingdom failed but there may have been a variety of factors that contributed to its demise, with famine caused by a series of low inundations perhaps one of the major ones (the scenes of starving people from the Fifth Dynasty pyramid complex of King Unas will be recalled here). Provincial officials or governors of the *nomes* (the forty-two provinces or districts of ancient Egypt that date back to the Early Dynastic Period or earlier) who held hereditary office also probably played their part, their power increasing as they broke away from the state to further their own ambitions in their petty kingdoms.

## THE FIRST INTERMEDIATE PERIOD

During the long history of ancient Egypt, there were three so-called Intermediate Periods, with the First Intermediate Period beginning after the decline of the Old Kingdom. The political situation was turbulent during this time and this is reflected in the rapid succession of kings who came and went during the Seventh and Eighth Dynasties. It is also evident that "nomarchs" (provincial governors) jostled aggressively for power during the earlier part of the First Intermediate Period. The previously mentioned tomb of Ankhtifi provides us with an important example of a burial place of one of these local rulers or warlords, as it contains valuable texts relating to the political turmoil of this time. The four pharaohs of the Ninth and Tenth Dynasties, which originated at Herakleopolis in Lower Egypt, may have ruled Egypt for about a hundred years. However, the writing was on the wall for the later Herakleopolitan kings with the emergence of the rival Eleventh Dynasty at Thebes in Upper Egypt, and its fourth king, Mentuhotep II, eventually became the ruler of the whole country. This was certainly achieved through military aggression, although whether Mentuhotep II's forces had to fight all the way to Herakleopolis to defeat the last Herakleopolitan king is not known. It may be that it was diplomacy rather than warfare that finally put Mentuhotep II on the throne of all Egypt, although archaeologists have found evidence indicating that the Herakleopolitan capital may well have been sacked shortly after this event.[26]

It is also clear that there were significant changes in material culture during the First Intermediate Period, as demonstrated by such things as new styles of pottery and the appearance of crude, wooden funerary models (e.g., offering bearers, boats, and even whole workshop scenes) that were made exclusively for burials. It was also common practice to cover the heads of mummies with colored "cartonnage" masks made from gypsum and linen. The first Coffin Texts also appeared during this time, taken from a group of over a thousand magical spells, most of which originated in the Old Kingdom.

## THE MIDDLE KINGDOM

The reunification of Egypt under Mentuhotep II marks the beginning of the Middle Kingdom and the establishment of the Eleventh Dynasty, which had Thebes as its capital city. At the start of the Twelfth Dynasty, King Amenemhat I made the significant decision to move the capital to the new site of Itjtawy in Upper Egypt. The city is now lost but it was probably located between the Lisht necropolis and Memphis, the location of the state capital for much of the Pharaonic Period. It is evident that Amenemhat I had to deal with invading forces of "Asiatics" in the Delta and this led to the region being protected by the "Walls-of-the-Ruler," which are a notable feature in the well-known ancient Egyptian tale *The Story of Sinhue*. As yet, however, no definite fortifications from the time of Amenemhat I have been discovered in the Delta.

During the later reign of King Senusret III there were a number of military campaigns in Nubia. These were apparently very brutal, with many men killed and women and children enslaved. A frontier had been established at Semna at the Second Cataract by Senusret I and a series of formidable fortresses were built in the region, both to protect the boundary and to act as trading posts.[27] Senusret III was also concerned with affairs at home, as he seems to have reigned in the power of the provincial no-marchs, who since the Old Kingdom had been a threat to royal power. It is not clear how Senusret achieved this, but the fact that he appointed three king's viziers to oversee all of Egypt's provincial affairs suggests that he did.

Senusret also made a significant break with earlier artistic convention when it came to royal statuary, as the statues of the king appear to show his real features; he is portrayed with a rather sad and aged face, and with rather large, jutting ears. When we look at these statues, it is quite likely that looking back at us is the actual face of an ancient Egyptian pharaoh who lived around four thousand years ago.

## THE SECOND INTERMEDIATE PERIOD

During the Thirteenth Dynasty, when the Middle Kingdom had begun to decline, groups of migrants began to settle in the eastern Delta. These people were known as the Hyksos ("rulers of foreign lands") to the Egyptians and it is probable that most of them originally came from Palestine. Subsequently, the Hyksos rose to power in the Delta, forming the Fifteenth Dynasty and establishing their impressive capital at Avaris (Tell el-Dab'a). In Upper Egypt, at Thebes, the native Sixteenth Dynasty had to sit by and watch the political influence of the Hyksos penetrating further into the country. However, this situation was checked by the last kings of the Seventeenth Dynasty[28] at Thebes, who decided that they had had enough of this foreign dynasty, and war was declared against the Hyksos. However, it was Ahmose I, the first ruler of the Eighteenth Dynasty, who eventually won the decisive victory and drove the Hyksos from Egypt.

Although the Hyksos were expelled from Egypt, they left their mark on the country, as they introduced innovations such as bronze work, an improved potter's wheel, humpbacked cattle known as "zebu," and new vegetables and fruit. The Hyksos also introduced important military innovations: the horse and chariot (important in Egyptian warfare), the powerful composite bow, helmets and armor, and a fearsome curved sword known as a *khepesh*. As has been noted, this is rather ironic, as the Egyptian adoption of this new military technology probably helped them to finally defeat and expel the Hyksos from Egypt.[29]

## THE NEW KINGDOM

The victory of Ahmose I and the founding of the Eighteenth Dynasty marks the beginning of the New Kingdom, and the creation of a true Egyptian empire that at its height stretched from Nubia to the banks of the River Euphrates in the far north of Lebanon. The power behind the empire was a succession of warrior pharaohs, the most belligerent of whom were probably Thutmose III and Amenhotep II. Thutmose III is sometimes referred to as the "Napoleon of ancient Egypt" (a name that was inspired as much by the mistaken belief that he was very small) and it was not until his forty-second regnal year that he eventually stopped campaigning in the Levant. It is clear that these campaigns could be very profitable: the spoils of war taken after the well-known battle fought at the town of Megiddo in Syria included nearly nine hundred chariots (two of which were gold plated), two hundred suits of armor, and over two thousand horses. Such rich rewards no doubt stimulated Thutmose III's fondness for campaigning in the Levant.

Amenhotep II also campaigned in Syria and during one campaign he is said to have executed the leaders of a Syrian uprising and then brought them back to Thebes, were they were hung on the city walls for all to see. If we are to believe the surviving Egyptian accounts, Amenhotep II was a powerful individual who was famed for his deadly prowess with the bow in battle. Interestingly, when the French Egyptologist Victor Loret excavated the tomb of Amenhotep II in the Valley of the Kings in 1898 he discovered that the king had been laid to rest in his sarcophagus alongside his longbow.

Another famous figure of the New Kingdom is Hatshepsut, who was the aunt of, and for fourteen years co-ruler with, Thutmose III. She was also the most powerful of Egypt's rare female pharaohs and she initiated many new building projects in Egypt. It was at western Thebes that she really left her mark, with the building of a magnificent memorial temple at Deir el-Bahri, which is undoubtedly one of the wonders of the ancient world. At this spectacular monument there are also many artistic delights, including scenes of marching soldiers involved in a trading expedition sent by Hatshepsut to the mysterious land of Punt.[30]

*Depiction of marching soldiers on an expedition to the mysterious land of Punt—from Queen Hatshepsut's magnificent mortuary temple at Deir el-Bahri on the Theban west bank.*

Any discussion of the New Kingdom must mention Egypt's most renowned ruler—Rameses II—who ruled for sixty-seven years during the Nineteenth Dynasty. He is said to have produced over one hundred children with his many wives and concubines during his lengthy reign. Rameses "the Great" is also renowned as a warrior pharaoh,[31] but his greatest legacy is the vast collection of fine monuments that he built throughout Egypt and Nubia, and no other pharaoh can match his remarkable building program. One of Rameses' most notable monuments is his mortuary temple on the west bank at Luxor (ancient Thebes), which is today known as the Ramesseum. His most famous monuments, however, are the magnificent rock-cut temples he built at Abu Simbel in Nubia.

Rameses II also made significant architectural additions to the magnificent Luxor and Karnak Temples on the east bank at Luxor, and created a new royal capital at Piramesse in the eastern Delta, which, to judge from the archaeological remains found there, would have been hugely impressive in its day.

Two of the most fascinating rulers of New Kingdom Egypt are Akhenaten the so-called Heretic Pharaoh (husband of the famous Nefertiti), who instigated a religious revolution in Egypt, and the world famous "boy-king," Tutankhamen, whose intact tomb in the famous Valley of the Kings remains

*The hugely impressive rock-cut facade of the Great Temple of Rameses II at Abu Simbel (Nubia), with its four colossal seated statues (twenty meters high) of Rameses II. In a remarkable feat of engineering the whole temple (and the nearby smaller temple of Queen Nefertari) was moved sixty-five meters to save it from the rising waters of the Nile caused by the construction of the Aswan High Dam. Photo, taken October 2004, courtesy of Przemyslaw "Blueshade" Idzkiewicz*

the world's most famous archaeological discovery. As we will see later, there is a considerable mystery surrounding the death of this young ruler whose time on the throne of Egypt was abruptly cut short. His tomb, which contains a huge collection of some of the most stunning artifacts to have ever survived from the ancient world, serves as a sad reminder of the numerous treasures that must have been lost as a result of the tomb robbery that took place in the valley in both antiquity and more recent times. In the Valley of the Kings "some 80 and more tombs and pits are currently known . . . and it is no exaggeration to say that the tombs of any of the *truly* great kings of Egypt—Thutmose III, Amenophis III, Sethos I, Rameses II, 'the Great,' would have put the child-pharaoh to shame."[32]

## THE THIRD INTERMEDIATE PERIOD

With the death of the last king of the Twentieth Dynasty, Rameses XI, the glory that had been the New Kingdom was ended, and the Third

The Great Pylon at Luxor Temple with its colossal statues (twenty-five meters high) of a seated Rameses II, and one of a pair of obelisks—the other now stands in the Place de la Concorde, Paris.

*Some of the massive decorated columns in the Great Hypostyle Hall at Karnak Temple, Luxor. Originally, they would have supported a roof, which is long since gone. Photo courtesy of Bjørn Christian Tørrisen*

Intermediate Period began. Although on the surface, Egypt seemed united under the Twenty-First Dynasty, the first king of which was Smendes, in reality, it was a divided and somewhat politically unstable country. The Twenty-First Dynasty was based at the city of Tanis in the Delta, but at Thebes in the south, a succession of army commanders, who were also high priests of Amun, ran Upper Egypt as an essentially separate state.

The power of the Theban aristocracy declined, however, and this coincided with the emergence of the Twenty-Second Dynasty in the Delta. Its first king was Sheshonq I, whose ancestors were the leaders of the "Meshwesh" (Libyans), and with the weakening in power of the Theban rulers he was able to install his son Prince Iuput as high priest of Amun, which was a policy followed by his successors. Sheshonq was also the first Egyptian king to campaign in the Levant since the Twentieth Dynasty. However, Thebes later split away as a separate kingdom and was wracked by civil war, while in the rest of Egypt a number of local kings ruled in parallel.

During the eighth century BC, the Kushites expanded into Egypt from Nubia and their king, Piy, intervened in a conflict between local rulers farther north. As a result of this intervention he achieved a viceroyalty that founded the Nubian Twenty-Fifth Dynasty, which unified Nubia and Egypt into a single kingdom.

## THE LATE PERIOD

The Late Period begins with the conquest of the north by Piy's successor, Shabaqo, who killed the last king of the Twenty-Fourth Dynasty, Bakenrenef, and established the Twenty-Fifth Dynasty as the ruling power in Egypt.[33]Although local independent rulers still wielded considerable power during this time, the unified Nubian and Egyptian state was a formidable one whose only serious rival was the growing power of Assyria.

It was only a matter of time before the Assyrians turned their gaze toward Egypt and in 676 BC King Esarhaddon invaded Egypt and subsequently became its first Assyrian ruler. He was followed by Ashurbanipal, but neither king was ever totally in control of the country and there were several uprisings against Assyrian rule, which effectively came to an end after Ashurbanipal was forced to withdraw from Egypt because of a serious uprising in Babylonia.

After the Assyrians withdrew from Egypt, the Twenty-Sixth Saite Dynasty[34] was founded by Psamtek I, who strengthened his position with the employment of Greek mercenaries and by establishing trade links with Greece and Phoenicia. Many of the Greek mercenaries, who swelled the ranks of the Egyptian army, lived in the city of Memphis. The strengthening of trade links led to the establishment of a major Greek trading colony at Naukratis in the western Delta, which was located close to the capital, Sais. The various excavations that have been undertaken at this well-known and important site have yielded much of interest, including the remains of temples dedicated to various Greek deities such as Apollo and Aphrodite, and a large workshop where faience scarabs (amulets, seals, or ring bezels in the form of the scarab beetle) had been made for export.

The Saite Dynasty was overthrown by Cambyses, who invaded Egypt in 525 BC and established the Persian Twenty-Seventh Dynasty. Cambyses was succeeded by Darius I, who appears to have made an effort to act as a real pharaoh. However, in 404 BC, the Egyptians revolted against Persian rule, and four years later, the Persians had been driven out of Egypt. The country was then ruled by a succession of native pharaohs of the Twenty-Eighth through Thirtieth Dynasties, though the Persians returned and took control again with the establishment of the Thirty-First Dynasty. Their time in power was brief, however, as in 332 BC, the legendary warrior-king Alexander the Great conquered Egypt and established the Macedonian Dynasty.

## THE GRECO-ROMAN PERIOD

Alexander the Great only stayed a short while in Egypt, but he found time to found one of the greatest cities of antiquity—Alexandria. Although archaeologists have not found much evidence relating to the early phases of Alexander's city, they have discovered remains from the later Ptolemaic and Roman Periods, including the Kom el Shugafa (an underground labyrinth of wonderfully decorated rock-cut tombs), part of a colossal statue of the goddess Isis,[35] and masonry from the famous Pharos lighthouse, one of the seven wonders of the ancient world.[36]

After the death of Alexander IV, Alexander's son, Egypt was ruled by a succession of Macedonian-Greek rulers belonging to the Ptolemaic Dynasty.[37] Subsequently, many Greeks settled in Egypt and they dominated the commercial and administrative spheres of the country. This Greek monopoly fueled the fire for several native uprisings that took place under the unpopular Ptolemaic kings. Nevertheless, the Greek rulers did rebuild many of Egypt's ancient temples and also added some new ones of their own, including the superb temple built to the goddess Hathor at Dendera in Upper Egypt and the Temple of Isis on the island of Philae in Lower Egypt.

Egypt officially became part of the Roman Empire in 30 BC, after Octavian Augustus appointed himself its new ruler following the defeat of his rival, the Roman general Mark Anthony (the lover and husband of the famous Cleopatra, last queen of the Ptolemaic Dynasty), at the naval battle of Actium.

During the Roman Period, Egypt was basically treated as a vast imperial estate that provided food and resources for Rome. Roman rule did not mean the end of traditional Egyptian culture, however, as new temples were built in the Egyptian style, Egyptian deities were incorporated into the Roman pantheon, the hieroglyphic script was still used, and many people still spoke Egyptian.

However, the arrival of the Romans and the subsequent emergence of Christianity in the later Roman Period did mark the final chapter in the long story of ancient Egyptian civilization, and with the division of the late Roman world into an eastern (Byzantine) and western empire in 395 AD this truly remarkable story was essentially ended.

## **2**

# FROM HAND AXES
# TO MUMMY PORTRAITS

## The Archaeology of Ancient Egypt


Each year, thousands of people visit the British Museum in London to gaze at the many wonders from the ancient world that are on display in its galleries. Undoubtedly, one of the most popular objects is the rather unprepossessing slab of dark gray basalt known as the Rosetta Stone, which measures about 112 centimeters high and features three horizontal registers of ancient text written in Greek and the Egyptian hieroglyphic and demotic scripts.[1]

It has been said: "The stone is one of the world's wonders, but it does not feature in the conventional lists of the Wonders of the World."[2] This statement is not mere hyperbole, as the decipherment of the hieroglyphic inscription on the stone by the renowned French scholar Jean-François Champollion ultimately provided the key that unlocked the secrets of ancient Egyptian civilization.

The Rosetta Stone takes its name from the port of Rashid (Rosetta) on the Mediterranean coast of the western Delta, where it was discovered in July 1799 by engineers working under the direction of Lieutenant Pierre François-Xavier Bouchard, an officer with Napoleon's invasion force, which had landed in Egypt the previous year. Bouchard had been ordered to strengthen Fort Saint Julien, a former Medieval citadel, in readiness for the expected counterattack from Nelson and the Royal Navy, and when he first set eyes on the stone after it had been uncovered by his engineers, Bouchard instinctively knew that it was something special. On examination

*The Rosetta Stone. One of the world's most famous ancient artifacts, and the key that unlocked the mysteries of ancient Egypt. © Trustees of the British Museum*

of the stone, it soon became evident that the top two Egyptian scripts were copies of the Greek text in the bottom register and that it recorded a decree issued by the Egyptian priesthood in honor of the Greek pharaoh Ptolemy V on the anniversary of his succession to the Egyptian throne. The French thus realized that this was a discovery of huge significance, as it meant that they were in possession of an artifact that could possibly lead to the deci-pherment of the ancient Egyptian language.

The Rosetta Stone was therefore soon on its way to the Institut d'Égypte in Cairo, where Napoleon's *savants* (scholars) naturally made copies of its texts. However, it was not in French hands for very long: two decisive na-val battles were fought in Aboukir Bay, east of Alexandria, and the British victors took the stone as one of their many spoils of war after the armistice of 1801. Nonetheless, because the French had made copies of the texts on the stone, Jean François Champollion was eventually able to crack its hiero-glyphic code and thus provide the foundation for the science of Egyptology.

## BURIALS OF THE OLD STONE AGE

As previously mentioned, there were people living in Egypt long before Pharaonic civilization emerged in the lush and fertile Nile Valley. When compared to the spectacular archaeological evidence from the time of the pharaohs, that left by its prehistoric communities pales. Nevertheless, this does not lessen its appeal or its importance, as the many remnants of Egyp-tian prehistory provide fascinating insights into a remote time. Included amongst this prehistoric evidence are a handful of rare and important buri-als dating to the Paleolithic, which are the oldest ones yet found in Egypt.

The earliest of these was discovered at the impressive site of Taramsa Hill, which lies on the Nile floodplain about one and one-half miles from the Temple of Hathor at Dendera in Upper Egypt. From the Early to late Middle Paleolithic, people visited Taramsa Hill to quarry extensive deposits of chert cobbles that provided the raw material for various stone tools such as hand axes and "Nubian points." Their extraction techniques were simple but effective, with pits and trenches (some of which were very large) dug to extract suitable cobbles from terrace deposits, and they also used quarry pits as working areas to make their stone tools.

The burial was discovered during an archaeological survey undertaken at the site in 1994 when Egyptologists stumbled across a weathered skull in an ancient extraction pit. A decision was made to excavate the pit immediately and the Egyptologists discovered a poorly preserved and fragile skeleton of a young boy or girl aged about eight to ten years old, who had been deliber-ately laid against the side of the pit with his/her face looking toward the sky and covered over with waste material from the pit. Subsequent examination of the bones suggested that the boy or girl was an anatomically modern hu-man who would have been much like us in physical appearance.

As is often the way with such ancient burials, it was not possible to ascertain a firm date for the skeleton, but it seems probable from evidence associated with the burial (e.g., the stone tools found scattered around it) that the boy or girl died around fifty-five thousand years ago during the late Middle Paleolithic. Although the skeleton is poorly preserved, it nonetheless provides a rare and poignant glance into the lives of Egypt's Middle Paleolithic communities and suggests that early modern humans may well have moved out of Africa via the Nile Valley.

Our next Paleolithic burial was found at the impressive site of Nazlet Khater 4 in Middle Egypt, another chert-quarrying site, though one that was somewhat different from Taramsa Hill. Here, people not only dug ditches and vertical shafts to extract chert cobbles, but also horizontal subterranean galleries that extended at least ten meters underground from the bottoms of some pits and trenches.

Radiocarbon dates obtained from various contexts (e.g., the remains of hearths) revealed that the Nazlet Khater miners lived in the Upper Paleolithic and that mining activities at the site were spread over a very lengthy period from around thirty-five thousand to thirty thousand years ago. Many pick marks can still be seen on the walls of the shafts and galleries and examples of actual picks made from the horns of gazelle and hartebeest were found in some of the underground galleries, which must have been oppressive and dangerous places to work in.

The most significant discovery at the site, however, was a grave close to the mine containing the burial of a young adult male, probably between seventeen and twenty years of age, who had been laid on his back. Next to his head was a stone axe, presumably placed there by those who buried him and perhaps intended for use in the next life. Interestingly, the young man's femur was found to display a curve that may be related to his having carried heavy loads since childhood, and his spine also showed signs of stress from heavy lifting. This evidence suggests that the Nazlet Khater man had not led a particularly easy life and that he spent a good deal of time working as a Paleolithic miner. Perhaps it points to an even darker possibility—that he was a slave who was worked to death in the mine?[3]

## PREHISTORIC CONFLICT AND MURDER IN THE NILE VALLEY

It is only in the last two decades or so that there has been an acceptance by the archaeological community that the prehistoric world was far more violent than was previously supposed.[4] Discoveries such as the one made at the cemetery of Gebel Sahaba, near the Nubian border, provide grim but fascinating evidence that argues against those who still cling to the idea of some kind of prehistoric "Golden Age," when violence and conflict were virtually unknown.

Excavations at the cemetery, which has been dated to the Late Paleolithic c.14,000–12,000 BP, uncovered fifty-nine individuals who had been interred in simple pits covered with sandstone slabs. It was clear that many of these people must have died very traumatic deaths:

> Out of the fifty-nine individuals, twenty-four showed signs of a violent death attested either by many chert points embedded in the bones (and even inside the skull) or by the presence of severe cut marks on the bones. The evidence of multiple burials (including a group of up to eight bodies in one grave) confirms the picture of violence.[5]

Almost 50 percent of the dead were women and children, and disturbingly, the children seem to have been executed by being shot in the head or neck with stone projectiles. We will never truly know the human story that lay behind this terrible act, but it is perhaps possible that it was related to conflict over a scarcity of land and resources brought about by exceptionally high Nile floods. However, anthropological studies of warfare in more recent non-state societies have shown that it could just as easily be ignited by other things such as revenge for a murder, or even simply by the desire to avenge an insult. Whatever the truth is, it seems that the harrowing evidence at Gebel Sahaba reveals a massacre, with a Late Paleolithic community perhaps taken unawares in a dawn raid on their settlement, which was a favored tactic in non-state warfare.

Further evidence that "Paleolithic life . . . in the Nile Valley was not entirely rosy"[6] comes from about one hundred miles farther north of Gebel Sahaba at Wadi Kubbaniya. Here, at the base of extensive occupation deposits ranging in date from c.23,000 to c.12,000 BP, the burial of a young man in his early twenties was unearthed. Like his later counterparts at Gebel Sahaba, he too had clearly died a violent death at the hands of armed aggressors. As well as receiving a spear-thrust to his back, he had been shot with two stone projectiles in the stomach, and furthermore, he had a healed stone projectile fragment embedded in his upper arm bone. The bone was only just healing around this wound, revealing that he had already been attacked—and survived—before he was killed.

Another individual from ancient Egypt who met an untimely and violent end is "Gebelein Man," who dates from the Naqada II (Gerzean) Period c.3400 BC. Gebelein Man was one of six naturally mummified bodies found in shallow desert graves on the slopes of the western hill[7] at Gebelein by Wallis Budge, keeper of Egyptian and Assyrian antiquities at the British Museum. As has been noted, the accidental discovery of such bodies by later Egyptians "may have helped to develop or reinforce religious ideas that linked the spiritual survival of the personality after death to the physical survival of the body."[8]

The Gebelein mummies were discovered in 1896, and by 1900, they were in the possession of the British Museum. Since 1901, Gebelein Man, or "Ginger," as he was originally named,[9] has been on display in the museum, one of the best-preserved mummies from the ancient world. Today, he lies in his reconstructed grave in a glass case in the middle of Room 64 and is one of the museum's most popular attractions. Some people find Gebelein Man rather unsettling as they come face-to-face with him and others find it downright wrong that a dead person should be on public display, but this is not the place to get bogged down in ethical debates.

In November 2012, the body of Gebelein Man was temporarily moved to Cromwell Hospital, London, for a CT scan, which revealed that he had been between eighteen and twenty-one years old when he died. The scan also threw up something of a nasty surprise, as it uncovered compelling evidence that Gebelein Man had been murdered with his killer catching him unawares. This evidence took the form of a stab wound in his back, just below his left shoulder blade, that had been made by a copper or flint dag-

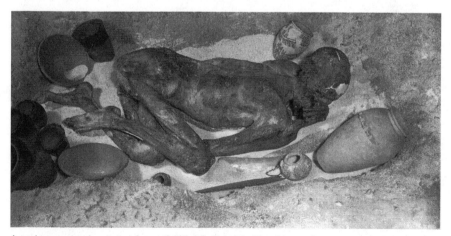

A prehistoric murder victim, from c.3400 BC. Gebelein Man lying in his reconstructed grave in the British Museum. © Trustees of the British Museum

ger. The blow that ended Gebelein Man's life had evidently been delivered with some force, as not only had it shattered one of his ribs, causing bone splinters to become embedded into his muscles, but it also penetrated his left lung. The fact that Gebelein Man has no defensive wounds present on his body lends further support to the theory that he was caught by surprise, although who stabbed him in the back, and why, will of course remain an ancient murder mystery.

## THE QURTA PETROGLYPHS

In 2005, a Belgian archaeological mission from the Royal Museums of Art and History (RMAH), Brussels, made a hugely important discovery relating to the people of Egypt's prehistoric past. On the high sandstone cliffs that run behind the modern village of Qurta in Upper Egypt, they found three separate panels of rock art that had been carved into the rock faces of the cliffs by Late Paleolithic communities over fifteen thousand years ago.[10]

Subsequent research (funded by Yale University) at the three sites has revealed a superb collection of finely engraved images or petroglyphs that depict various wild animals and a small number of nonfigurative or abstract symbols (there are about 180 petroglyphs in total). The most common animal depicted in the Qurta rock art panels is the rather fearsome aurochs, the now extinct ancestor of today's domestic cattle. Other animals depicted are waterfowl, hippopotami, gazelle, hartebeest, and fish. The naturalistic depictions of the animals stands in marked contrast to the highly stylized carvings of human figures also found at the Qurta sites. These show side views of possible females with exaggerated and well-rounded buttocks.

Interestingly, the Qurta rock art finds close stylistic parallels to that produced by contemporary Upper Paleolithic artists in Europe, which at this time was largely in the grip of an ice age. Although it is perhaps unlikely, the idea that these parallels reveal intercontinental contact between Late Paleolithic communities in ice-bound Europe and arid North Africa is an intriguing one nevertheless. As with all Upper Paleolithic art, the true meaning of the Qurta petroglyphs can never be known, but it seems likely they are somehow connected to Late Paleolithic beliefs and the world of ritual and religion.

In 2010, the Belgian mission from the RMAH discovered a further forty-nine rock art sites near the village el-Hosh in Upper Egypt, with the majority dating to the end of the Paleolithic, or "Epipaleolithic" (c.10,000–7000 BP).[11] Included amongst the rock art repertoire seen at the various sites are fish-trap designs, ladder-shaped motifs, human figures (obviously male), crocodiles, harpoon-like objects, and an isolated and highly complex geometric motif, which so far is unique in Egyptian rock art.

## DISCOVERIES FROM THE CITY OF THE FALCON-GOD

We have an abundance of finds from the Predynastic and Early Dynastic Periods, but those found at the end of the nineteenth century at Hierakonpolis ("City of the Falcon-God") in Upper Egypt undoubtedly rank among the most notable. Hierakonpolis was the name the Greeks gave to this large settlement (which lies about fifty miles south of Luxor), which in preclassical times had been named Nekhen, as it was the home of the early falcon-god Nekheny, who later became assimilated with the major sky-god, Horus.

The discoveries were made by the English Egyptologists James Edward Quibell and William Green, who carried out two seasons of excavation at Hierakonpolis between 1897 and 1899. Although the ancient town and associated cemetery had fallen prey to both local treasure hunters and unscrupulous antiquities dealers from Luxor, Quibell and Green found a wealth of artifacts. Some of the finest items were recovered from chambers located within the Old Kingdom temple area, and a brick-lined pit in the third chamber of the temple yielded a superbly made and rather fierce-looking sheet-gold falcon head (probably dating from the Sixth Dynasty) featuring lifelike obsidian eyes and a tall, double-plumed headdress. In the fifth chamber, two striking, copperplate statues of the Sixth Dynasty king Pepy I were found buried beneath the wall: one statue was life-size and depicted the king as an adult, while the other, smaller statue (which was found inside the larger one) was a representation of Pepy as a youth. Also found with the copper statues were a charming pottery lion figurine (probably Third Dynasty in date) and a finely carved greenstone statue of Khasekhemwy, last king of the Second Dynasty. Although half of the king's face was missing, the statue's base carried a fascinating description recording that the king had killed over forty-seven thousand Lower Egyptian rebels. If this number of dead reflects reality rather than royal rhetoric, then Khasekhemwy appears to have been a force to be reckoned with.

To the east of the temple area, Quibell and Green discovered a third, larger cache of material buried underneath the walls of a mud-brick building in the so-called Main Deposit. It seems that at some point during the Old or Middle Kingdom, the objects in the Main Deposit were buried as votive offerings by priests who had removed them from the ancient shrine of Horus at Hierakonpolis.

Although the Main Deposit contained many interesting objects (e.g., various stone vessels, ivory and faience statuettes, and another broken statue of Khasekhemwy featuring an identical inscription to its above counterpart), it is most notable for a handful of artifacts relating to the late Predynastic/ Early Dynastic Period, the most famous of which is the Narmer Palette.

This impressive and very large shield-shaped palette (sixty-four centimeters in height) made from dark-green siltstone is decorated on both sides with finely carved scenes and has been referred to as "the earliest historical record from Egypt."[12] This ceremonial object, which has its antecedents in the smaller, plain cosmetic palettes of the Naqada culture, may have been commissioned in order to celebrate the military victories of King Narmer (whose name appears on both sides of the palette between opposing heads of the cow-goddess Bat) and the subsequent unification of Egypt. The king's figure is most dominant on the lower side of the palette, where we see him wearing the white crown of Upper Egypt, as a towering figure who is about to put paid to a fallen enemy (perhaps a Delta chieftain or an

*The Narmer Palette. This impressive and intriguing artifact may depict the military victories and subsequent unification of Upper and Lower Egypt by King Narmer.*

Asiatic from northern Sinai) with his upraised mace. This depiction of the king smiting his foe subsequently became an important and standard motif in Egyptian royal iconography right down to Roman times. Above Narmer, to the right, the falcon-god can be seen perched atop a papyrus thicket (possibly symbolic of the Delta marshes) holding a rope in one of its talons, which appears to be attached to the nose of a prisoner who emerges from the thicket. In the bottom panel, a further two fallen enemies lie sprawled below Narmer's feet.

On the upper side of the palette, Narmer wears the red crown of Lower Egypt and can be seen with his standard-bearers approaching two rows of decapitated captives, whose heads lie at their feet. The central panel of the palette shows two fantastical creatures with their necks entwined to form the central well where cosmetics could be ground. These creatures, each of which is held on a leash by a retainer, are referred to as "serpopods" and were borrowed from contemporary Mesopotamian royal iconography, and it is possible that they symbolize the unification of Lower and Upper Egypt. Beneath the serpopods, Narmer is depicted as a raging bull attacking a fortified town while trampling an enemy underfoot.

Whether this extraordinary artifact actually provides us with a record of specific events is open to question and nowadays, more scholars are perhaps of the opinion that the scenes on the Narmer Palette essentially symbolize the power of the king and the central role he played in defeating the forces of chaos. They may well be right, and the palette could simply be an early example of Egyptian royal iconography—albeit on a small scale. Nonetheless, it seems hard to believe that warfare did not figure in some way during the power struggles that must have taken place during the late Predynastic Period when early Egyptian kings sought to outdo each other and become top dog in the incipient state. Furthermore, it may or may not have been Narmer who was the first ruler to unify both Upper and Lower Egypt, but the imagery that appears on both sides of the palette "might . . . be taken as evidence that he is at least claiming to be the king of the whole of Egypt."[13]

Another significant artifact found in the Main Deposit was the pear-shaped, ceremonial limestone mace head that features relief decoration depicting an early king wearing the white crown of Upper Egypt, who is involved in a ceremony celebrating either the foundation of a temple or the initiation of an irrigation project. In front of the king's face there is a scorpion hieroglyph, and this has led to his being dubbed "King Scorpion," although it is possible that King Scorpion and King Narmer are actually one and the same person. Running around the top of the mace head is a decorative frieze depicting lapwings hanging by their necks from vertical standards. As the lapwing was used as a hieroglyph meaning "common people," it is possible that they allude to the various enemies that the king had conquered.

The other notable late Predynastic/Early Dynastic objects from the Main Deposit are the "Two-Dogs Palette" and the "Narmer Wedding Mace-head." Although smaller than the Narmer Palette, the raised relief decoration on the Two-Dogs Palette is as fine as that seen on the former, and the mythical and real animals seen attacking each other on its two sides may again point toward the conflicts that took place during the unification of Lower and Upper Egypt. On the Narmer Wedding Macehead, the king is depicted on a dais awaiting the arrival of a female figure in a carrying chair. It has been suggested that this scene could perhaps commemorate the wedding of the southern king Narmer to a northern princess, which helped to consolidate a newly unified country by creating a royal family drawn from both Lower and Upper Egypt.[14]

Another significant discovery made during Quibell and Green's excavations was the decorated "Tomb 100," which was located on the eastern edge of the settlement. This subterranean mud-brick tomb was probably the final resting place of a late Predynastic chieftain or king of the Gerzean/Naqada II Period. As well as containing various artifacts such as stone and pottery vessels and a finely worked forked flint spearhead, one of its walls was decorated with a remarkable painted scene (later removed to the Egyptian Museum in Cairo by Green). Included in this rare and ancient artwork are depictions of a conqueror threatening bound captives with a mace, figures wearing kilts, who seem to be dancing, various animals (e.g., gazelle and lions), and distinctive bow-shaped ships with high prows and sterns that carry passengers. It has been noted that the tomb "is important as an indicator of the growing social stratification of Egyptian society [during the late Predynastic], as well as a document showing the conventions and motifs of Egyptian art in process of formation."[15] It has also been argued that "the person once buried in the decorated tomb deserves consideration as one of the legendary kings of Upper Egypt."[16]

## A WAR GRAVE FROM THE MIDDLE KINGDOM

Many of the countless visitors who flock to the mortuary temple of the famous Egyptian queen Hatshepsut, at Deir el-Bahri on the west bank at Thebes, are probably unaware that in the earlier twentieth century, a gruesome discovery was made in the steep cliffs that form a spectacular backdrop to this magnificent monument. The story of the find begins in the spring of 1923, when a team from the Metropolitan Museum of Art in New York, led by Herbert Winlock, found a previously unknown tomb directly above the mortuary temple of Mentuhotep II (which lies adjacent to Hatshepsut's temple), and next to that of Khety, the king's chancellor.

As it was the end of the season, the team from the Met made only a cursory inspection of the tomb, discovering that although it had long since been plundered it still contained many corpses, and in 1925, they returned to make a more thorough investigation of the dead bodies. At first, it was thought that they might be those of early Coptic Christians, but the team soon changed their minds when they realized that that some of the linen mummy wrappings stripped from the bodies featured typical Middle Kingdom names such as Ameny, Sebebekhotep, and Sebekhnaht.

The anatomist Dr. Douglas Derry subsequently arrived from Cairo to lead the examination of the dead. The fact that they were all young males, and had short bobbed hairstyles similar to those seen on the wooden models of Middle Kingdom soldiers found in 1893 in Prince Meseheti's tomb at Asyut, made Winlock and his colleagues wonder whether they were soldiers too. They soon found out that not only was their theory correct, but the soldiers had clearly died on the battlefield:

> We . . . had methodically measured the first nine bodies when the tenth was put on the table and Brewster noticed an arrow-tip sticking out of its chest . . . Up to that time our work-tent had been a mere laboratory. From this moment onward it took on some of the gruesomeness of a field dressing-station—only the front was four thousand years away.[17]

At least ten of the men had been hit or killed by ebony-tipped arrows, and about thirty others displayed serious or lethal head wounds. The massive injuries seen on several skulls showed that the enemy had also viciously clubbed some of the soldiers on the left side of the face as they lay on the ground, and small, depressed fractures seen on others pointed to the use of slingshots. It was also clear that vultures or other carrion birds had scavenged at least six of the bodies, indicating that the dead men had lain for some time on the battlefield before they were retrieved by their comrades. Several bracers (archer's wrist guards that protect from the lash of the bowstring) were found amongst the dead, one of which was still tied around the wrist of its owner, suggesting that at least some of the dead had been part of an Egyptian archery unit.

The location of the battlefield on which these soldiers lost their lives can never be known for sure, but it could be that they died storming a fortress during the last phase of the civil war between the southern Theban Dynasty and the northern Herakleopolitan Dynasty. This war ended in victory for Mentuhotep II, who reunited the country not long after the death of Merykara, the last significant Herakleopolitan ruler. It is perhaps even possible that these soldiers were heroes of an assault on the city of Herakleopolis itself and were thus accorded the honor of being buried close to Mentuhotep's temple. Alternatively, it may be that the soldiers were killed in a conflict closer to home and at a somewhat later date in the Twelfth Dynasty. Whatever the truth is, there can be no doubt that their bodies provide a graphic testimony to a savage encounter that took place somewhere in ancient Egypt during the Middle Kingdom.

## THE DEIR EL-BAHRI CACHE

As darkly fascinating as the soldiers' tomb is, it cannot compete with the hugely important discovery also made at Deir el-Bahri in the later nineteenth century. In 1871, a notorious local tomb robber Ahmed Abd el-Rassul, who was perhaps looking for a lost goat that had strayed, or, more probably, looking for new "business opportunities," discovered a previously undiscovered tomb (designated as Tomb DB320) belonging to the Theban high priest of Amun Pinudjem II (who was effectively the ruler of southern Egypt in the late New Kingdom) and his family.

The Pinudjem family still lay in their coffins, untouched, like the many grave goods (there were around six thousand, although the majority were *shabti* figures placed in the tomb to "magically" serve Pinudjem and his family in the afterlife) that were stacked high in their tomb, and el-Rassul must have been mightily pleased with his "accidental discovery." He must have been even more pleased with the fact that the corridors and side chamber were also stacked high with numerous coffins, some of which were adorned with the royal *uraeus*, or cobra. He soon discovered, however, that their royal occupants had long since been stripped of the valuable amulets and jewelry that would have covered their bodies. Undeterred by this loss, over the next decade, Ahmed and his brothers gradually leaked artifacts from the tomb on to the Luxor antiquities market.

Unsurprisingly then, the authorities became ever more suspicious that locals had found a new and important tomb, and it is no surprise that Ahmed and his family were the chief suspects. Thus, in 1881, Ahmed and his brother Hussein were finally arrested and subsequently sent to Qena, where they were interrogated and tortured, but they bravely refused to give up their secret. However, their fortitude was in vain, as their elder brother Mohammed confessed all and was rewarded with a lump sum and, rather ironically, a job with the Antiquities Service.

After hearing of Ahmed's confession, Émile Brugsch, assistant to the newly appointed director of the Antiquities Service, Gaston Maspero (who was in Paris at the time), set out to investigate this hugely exciting new tomb and was obviously impressed with what he found after being lowered inside the ancient sepulcher:

> Soon we came upon cases of porcelain funerary offerings, metal and alabaster vessels, draperies and trinkets, until reaching the turn in the passage, a cluster of mummy cases came into view in such a number as to stagger me.
>
> Collecting my senses, I made the best examination of them I could by the light of my torch, and at once saw that they contained the mummies of royal personages of both sexes; and yet that was not all. Plunging on ahead of my guide, I came to the [end] chamber . . . , and there standing against the walls or here lying on the floor, I found even a greater number of mummy-cases of stupendous size and weight.
>
> Their gold coverings and their polished surfaces so plainly reflected my own excited visage that it seemed like I was looking into the faces of my own ancestors.[18]

It was an incredible discovery, as interred in the tomb was a collection of mummies belonging to various Egyptian kings, queens, lesser royals, and courtiers. Included among the collection were the mummies of Rameses I–III and IX, Sety I, Thutmose I–III, and Amenhotep I and his mother, Queen Ahmose Nefertari. The reason so many renowned Egyptian rulers and members of the royal court had ended up buried in a tomb ill-befitting their status was simple—robbery. The end of Egypt's most glorious period—the New Kingdom—was marked by instability and the gradual disintegration of the country. As a result, security within the Valley of the Kings (and elsewhere) was weak and the royal tombs were virtually unprotected from looting and desecration. The end result was that the priesthood at Thebes gathered together the mummies, and transferred them to Pinudjem's tomb, but probably not before they themselves had stripped them of much of the valuable jewelry that covered their bodies.

Gaston Maspero was given the honor of unwrapping the royal mummies from the Deir el-Bahri cache and he began with that of Thutmose III, but the king was in a sorry state, as tomb robbers had cut his head and limbs from his body and his penis was also missing. His face, though, was in a better condition and it showed that Thutmose had buckteeth and was a bald old man when he departed for the Egyptian afterlife.

After he unwrapped the mummy of Egypt's greatest pharaoh, Rameses II, Maspero found that the body of the famous king was well preserved. He tells us: "The eyebrows are thick and white, the eyes are small and close together; the nose is thin and long like the hooked noses of the Bourbons and slightly crushed at the tip by the pressure of the bandages."[19] Although Rameses' hair had gone white in his old age (he was around ninety when he died), it had originally been red, which would have been very uncommon in ancient Egypt, and in his prime he must have been a very striking individual.

However, the mummy of Rameses III was not in a good condition, as it was coated with a thick black embalming resin that had to be chipped away. That of Queen Ahmose Nefertari was in an even worse state, as the body of the famous queen[20] deteriorated when exposed to the humidity of Cairo and smelled so bad that it had to be buried underneath the museum storehouse until the smell had dissipated.

Also included in Tomb DB320 was the body of an unknown male, rolled up in dirty sheep or goat skin in a simple, undecorated wooden coffin. The man's feet and hands were bound and his "face was twisted in a grimace of unspeakable anguish"[21]; his body also showed no signs of mummification. Was this man a tomb robber who had been caught by the necropolis guards and who subsequently paid the ultimate price for his sacrilege? Alternatively, it is conceivable that the body is that of the executed Prince Pentawere, one of Rameses' sons, and one of the chief conspirators of the famous "Harem Conspiracy" in which Rameses III was probably assassinated. It has to be said that although the young man's "grimace of unspeakable anguish" was more probably caused by natural postmortem changes, the idea that he died horrifically (perhaps even being buried alive) should not be ruled out.

There is some debate as to whether Rameses III was actually murdered during the failed palace coup in 1155 BC that involved members of his harem.[22] However, a recent scientific examination of Rameses III's mummy by Zahi Hawass and his colleagues[23] strongly indicates that the king was indeed murdered. The team found that Rameses had a large deep wound in his throat directly under the larynx, probably caused by a sharp blade of some sort. They also found that the ancient Egyptian embalmers had inserted an Eye of Horus amulet (used as a healing charm), suggesting that the wound was already present before the embalming process began. Hawass and his team also examined the body of the unknown man from

DB320, and interestingly concluded from their DNA analysis that he was very probably Rameses' son, and furthermore, that it was possible that he died through strangulation.

The Deir el-Bahri cache was not alone, as in 1898, the French Egyptologist Victor Loret discovered another one in KV35—the tomb of Amenhotep II. Included in this second collection of Egyptian royals was not only Amenhotep II's mummy, but also those of Thutmose IV, Amenhotep III, Merenptah, Sety II, Siptah, and Rameses IV–VI. Hieroglyphic inscriptions on labels found attached to some of the mummies show that they had been removed for safety to KV35 on the orders of Pinudjem, high priest of Amun.

## DISCOVERIES FROM THE CITY OF THE SUN-GOD

One of the most famous (or infamous) figures from ancient Egypt is the so-called Heretic Pharaoh, Akhenaten, the architect of a radical religious experiment that saw the traditional gods and goddesses of the Egyptian pantheon replaced by a solar religion that centered on the worship of the Aten ("the sun-disc"). In the fifth year of his reign, Akhenaten turned his back on the ancient religious and administrative capitals of Thebes and Memphis and founded a new royal city on the east bank of the Nile that lay about midway between the two ancient cities. The new capital was known as Akhetaten ("horizon of the Aten"), although today, the site is known as Amarna, after the modern village located nearby. Archaeological work at Amarna has been ongoing since the late nineteenth century and this has provided us with an unrivalled picture of life in a New Kingdom city in ancient Egypt—albeit a short-lived one (Amarna was abandoned after Akhenaten's death and was only occupied for about thirty years). These various archaeological investigations have yielded many fascinating reminders of the city's occupants, but a handful of finds stand out above all others.

The first—and most famous—of these is the Nefertiti bust, which was discovered in the early twentieth century during excavations carried out at Amarna by a team from the Deutsche Orient-Gesellschaft (German Oriental Society), who were led by one of early Egyptology's noteworthy figures—Ludwig Borchardt. The bust was unearthed in the studio of Thutmose, "the Chief of Works, the Sculptor," whose ruined mud-brick villa lies in the southern suburbs of Amarna, the location of the workshops that were engaged in the production of various items for the palaces and temples of Akhenaten's new city.

Along with the Nefertiti bust, there was a collection of superbly sculpted stone heads depicting Nefertiti and also other members of the Amarna

A face from the past. A haunting mummy portrait of a priest of the Greco-Roman god Serapis, from a Roman Period burial (c.140–160 AD) found at Hawara. © Trustees of the British Museum

royal family and court (e.g., the daughters of the king and queen, and Kiya, Akhenaten's secondary wife). Over twenty plaster casts that served as prototypes for the finished stone versions were also found along with carved stone limbs that like the stone heads were made for composite statues.

The Nefertiti bust measures forty-eight centimeters high and is made from rather fragile limestone, with its irregularities smoothed out with a layer of gypsum plaster. This would have provided a good surface on which to paint the details of Nefertiti's face, and these have survived remarkably well given that Thutmose made the bust well over three thousand years ago. On her head, Nefertiti wears her distinctive blue flat-topped crown, around which are wrapped colored streamers of gold, red, and blue, and these are mirrored in the beautiful bead necklace she wears around her slender (and exaggerated) neck. Her face is painted a pale pink-brown color, which nicely sets off the deep red-brown of her lips, the black of her slim, arched eyebrows, and the kohl makeup that rings her "eyes" (only one rock crystal eye actually survives; the other one was already missing when the bust was found).

There can be no denying that this royal face from the ancient world is a beguiling sight, yet the Nefertiti bust may not be actually a true reflection of the queen's appearance, and rather could be an idealized image of royal beauty such as can be seen in the many surviving statues depicting Egypt's kings. Nevertheless, in many people's eyes, the famous queen remains one of the most beautiful women of the ancient world, and doubtless, she will continue to enjoy this reputation in the future.

As impressive as the finds from the workshop of Thutmose are, they are not as significant—at least in historical terms—as the so-called Amarna Letters. These small but famous artifacts were discovered in 1887 by a local woman digging out decayed mud-bricks or *sebakh* from the ancient mud-brick buildings at Amarna (decayed mud-brick makes a very good fertilizer as it is rich in phosphates). The letters take the form of small pillow-shaped clay "cuneiform" tablets (around four hundred of which now survive in various museums and private collections around the world) bearing inscribed texts in the wedge-shaped cuneiform script that was commonly used throughout the ancient states of the Near East for recordkeeping and diplomatic correspondence.

We will look at the Amarna Letters in more detail in chapter six, but it is worth noting that they were recovered from the remains of a mud-brick building, some of which were stamped with the legend: "The House of Correspondence of Pharaoh, life! prosperity! health!" It appears that this building had originally been the equivalent of the "Foreign Office" at

Amarna, where incoming cuneiform letters from Egypt's various allies and vassal states were filed away, and was the place where busy scribes had also presumably worked on the outgoing ones sent to these foreign kingdoms.

The first scientific excavations at Amarna took place in 1891–1892 and were directed by the famous English Egyptologist Flinders Petrie, who was assisted by the young Howard Carter, whose own fame would later eclipse Petrie's as a result of his spectacular discovery of the tomb of Tutankhamen. As well as locating the Foreign Office, and several further Amarna letters, Petrie made many other exciting discoveries, such as the remains of pottery vessels that had been imported from the kingdom of Mycenae in Greece.

Petrie's greatest achievement at Amarna, however, was to uncover the remains of exquisite paintings that had adorned its royal buildings. The most famous of the paintings came from the building dubbed the "King's House," where Petrie found part of a rather touching wall scene depicting Akhenaten, Nefertiti, and two of their daughters, who show the distinctive elongated skulls that are a characteristic feature of Amarna art. This fragmentary yet extraordinary artwork is rightly viewed as one of the greatest to have survived from ancient Egypt.

In the nearby building known as the Great Palace, Petrie discovered further stunning paintings surviving in varying states of preservation on three pavements located in two large rooms in the areas known as the North Harem and the Main Hall. In total, around 210 square meters of paintings survived, with the best preserved being those seen on the Great Pavement in Room E of the North Harem. Here, artists had painted captured Nubians and Syrians on the central pathway that divided the room in two (thus allowing the king to symbolically trample his enemies underfoot) and two rectangular ponds bordered by marsh plants, with ducks flying over the ponds and charming calves gamboling amongst the vegetation. The painted pavements found in Room F and the Main Hall were similar to those in Room E, with rectangular fish-filled pools flanked by duck and marsh scenes with leaping bulls (one attacking a lion), calves, and a kingfisher; central pathways depicted defeated Nubians and Syrians; bordering the pavements were depictions of bouquets and offering stands.

After Petrie had cleaned and stabilized the paintings by covering them with a thin coating of tapioca water, a shed was built over the Great Pavement to further protect this remarkable yet fragile reminder of the short-lived glory of Amarna. Tragically, though, the painted pavements in the Great Palace were hacked up by a local farmer perhaps fed up with his fields being trampled by the many tourists who had to cross his land to see them (the Egyptian Antiquities Department had not provided a footpath to

the site, but it is also possible that they were destroyed as the result of a local feud). Fragments of the paintings were fortunately salvageable and can
be seen today in the Egyptian Museum, but although these fragments are
still beautiful to look at, they provide a sad reminder of the greater artistic
treasures that were lost when the painted pavements were vandalized.

## BURIAL PLACE OF THE SACRED APIS BULLS

In the first century BC, the Greek geographer Strabo wrote of the Serapeum, the burial place of the Apis bulls at the Saqqara necropolis near
Cairo. These sacred animals were seen by the ancient Egyptians as the
physical embodiment or "messengers" of Ptah, the creator-god associated
with nearby Memphis, the capital of Egypt for much of the Pharaonic Period. However, in time, the desert sands completely covered the Serapeum
and it became lost, with Strabo's words all that remained to testify to its
existence. In the nineteenth century, Napoleon's *savants* searched for the
Serapeum to no avail, but some fifty years later, another Frenchman struck
luck and found the famous cult site, in the process revealing one of the true
wonders of ancient Egypt.

The Frenchman in question was Auguste Mariette, one of the most notable figures in the early story of Egyptology. In 1850, Mariette traveled
to Cairo on behalf of the Bibliothèque nationale in Paris to acquire early
Christian Coptic manuscripts, but he also intended to search for ancient
Egyptian antiquities while he was in Egypt. This was not surprising given
that he was junior curator at the Louvre Museum and was passionate about
ancient Egypt.

After his attempts to acquire manuscripts met with no success, Mariette
was thus able to turn his full attention to ancient Egypt. After seeing sphinx
statues that had come from Saqqara, in both Alexandria and Cairo, he began to wonder whether they could have come from the avenue of sphinxes
that Strabo mentioned in his account of the Serapeum. He soon found out,
as shortly afterward, while planning tombs at Saqqara, Mariette stumbled
across a statue of a sphinx buried up to its neck in the sand. Realizing that
this statue was probably still in its original location, Mariette assembled a
team of local workmen to search for more. Within a short space of time they
had uncovered over a hundred more sphinxes that lined a great proces-
sional way, at the end of which, nearly a year later, Mariette discovered the
remains of the Serapeum temple, and the entrance to the sacred catacombs
of the Apis bulls lay beneath it.[24]

We can only imagine Mariette's excitement as he and his workmen explored the dark and echoing spaces of the Serapeum by torchlight, the first people to do so in a very long time, but it must have been a remarkable and somewhat eerie experience. Their explorations revealed a truly impressive subterranean building, with its major architectural component (the "Greater Vaults") a wide and lofty gallery with side chambers containing twenty-four massive granite sarcophagi (weighing as much as eighty tons). These contained the mummified burials of the sacred Apis bulls dating from the reign of Psamtek I of the Twenty-Sixth Dynasty to the late Ptolemaic period.

Unfortunately, the stone coffins had all been plundered in antiquity, but early in 1852, more smaller galleries with side chambers were discovered. Here in the "Lesser Vaults," bull burials dating from the New Kingdom to the Third Intermediate Period were placed in wooden rather than stone coffins, and remarkably, one survived intact. This was inscribed with the titles of Rameses II's son, Khaemwaset, and inside the coffin was a sheet-gold anthropoid mask lying among poorly preserved bones. Mariette thus concluded that rather than an Apis bull, the coffin had contained Khaemwaset, who was involved in the construction of some of the Serapeum's vaults. Although not all Egyptologists agree, and some argue instead that the badly decayed remains were actually those of an Apis bull, many have nevertheless followed Mariette's lead.

As Mariette continued his exploration of the Serapeum he unearthed a third series of bull burials in smaller vaults dating to the Eighteenth and Nineteenth Dynasties of the New Kingdom, and Mariette was again highly fortunate to discover an intact burial in one of these. As well as recovering fragmented (and perhaps cooked) skeletons of two bulls from two huge coffins, Mariette also found many interesting funerary goods of a high quality. These included two decorated shrines (each of which contained four faience statues dedicated by the vizier Paser) depicting Rameses II and Khaemwaset making offerings before the Apis bull, a tall wooden statue of Osiris[25] gilded with gold leaf, and four large alabaster Canopic jars containing the embalmed viscera of the bulls. Set in the floor of the burial chamber were some 250 *shabti* figures made from calcite and faience, and also found were fifteen bull-headed *shabtis*, various items of gold jewelry including a superb gold pectoral ornament of a falcon with a ram's head, and stone amulets. Perhaps, though, it was the footprints that were still clearly visible in the sand on the floor of the chamber that were the most remarkable find of all. These had survived for some four thousand years, a ghostly reminder of the priests responsible for the burial of the two sacred bulls.

## THE ROYAL BURIALS AT TANIS

Given the huge range of stunning artifacts found inside Tutankhamen's tomb, it is hardly surprising that it is often seen as the greatest archaeological discovery ever made. However, at the ancient city of Tanis in the Delta, the French Egyptologist Pierre Montet discovered a series of royal burials that come a close second to that of Tutankhamen. Despite this, these burials are not well known outside Egyptological circles, as their discovery during the early years of World War II, when the eyes of the world were obviously elsewhere, meant that they did not receive the full attention they deserved. The fact that the burials were subsequently published in French (*La nécropole royale de Tanis*, 1947–1961) has not helped in this regard either.

Pierre Montet began his excavations at Tanis in 1928, assuming that he was excavating Pi-Ramesses, the new capital built by Sety I and his successor, Rameses II. This was understandable given that many monuments attributed to the latter were strewn all over the site. However, Egyptologists have since realized that the actual site of Pi-Ramesses is at Qantir, some thirteen miles from Tanis, and that the Libyan kings of the Twenty-First and Twenty-Second Dynasties had simply recycled monuments from Qantir to be used in their new capital in the Delta.

It was not until 1939, when Montet was excavating in the area of the Great Temple of Amun, that he fortuitously found a deep hole leading to the underground burial chambers of the Tanite kings. The first tomb he found was that of Osorkon II, which contained a marvelous Middle Kingdom sarcophagus belonging to his father, Takelot I, and other objects such as hundreds of *shabti* figures.

After Osorkon's tomb had been cleared, Montet discovered an adjoining burial chamber, but this one had escaped the attention of the tomb robbers and inside it, lying on the floor, was an extraordinary falcon-headed coffin made from solid silver. Also in the tomb were four enchanting miniature silver coffins that were receptacles for the king's internal organs, which were removed from his body during the mummification process (Canopic jars were normally used as the containers for royal viscera).

Inscriptions on the walls of the tomb attributed it to Psusennes I. However, it soon became evident that another king was its occupant, as three days later, the coffin was opened in front of Egypt's King Farouk and inside lay a mummy wearing a beautiful golden face mask adorned with exquisite jewelry inscribed with the cartouches (royal titles) of a previously unknown king, Sheshonq IIa. On his feet, the king wore a pair of simple but fine funerary sandals made from sheet gold, and around his wrists he wore two gold bracelets inscribed with the eyes of Horus, the falcon-god who watched over and protected Egyptian kings, in lapis lazuli and carnelian. These had originally belonged to his ancestor, Sheshonq I.

In 1940, after having worked his way through more plundered burial chambers, Montet discovered an intact tomb sealed by a huge granite plug, which took his workmen nearly a week to breach. It had been worth the wait, though, as inside was the intact burial of king Psusennes I, who lay inside a beautiful silver coffin contained inside a black granite coffin. This, in turn, lay inside a huge stone coffin with a magnificent carved lid, all usurped from the burial of the pharaoh Merenptah (the fourth king of the Nineteenth Dynasty).

King Psusennes was accompanied in death by a superb range of artifacts, the most spectacular of which was the golden funerary mask covering the king's face. This mask bears witness to the great technical skills and patience possessed by ancient Egyptian goldsmiths, as does the gold collar made of five thousand separate rings that Psusennes wore in death. Two other gold collars were found on his mummy along with other exquisite items of jewelry such as an elegant arm bracelet dedicated by Smendes II, high priest of Amun at Thebes, and a scarab amulet made from green jasper and gold that had been placed with the burial to help ensure the king's admittance to the afterlife.[26] The king's fingers and toes were fitted with gold sleeves and the incision in his abdomen where the ancient embalmers had removed his internal organs during the mummification process was covered with a fine gold plaque inscribed with the Eye of Horus. A simple but beautiful lotus-shaped chalice made from gold was also recovered, along with a silver bowl with incised decoration symbolizing a pool filled with lotus flowers. A ritual brazier made in the time of Rameses II, over three hundred years previous, was also included amongst the king's grave goods.

Somewhat remarkably, Montet also discovered two further undisturbed tombs, one in 1940 and the other in 1946 when he returned to the site after the end of the war. The tomb found in 1940 contained the burial of Psusennes' possible son and successor, Amenemope, in a chamber intended for Psusennes' wife, Mutnedjmet. Amenemope's wooden coffin was gilded with gold and his mummy was accompanied by an array of beautiful jewelry including a marvelous Horus-falcon pectoral, its outstretched wings inlaid with hundreds of pieces of colored carnelian and faience.

In contrast to the earlier undisturbed tombs, the one found in 1946 did not contain a royal burial, but rather that of Psusennes' general, Wendjbaendjed. The fact that the general was accorded the privilege of being buried in the same royal funerary complex as Psusennes and other Tanite royalty reveals that his king must have thought very highly of him. This is further revealed by the beautiful and unusual bowl that was found in the general's richly equipped tomb, which features an inscription around its inner edge proclaiming it was a gift from Psusennes. The main body of the bowl is made from silver and in its center is a chrysanthemum motif made from inlaid glass paste, which is surrounded by a sheet-gold relief depicting four young women catching ducks in a fish-filled pool covered with lotus flowers. Other star finds from the general's tomb were his simple, but beautiful, sheet-gold funerary mask, and a ring with a lapis lazuli seal inscribed with the name of Rameses IX, who had died around two hundred years earlier.

## VALLEY OF THE GOLDEN MUMMIES

One of the most spectacular discoveries from ancient Egypt was made more recently at Bahariya Oasis in Egypt's Western Desert. The story of this discovery starts in 1996, when an antiquities guard from the Temple of Alexander the Great was riding his donkey in the desert not far from the oasis' capital, Balat, when the donkey tripped and caught its leg in a hole. Getting off to look, the guard discovered the entrance to a tomb in which he could glimpse gold.

This chance discovery led local antiquities inspectors to the site and they discovered four subterranean rock-cut tombs, but these were not excavated until 1999, by Zahi Hawass and his colleagues. They turned first to Tomb 54, uncovering eight steps leading down into a small room and two connecting burial chambers, with a small "delivery" room the place where mourners handed over the deceased for internment in the tomb. In each burial chamber, there were two opposing niches cut into the sandstone walls above floor level and these formed bench-like platforms on which forty-three mummies had been laid, or in some cases actually stacked one on top of another. Poignantly, included among these mummies were those of a little boy and girl lying next to each other. It is quite probable that they were brother and sister who both died when they were only about five years old, and it also seems likely that Tomb 54 was a family tomb used over several generations (as appears likely for many other tombs in the cemetery).

Tomb 55 was quite different in plan from the above and consisted of a rock-cut shaft (about ten feet deep) at the bottom of which was a burial chamber set into each of its four walls. Seven poorly preserved mummies and a few burial goods (e.g., two pots, a copper anklet, and a faience-bead necklace) were found in two of the chambers and one well-preserved one was found on its own in a discrete niche. This mummy was later X-rayed and turned out to be a male around forty years of age who had had two of his molars extracted, indicating that there were dentists practicing in the oasis in ancient times.

Tomb 62 is the largest one yet found, and although similar in plan to Tombs 54 and 64, its thirty-two mummies were interred in shafts cut into the walls of the burial chambers rather than niches. Most of the mummies were simply wrapped in linen, although some were covered in cartonnage (a type of thin plaster consisting of layers of glued or plastered linen or papyrus), and some lay in wooden coffins. Pottery vessels and Greek and Roman coins were also found with the mummies interred in Shaft A in the first burial chamber.

In tomb 64, a total of eighteen mummies were found in burial niches and in two shafts cut into the walls on either side of the steps leading down into the delivery room. In the left-hand shaft there was a linen-wrapped child's mummy, and another child's mummy, with a gilded mask onto which a simple face had been painted, was discovered with five poorly preserved adult mummies in the right-hand shaft.

Tomb 1 only contained five mummies (four in clay coffins, one in an anthropoid coffin in the top of the tomb shaft), but various types of pottery vessels were found in a chamber between the delivery room and burial chamber, which may have been an offering room used by relatives who came to visit the deceased. Two small paintings of the god Anubis (protector of the dead) were painted on either side of the entrance to the burial chamber.

As well as the artifacts mentioned above, many other interesting grave goods came from the tombs, such as a carved wooden head of the lion-goddess of war, Sekhmet, and four clay statuettes of mourning women with their hands placed on their heads or over their eyes. Even more touching are the toys placed with the children's mummies, which included a charming model of a terracotta pony or horse. Along with many large pottery vessels, there were small glass vessels with long necks that may have held some type of liquid (e.g., wine) or perhaps an ointment of some sort (e.g., kohl for eye makeup), and a small but lovely pottery vessel painted with lotus flower decoration.

It is clear from the slightly crude but nonetheless striking and complex decoration seen on the mummies found in this oasis cemetery (and from the artifacts that accompany them) that they date to the Greco-Roman Period (first and second centuries AD). Hawass has identified four distinct types of mummies, with the first featuring impressive face masks gilded with gold leaf and gilded and embossed cartonnage, and chest plates that depict various Egyptian deities. Several of these mummies also have striking headbands containing colored inlays of faience and semiprecious stones. The second mummy type also have golden facemasks, but their upper bodies are usually covered in a thick layer of cartonnage that is brightly painted with religious imagery. The third type are not painted or gilded, but are tightly wrapped in dyed linen that has often been carefully arranged around the body to form quite complex geometric patterns. In marked contrast to the above is the fourth mummy type, which are poorly wrapped and undecorated, with bodies often badly preserved as a result. The differences in mummy types point strongly toward marked social divisions in the communities of Bahariya Oasis, with an elite who were probably wealthy landowners and merchants who had grown rich on the many products the oasis produced (e.g., wine, figs, and dates), and a middle and working class below them.

The handful of Greco-Roman tombs mentioned here are just the tip of the iceberg, as astonishingly, it has been estimated that they are located in a cemetery that could cover as much as four square miles and contain as many as ten thousand mummies. The further discovery of the burial of a Twenty-Sixth Dynasty governor of Bahariya Oasis has also revealed that not all of its occupants date to the Greek or Roman Period. The cemetery has since become known as the Valley of the Golden Mummies after the large depression in which it is located, and no doubt many ancient treasures are still waiting to be discovered beneath its sands.

We will leave the Valley of the Golden Mummies with the words of Zahi Hawass, which capture what was obviously a memorable and sometimes unsettling experience for those who carried out the initial excavations at this huge, ancient necropolis:

> As you slowly brush sand away from around a mummy, you never quite know the exact moment when the mummy's features will emerge. Suddenly its eyes will pop out from the sand, staring directly at you. These eyes are beautifully crafted and inlaid with white marble around a black obsidian iris . . . at midday they reflect light in a way that gives them a kind of glint. In some cases, the eyes are even set in bronze or copper with thin spikes for eyelashes, which makes the effect even more uncannily realistic. In a few of the mummies the eyes had somehow shifted so that they pointed in different directions, and the effect that they made, looking every which way out of the sand as we worked, was quite unnerving.[27]

## PORTRAITS FROM THE PAST

Although the burials from the Valley of the Golden Mummies may have given Hawass and his colleagues the jitters from time to time, there are mummies from the Faiyum that are truly haunting, as they allow us to gaze into the actual faces of people who lived and died in this fertile region some two thousand years ago.

What makes these mummies so special is that they were found with life-like portraits of the dead that are painted on attached wooden boards, or on the actual linen of the mummy wrappings.[28] That the so-called Faiyum Portraits are Roman in date is clearly shown by the hairstyles, dress, and jewelry of the people who are portrayed, and they can be compared with paintings and mosaics found at other Roman sites such as the world-famous Pompeii in Italy. Similar mummy portraits have been found at other sites in Egypt, such as the city of Antinoopolis (founded by the emperor Hadrian in 130 AD), but the majority have come from the Faiyum.

The Faiyum Portraits were known about as early as the beginning of the seventeenth century, when the traveler Pietro della Valle brought back examples to his native Italy. In the later nineteenth century, an enterprising Austrian antiquities dealer named Theodor Graf bought many examples from locals, who had dug them up from a Roman cemetery near the town of el-Rubaiyat. He subsequently sold and exhibited them worldwide, and some examples made their way into the hands of famous figures such as Sigmund Freud, the famous founder of psychoanalysis.

In 1888, Flinders Petrie was at Hawara in the southeast of the Faiyum, excavating the pyramid complex of the Middle Kingdom pharaoh Amenemhat III, and accidentally discovered an extensive cemetery of Roman mud-brick tombs. He was not particularly concerned with the Roman tombs, but a day after this discovery—just as he was about to turn his attentions elsewhere—a mummy with a painted portrait on a wooden panel was found, showing "a beautifully drawn head of a girl, in soft grey tints, entirely classical in its style and mode."[29] Another portrait was soon unearthed and showed a "young married woman of about 25; of a sweet but dignified expression; with beautiful features and a fine complexion. She wears pearl earrings and a gold necklace."[30] The cemetery yielded up many more mummy portraits, and in total, Petrie recovered sixty; when he returned to the site a few years later he was rewarded with a similar number.

These ancient faces from the past are more than just portraits, however, as "in addition to depicting the deceased, [they] convey a host of other information: age, sex, religious affiliations, and social status."[31] For the most part, the portraits are of wealthier Greeks and Romans who followed the Egyptian cults of the god and goddess Osiris and Isis, and also the Greco-Roman god Serapis. It may be possible, as Petrie suggested, that some of the portraits had originally been framed and hung on the walls of houses during the lifetime of the deceased whom they commemorated. It could perhaps even be possible that some of the portrait-mummies themselves were kept on display in houses for several years before burial.

It is evident that not all of the Faiyum portraits are true likenesses of the dead, as separate portraits have been discovered showing individuals who have almost identical faces and clothing, and such paintings thus represent "absolutely standard production-line pieces"[32] produced by separate workshops in the Faiyum. However, there can be no doubt that many of the faces that stare back at us from the Faiyum Portraits are the ones that their owners would have seen if they looked in a mirror some two thousand years ago.

## KING KHUFU'S SKY BOATS

In 1954, an inspector with the Egyptian Antiquities Service named Kamal el-Mallakh was undertaking routine excavations around the Great Pyramid of Khufu at Giza and stumbled across a pair of long, rectangular pits oriented east to west, lying end to end immediately to the south of the pyramid. On closer inspection, el-Mallakh discovered that both pits had been covered over with massive limestone slabs (weighing around sixteen tons each) and that one of the slabs in the eastern pit had been inscribed with a cartouche containing the name of Khufu's son and successor, Djedefre, suggesting that he had ordered the pit to be covered over with the massive slabs.

It was possible, then, that the two pits could well contain something special, and after overcoming the reluctance of his superiors, who believed that they were actually part of the pyramid's foundations or a paved courtyard, el-Mallakh made a hole in one of the slabs covering the eastern pit. Inserting his torch into the hole, he was amazed to see its beam illuminating the remains of a full-size dismantled boat lying in the pit. In total, there were 1,224 separate pieces of timber, carefully piled up in thirteen layers, as well as six pairs of oars. George Reisner had previously discovered another three boat pits on the eastern side of the Great Pyramid, but unfortunately, these only contained badly decayed fragments of wood inlaid with fragments of gold leaf—hinting at the former splendor of the boats.

Luckily, the roofing slabs had provided an airtight seal, which provided excellent conditions for the preservation of the boat, and its timbers were generally found to be very well preserved, leaving the way open for its reconstruction. This was carried out by the highly skilled Egyptian conservator Hag Ahmed Youssef, who, after over a decade of extremely painstaking work, was finally able in 1968 to present to the world a fully reconstructed royal boat or "barque" of the Fourth Dynasty. This measures some forty-four meters in length, around six meters across at its widest point, and weighs in at around forty-five tons, with its curved bow and stern rising to around seven meters in height. The boat also has a large cabin, which is divided into two separate compartments by a wooden partition. Examination of the boat's separate components revealed that although a variety of different woods had been used in its construction, the majority of the boat was made from cedar imported from Lebanon. Today, this superbly reconstructed ancient vessel can be seen in the museum that was specifically built for it alongside the Great Pyramid at Giza, and every year, many thousands of visitors come to gaze on this amazing relic from the ancient world.

The presence of a second boat was suspected in the western pit but was not confirmed until 1987, when Japanese archaeologists drilled a hole through one of its covering limestone slabs, inserting a camera to reveal its dismantled cedar planks. Unfortunately, when a team from Waseda University scientifically analyzed the dismantled boat in 1992 and 1993, they found that it had been getting seriously damaged. This damage was being caused by water leaking into the pit from the nearby museum in which its counterpart was housed, and also by insects and fungi that had entered the pit when it was breached. It thus became a priority to remove and restore the boat in the western pit before it became irreparably damaged. However, it was not until 2011 that the huge slabs covering the pit began to be removed by the Waseda team, and it was another two years before the boat began to be removed from its ancient burial place. A cartouche bearing the name of Khufu was found on part of the boat and radiocarbon dates taken on its timbers suggest that it was over 4,500 years old.

It is hoped (perhaps optimistically) that the study, preservation, and reconstruction of the boat can be achieved within five years, and it will then be displayed on the entrance to the Giza Plateau and the great pyramids, providing visitors with an impressive welcome to one of the world's most famous ancient sites.

Several other boat burials have been found at various royal and non-royal funerary sites in Egypt. These include the six found in the late nineteenth century by the French Egyptologist Jacques de Morgan at the Middle

The magnificent royal boat found alongside the Great Pyramid of King Khufu at Giza, where it can now be seen in its purpose-built museum. Photo, taken 3 November 2010, courtesy of Berthold Werner

Kingdom pyramid complex of Senwosret III at Dashur, the two boats buried in chambers on top of the Sixth Dynasty mastaba tomb of the vizier
Kagemni at Saqqara, and most notably, the fleet of fourteen Early Dynastic (c.3000 BC) vessels uncovered at Abydos in 2000 by the University of
Pennsylvania. However, none of the boats found at these or any of the other
sites can match the splendor of the one found by Kamal el-Mallakh at the
Great Pyramid, and it is perhaps unlikely that a comparable vessel will ever
be discovered beneath Egypt's sands.

There are a number of theories regarding the meaning of the Egyptian
boat burials, with perhaps the most popular—at least in regard to the royal
examples—being that the boats were solar barques used by the king to
eternally sail across the sky after he had been united with the sun-god Ra,
illuminating both the land of the living and the dead as he traveled from
east to west by day, and west to east by night. Another popular idea is that
the royal boats were simply used to ferry the dead king's body downstream
on a pilgrimage to the tomb of the god Osiris at Abydos, and then back
upstream to his final resting place in his pyramid. However, it is probably more likely that the boats did have a spiritual rather than a practical
purpose, and that they were provided for pharaohs and the non-royal elite
alike, as otherworldly craft in which they could make journeys across the
day and night sky.

## WONDERFUL THINGS

> We had now dug in the Valley for several seasons with extremely scanty re-
> sults, and it became a much debated question whether we should continue the
> work, or try for a more profitable site elsewhere. After these barren years were
> we justified in going on with it? My own feeling was that so long as a single
> area of untouched ground remained the risk was worth taking. It is true that
> you may find less in more time in the Valley than in any other site in Egypt,
> but, on the other hand, if a lucky strike be made, you will be repaid for years
> and years of dull and unprofitable work.[33]

On 4 November 1992, the English archaeologist Howard Carter made the
greatest archaeological discovery the world has yet seen when he found the
tomb (KV62) of Tutankhamen in the Valley of the Kings. It all began when
Carter's workmen stumbled across the steep, sunken stairway leading to
the tomb's outer entrance while they were clearing ancient huts, probably
belonging to workmen who had built Rameses VI's tomb. The tomb had

*The Valley of the Kings. Burial place of Egypt's New Kingdom pharaohs and the location of the world's most famous archaeological discovery—the tomb of Tutankhamen. Photo courtesy of Bjørn Christian Tørrisen*

fortuitously been hidden by the debris brought down into the valley as the result of a powerful flash flood that probably took place not long after its entrance had been sealed following the funeral. It is also now evident that the same flood covered the entrances to the recently discovered Tomb KV63, which we will examine below, and the controversial KV55, which we will return to in chapter four.

After they had cleared the mass of ancient debris filling the stairway (which contained many ancient potsherds and broken boxes), they encountered the sealed entrance, and excitingly, it bore seal impressions naming Tutankhamen, strongly suggesting that his intact royal tomb lay beyond. Carter's excitement was tempered by closer inspection of the doorway, as it had clearly been breached twice by tomb robbers from before the time of Rameses VI, with the robberies very probably taking place shortly after the burial. However, the fact that the doorway had subsequently been resealed indicated that the robbers had not plundered the tomb wholesale. Carter was thus understandably itching to break through into the tomb to see what treasures still lay inside, but he had to contain himself until his benefactor, Lord Carnarvon (who had previously carried out several excavations in and around the Valley of the Kings with Carter), arrived from England with his daughter, Lady Evelyn Herbert.

On 26 November, on the "day of days," Carter discovered a second sealed doorway that again bore seal impressions naming Tutankhamen. With Lord Carnarvon, Lady Evelyn, and Carter's friend A. R. Callender[34] looking on, Carter made a small hole in the upper left-hand corner of the doorway, inserting a candle to check that no dangerous gases lay within. Carter then widened the hole and inserting the candle farther, and he took his first look inside the tomb of Tutankhamen:

> At first I could see nothing, the hot air escaping from the chamber causing the candle flame to flicker, but presently, as my eyes grew accustomed to the light, details of the room within emerged slowly from the mist, strange animals, statues, and gold—everywhere the glint of gold. For the moment—an eternity it must have seemed to the others standing by—I was struck dumb with amazement, and when Lord Carnarvon, unable to stand the suspense any longer, inquired anxiously, "Can you see anything?" it was all I could do to get out the words, "Yes wonderful things."[35]

Wonderful things were indeed found inside this first room (the antechamber) after the blocking of the doorway was removed the next day, for it was packed full with a diverse array of artifacts, many of them very beautiful.[36] The largest objects from the antechamber are the three magnificent gilded wooden couches or beds that have fantastical-looking animal side-sections (Carter's "strange animals") supported on sturdy, rectangular frames. The side-sections of the first couch take the form of lionesses with rather friendly faces and curling tails, while the second couch has cow-headed side-sections (representing the goddess Mehetweret), again with curling tails. The third couch depicts the composite goddess Ammut ("the devourer"), who was part lioness, part hippopotamus, and part crocodile. As the antechamber only measured about twenty-six by twelve feet, the couches had been made in kit form, which enabled them to be brought into this small room and fitted together at the time of the burial by the funerary party.

The statues Carter had seen turned out to be two rather eerie, life-size figures of Tutankhamen carved from wood, their bodies painted with a shiny black resin, and their royal headdresses, broad collars, and kilts gilded with gold and inscribed with the names and titles of Tutankhamen. Blocked-up hollows in the bottom of the kilts probably reveal the hiding places for papyri featuring religious texts, but unfortunately none were forthcoming when Carter examined them and their whereabouts remain a mystery.

Several smaller pieces of funerary furniture were stored in the antechamber, including a charming little chair featuring decorated panels of ebony, ivory, and gold, probably used by Tutankhamen when he was a boy. There were also various decorated stools, feline-footed wooden beds, and a rush or wicker chair that would not look out of a place in a modern home. Best of all was the "Golden Throne" found wrapped in black linen beneath the Ammut couch. Although this throne is actually an elaborate armchair, it is undoubtedly one of the most beautiful artifacts from ancient Egypt, with superbly carved legs (leonine in form, with the front two topped by lion's heads) and openwork side panels consisting of winged, protective cobras. The chair also features an exquisite and touching scene inlaid in its sloping back. This depicts Tutankhamen and his young queen, Ankhesenamen, relaxing in one of the rooms of the royal palace:

> Through a hole in the roof the sun shoots down his life-giving protective rays. The king himself sits in an unconventional attitude upon a cushioned throne, his arm thrown carelessly across its back. Before him stands the girlish figure of the queen, putting, apparently, the last touches to his toilet: in one hand she holds a small jar of scent or ointment, and with the other she gently anoints his shoulder or adds a touch of perfume to his collar. A simple homely little composition, but how instinct with life and feeling it is, and with what a sense of movement![37]

Numerous boxes and chests also filled the antechamber, although having been ransacked by thieves—and the remaining objects subsequently bundled back into them by the necropolis officials who tidied up the chamber after the thefts—it was hard to make sense of their original contents. Nonetheless, many fine objects were found inside these boxes, including several faience vases and cups, two boomerangs made from electrum, a beautiful carved ivory casket, a calcite wine strainer, an elaborately woven garment, and a splendid ceremonial corselet featuring many thousands of inlaid pieces of gold, glass, and faience. Also found stuffed into some of the boxes were items of clothing such as the king's linen shirts and undergarments, decorated robes, and several pairs of sandals. In one of the caskets, there was a leopard-skin priest's robe decorated with gold and silver stars and a gilt-gold leopard head, an impressive scarab beetle made from gold and lapis lazuli, and a solid gold scepter.

*The beautiful and touching depiction of Tutankhamen and his queen, Ankhesenamen, inlaid in the back of the Golden Throne found in Tutankhamen's tomb by Howard Carter and Lord Carnarvon. Photo courtesy of Richard Seaman*

Many of the boxes and chests are finely decorated, but the most impressive example has to be the superb "Painted Box," with its entire surface covered with highly detailed and beautifully painted scenes (on gesso). On its sides, Tutankhamen fires arrows from his chariot at massed ranks of Syrian soldiers; on its curved lid, the king once again poses in his chariot, but this time he is hunting animals in the desert rather than battling Syrians; on the ends of the box, the king is shown as a rampant lion trampling his foes beneath his feet. Among the miscellaneous objects jumbled inside were three pairs of gold-covered sandals, a gilt headrest, and more decorated robes, one of which had been covered with around three thousand gold rosettes.

Four dismantled chariots were also found at the southeastern end of the antechamber, and three of these were lavishly and superbly decorated with gold leaf and brightly colored inlays of glass and semiprecious stones. The inner surface of one of the chariots is covered in fine raised relief decoration that features depictions of bound and kneeling Nubian and Asian captives who are flanked by royal sphinxes. It is likely that these chariots were used by Tutankhamen on state occasions, unlike the fourth, which was undecorated, and may well have been used by the king when he went on hunting expeditions.

During the preliminary investigation of the antechamber, a robber's hole was noticed underneath one of the animal couches in a small sealed doorway (around four feet high), which led to a side chamber that was subsequently dubbed the Annexe by Carter. It had obviously been ransacked by the tomb robbers: "The state of this inner room (afterwards called the Annexe) simply defies description. In the antechamber there had been some sort of attempt to tidy up after the plunderers' visit, but here everything was in confusion, just as they had left it."[38] Nevertheless, despite the tomb robbers' visit to the Annexe, over two thousand artifacts still remained inside this small chamber, many of which display exquisite workmanship. For example, there was another wonderfully decorated box and a rush-work hassock elaborately decorated with colored beadwork that features a depiction of a bound and sprawling captive. Also found amongst the confused jumble was the so-called Ecclesiastical Throne, which is actually a folding footstool made from ebony that is decorated with gold foil and inlays of faience, glass, and colored stones. There was also an impressive bed with a carved ebony frame that is entirely covered with gold leaf, and four elegant headrests inscribed with the names of Tutankhamen.

Also included in the huge collection of objects from the Annexe was a small white chair with a high back and carved animal feet that Tutankhamen had probably sat in as a child, as well as game boards.[39] There were also bows, shields, arrows, numerous alabaster vessels and wine jars, stools, baskets still containing fruit, and a box filled with what appear to have been "the knick-knacks and playthings of Tutankhamen's youth." Inside it was a miscellaneous assortment of objects: pocket-game boards, slingshots, bracelets and anklets, mechanical toys, and paint pots and pigments.

Excitingly, it was found that the two life-size statues of the king in the antechamber stood to either side of an inner sealed doorway, apparently guarding it, but Carter and his companions were rather dismayed to discover that the tomb robbers had breached it near the bottom. However, the fact that it had been resealed in antiquity gave them hope, as it indicated that the necropolis officials responsible for plugging this robber's hole believed there was something still worth protecting behind the doorway. Even so, they cannot have been prepared for the astonishing objects that were discovered behind it after its blocking had been carefully dismantled following the even more careful clearance of the antechamber, which Carter referred to as "like playing a gigantic game of spillikins" (pick-up sticks).

The dismantling of the doorway took place on Friday, 17 February 1923, in front of an assembled throng of various dignitaries, and it was not long before Carter, who was trembling with nervous excitement as he began his work, had made a hole large enough to poke a flashlight through:

> An astonishing sight its light revealed, for there, within a yard of the doorway, stretching as far [as] one could see and blocking the entrance to the chamber, stood to what all appearances was a solid wall of gold. . . .
>   We were at the entrance of the actual burial chamber of the king, and that which barred our way was the side of an immense gilt shrine built to cover and protect the sarcophagus. It was visible now from the antechamber by the light of the standard lamps, and as stone after stone was removed, and its gilded surface came gradually into view, we could, as though by an electric current, feel the excitement which thrilled the spectators behind the barrier.[40]

This stunning piece of funerary equipment, which measures approximately five by three and one-half meters and stands almost three meters high, was subsequently found to be the outermost of a nest of four beautiful gilded wooden shrines. Like their larger counterpart, the three smaller shrines are superbly decorated all over with religious iconography incised into the gold leaf that covers both their outer and inner surfaces. All the shrines have double-folding doors at their eastern ends that were shut with ebony bolts slid between two huge silver-coated staples, and the doors of the second and third shrines were found to have knotted ropes with attached necropolis seals still in place.

Lying between the third and fourth inner shrines were ceremonial bows and arrows as well as two lovely decorated fans that are gilded with gold leaf and have semicircular head pieces or "palms" mounted on long handles (approximately one meter in length). One of the fans depicts Tutankhamen out hunting in his chariot accompanied by his favorite dog, and on its reverse side he can be seen returning triumphant from the chase, with two ostriches being carried by his servants. The decayed remains of the brown and white ostrich feathers that had once adorned the top of the fans were still in place, and an inscription on the handle of the fan depicting the king in his chariot records that he obtained them "while out hunting in the desert east of Heliopolis."

Within the fourth and smallest shrine, Carter and his colleagues were thrilled to find the king's magnificent sarcophagus still in place. Made from a single block of yellow quartzite measuring three by one and one-half meters, and one and one-half meters in height, it has a curved or "cavetto cornice" top, and its surfaces are superbly decorated with deeply incised hieroglyphs and various protective symbols such as the *wedjat* eye. However, it is the guardian goddesses, Isis, Nephthys, Neith, and Selkis, who are carved in high relief on each of its four corners, with their outstretched and touching wings enveloping its sides, that provide the most striking testimony to the supreme talent of the sculptor of this masterpiece in stone.

After successfully dismantling the four shrines, the sarcophagus lid (which weighed around a ton and a quarter) was ready for lifting, but unfortunately, it was cracked, and a relatively easy task was thus made a lot more complicated. However, this problem was overcome with an elaborate pulley system, and Carter takes us back to the hugely exciting moment when the lid was lifted:

> I gave the word. Amid intense silence the huge slab, broken in two . . . rose from its bed . . . A sight met our eyes that at first puzzled us. It was a little disappointing. The contents were completely covered by fine linen shrouds. The lid being suspended in mid-air, we rolled back those covering shrouds, one by one, and as the last was removed a gasp of wonderment escaped our lips, so gorgeous was the sight that met our eyes: a golden effigy of the young boy king, of most magnificent workmanship, filled the whole of the interior of the sarcophagus.[41]

What they had found was a superbly decorated anthropoid coffin, which was the first of a series of three "that were contained one within another like so many Russian dolls." All three of the coffins are decorated all over with the *rishi* or feathered pattern and covered in layers of shining leaf and sheet gold, with inlays of precious stones and colored glass. Although they vary in their smaller details, the lids show Tutankhamen in a typical kingly pose, represented as the god Osiris with his arms crossed, the twin emblems of kingship—the crook and flail—grasped in his hands. On his head, he wears the distinctive *nemes* crown, which was actually a striped headdress adorned on the brow with figurines of the sacred cobra of Lower Egypt and the vulture goddess of Upper Egypt (Wadjit and Nekhbet). The first two coffins were constructed from wood, but the innermost example was made completely from heavy gold sheet and is "perfect both in its proportions and in the standard of craftsmanship it displays."[42] Today, the scrap value of this coffin is likely to be in the region of at least two million dollars.

With the unfastening of the lid of the third coffin, Carter was able to gaze down on the mummy of Tutankhamen, which had last been seen some three thousand years previously by the Necropolis priests who buried the young king. Sadly, the mummy wrappings were in poor condition and were blackened and cracked by the resin libations that had been liberally poured over the mummy. The later autopsy carried out on 11 November 1923 by Dr. Douglas Derry, professor of anatomy at the University of Cairo, re-

*A remarkable testimony to the skills of ancient Egyptian metalworkers. The exquisite golden funerary mask that covered the face of Tutankhamen in his coffin. Photo courtesy of Bjørn Christian Tørrisen*

vealed that Tutankhamen's body had fared little better, and was now little more than a skeleton. Derry was able to ascertain, however, that the king had been a slightly built youth who died around eighteen years of age. Unlike the young king's body, the golden portrait mask that covered his face had not suffered from the ravages of time and "stands without parallel as a masterpiece of the Egyptian metalworker's craft."[43] Made from two separate sheets of skillfully hammered gold, and inlaid with lapis lazuli, blue faience, glass, and carnelian, the mask again shows Tutankhamen wearing the *nemes* headdress, although the royal cobra and vulture on the brow are made from solid gold. Quartz and obsidian were used to model the king's eyes and heighten the lifelike appearance that the mask undoubtedly possesses.

The burial chamber was the only room in the tomb that featured decorated walls, and although the paintings found there are not particularly fine, they still possess a certain simple charm. As in other tombs in the Valley of the Kings, they comprise religious imagery; on the north wall, for example, Tutankhamen is seen being welcomed into the underworld by Osiris (into whom he and all other Egyptian kings were transformed at death), and on the west wall is an extract from the Book of Amduat (a collection of religious texts basically concerned with the nocturnal journey and rebirth of the sun-god), showing twelve baboon deities and the solar barque or boat. On the east wall, the mummified body of Tutankhamen is depicted lying in a tall decorated shrine being pulled by twelve men, two of whom are the chief ministers or viziers of Lower and Upper Egypt.

During their first entry into the burial chamber Carter and his colleagues were surprised to find a low open doorway in its eastern side that led into another small chamber. Carter says:

> We were able from we stood, to get a clear view of the whole of the contents, and a single glance sufficed to tell us that here, within this little chamber, lay the greatest treasures of the tomb. Facing the doorway on the farther side, stood the most beautiful monument that I have ever seen—so lovely that it made one gasp with wonder and admiration.[44]

What had so enthralled Carter was a decorated Canopic shrine standing against the east wall of the treasury, its top almost touching the roof of the small chamber (it measures around seven feet high). This stunning piece of funerary furniture is covered all over in gold leaf and features religious imagery in sunken relief. Around its top runs a frieze of rearing *uraei* (royal cobras) and on each of its four sides there are carved figurines of the goddesses Isis, Nephthys, Neith, and Selquet, who face inward with their arms raised in a protective gesture. Two of the goddesses are unusually depicted glancing over their shoulders, as if keeping watch for intruders. Inside the shrine itself, there was a chest containing four cylindrical hollows topped by superbly modeled calcite stoppers in the form of the king's head wearing the striped *nemes* headdress. Inside each hollow was a beautifully decorated miniature coffin containing the internal organs of the king, with the names of the deities responsible for protecting them inscribed on a central vertical band on the coffin lids: Imsety (liver), Hapy (lungs), Duamutef (stomach), and Qebhsenuef (intestines).

Although the shrine is undeniably an object of great beauty, the most striking artifact from the treasury is arguably the life-size image of the jackal-like god Anubis that sat on top of a gilded shrine in the form of a pylon (temple facade), which was mounted on long carrying poles. The pylon was located in the center of the room in front of the Canopic shrine, with Anubis facing the doorway, obviously set there to guard both the shrine and the burial chamber. The figure is carved from wood and covered in a shiny black resin, with the eyes, ears, and collar around his neck highlighted with gold leaf. When found by Carter and his team, the figure had a fine linen scarf and shawl around its neck and shoulders, and an outer linen shirt almost completely covered it. The head of Anubis was still visible, though, and his fierce, lifelike gaze was directed at those who dared to desecrate the burial chamber.

Numerous smaller items were found in the treasury, including many gilded wooden statuettes found inside the twenty-two small shrines mounted on wooden sledges that were stacked along the south wall. The statuettes (which were wearing linen shawls when Carter found them) depict Tutankhamen and various gods and goddesses. Notable examples include the two showing the king standing upon the back of black leopards, the one depicting him being borne aloft on the head of the goddess Menkeret, and the two that depict him standing on papyrus-reed rafts, his arm held aloft in the ritual act of spearing the god Seth, who is shown in the form of a hippopotamus.[45] Amongst the many other objects found in the treasury were model wooden boats, many caskets and chests still containing numerous pieces of fine jewelry, a scribe's writing kit, large numbers of *shabti* figures, a beautifully decorated bow case that would once have been attached to the king's hunting chariot, and a miniature coffin containing a lock of the hair of Tutankhamen's grandmother, Queen Tiye.

An unexpected and rather sad discovery from the treasury was the two mummified fetuses found in two miniature coffins placed inside a plain wooden box. Dr. Douglas Derry examined them and concluded that they were both baby girls, around five and seven months old, respectively, although Professor Ronald Harrison and his colleagues subsequently revised the age of the latter upward to eight or nine months.[46] More recently, however, it has been argued that the two girls did not represent two separate stillbirths, but rather were actually stillborns from a twin pregnancy.[47] Whatever the truth, it seems likely that these two girls were the daughters of Tutankhamen and Ankhesenamen.

## TOMB KV5—MAUSOLEUM OF THE SONS OF RAMESES II

The tomb of Tutankhamen may have contained the most spectacular assemblage of royal burial goods ever found in the Valley of the Kings, but the final resting place of the famous king and all the other royal tombs of the valley are truly dwarfed by the amazing Tomb KV5, which was discovered by the eminent American Egyptologist Kent Weeks in 1987. I say "discovered," but KV5 had probably been known about since the eighteenth century, and had seen limited excavations by James Burton in the early nineteenth century, with Howard Carter also making a cursory inspection of the tomb in the early twentieth century. However, not long after Carter's brief examination of the tomb, it joined the list of other tombs in the Valley of the Kings that have been mapped by earlier explorers and Egyptologists but have since been unfortunately lost.

Nevertheless, these maps showed Weeks that KV5 was probably located near the valley's entrance, and in 1989, just as his Theban Mapping Project[48] was coming to an end, he was handed an urgent reason (and an opportunity) to find the lost tomb: the Egyptian Antiquities Organization (EAO) had decided to widen the entrance to the valley to ease the problem of tourist traffic, thus raising the threat of serious damage to KV5. Weeks was thus given the green light by the EAO, and after some time and a lot of hard digging by Weeks' skilled local workmen, the debris-choked entrance and first chamber were revealed, with the channel that Burton had cut through the debris still clearly visible.

Burton was only able to partially excavate three chambers, and although he knew that more were to be found in KV5, he would surely have been staggered at what has since come to light as a result of the painstaking and backbreaking work carried out by Weeks and his team since their rediscovery of the tomb. What they have uncovered so far is an enormous underground labyrinth that "probably contains more than 150 corridors and chambers"[49] along with a huge central hall with sixteen columns, upon the ceiling of which Burton left his autograph in candle smoke. The massive scale of the tomb, coupled with the fact that it is filled with extensive amounts of debris brought in by at least six major flash floods, and that there have also been numerous ceiling collapses, means that it will be many years before the true size and plan of the tomb are known for sure. We can be in little doubt, though, that this future work will reveal many more chambers and also increase our admiration for the builders of this magnificent tomb.

Many of the walls of the tomb's corridors and chambers are decorated with fine relief carvings, with some still carrying traces of the paint with which they had originally been brilliantly colored (red, white, and blue were the dominant colors used). Undoubtedly, one of the most notable carvings from the tomb is the statue of Osiris, god of the underworld, discovered in 1995. Standing in a niche at the junction of the corridor complex that leads off the central hall, the statue is finely carved from the rock face and stands a little over five feet high. Traces of the dark gray-green paint (often seen on statues of Osiris) that originally covered the statue remain, although its face was broken off in antiquity—probably as a result of a deep crack that had run through the wall. It seems that an ancient artisan—perhaps even the sculptor himself—had tried to put Osiris' face back on, as mortar can still be seen in this crack.

The scenes and accompanying inscriptions on the decorated walls of KV5 reveal that this giant sepulcher was built for a number of Rameses II's principal sons, including Amun-her-khepeshef, the first son of Rameses, and the king's second son, Rameses, who was dubbed "Junior" by Weeks and his team so as to avoid confusing him with his more illustrious father. It is not certain how many sons Rameses actually had, but his various royal wives probably provided him with at least fifty male offspring and the same number of daughters. There are some twenty representations of the royal sons on the walls of KV5 and thus it appears probable that there were at least this number interred within the extensive confines of its walls and chambers.

As yet, actual physical evidence of these sons has been rather thin on the ground, although an interesting collection of skeletal remains was discovered in a pit in Chamber 2 in 1997. After it was excavated in 1998, it was found to contain three male skulls lying on top of a complete male skeleton along with the mummified foreleg of a young cow. Although the pit probably did contain a burial in a wooden coffin, the skeletal remains found in the pit in 1997 appear to be intrusive. The skeleton may well have been washed into the pit by a flash flood, although it is perhaps possible that the three skulls were hacked from royal mummies by tomb robbers searching for precious gold and jewelry, and then callously tossed into the pit. Interestingly, the largest and most male-looking of the skulls had a healed scar above the right eye, which could be evidence of a serious but nonfatal axe or sword blow received in battle.

The fact that the tomb had been robbed several times in antiquity, and then cleared of any remaining valuables by necropolis guards at the end of the New Kingdom, meant that there were no spectacular discoveries from KV5, but nevertheless, many interesting artifacts have been recovered from the tomb. For example, there is the base of a broken amphora imported from Canaan that had been used as a paint pot by one of the tomb artists. The pot still contained blue pigment when found and it was evident that the artist, or someone else, had clumsily knocked it over at some point, as there was a large blue stain next to it on the floor. Another object providing us with a fascinating link to the KV5 workforce is the limestone flake or ostracon on which someone had recorded the delivery of two hundred oil lamps to the tomb. *Shabti* figures, hundreds of faience beads, amulets, alabaster jars, broken glass vials, furniture and statue inlays, coffin fragments, numerous fragments of painted plaster, and many thousands of potsherds have also been recovered from KV5. Although it seems unlikely (but not impossible) that finds of a more spectacular nature will be recovered from KV5 in the future, we can be sure that this amazing underground mausoleum has much more to reveal.

## KV63: A NEW "TOMB" IN THE VALLEY OF THE KINGS

In 2005, Dr. Otto Schaden, director of the Amenmesse Project of the University of Memphis, was searching for foundation deposits near the entrance to the tomb of Amenmesse (KV10) in the Valley of the Kings when he located the top of a filled-in shaft, presumably leading to a previously unknown tomb—the first to be found in the valley since the discovery of Tutankhamen's in 1922.

The subsequent excavations revealed an intriguing collection of objects in a small L-shaped chamber, but no actual burials, although the chamber may originally have contained one. The most significant relics are the seven decorated wooden anthropoid coffins that were gathered together in one corner of the chamber. All of them are covered in a thick, black coating of resin, and at least three of the coffins have yellow faces or masks, possibly indicating that their occupants were female, as females are often depicted with yellow skin in Egyptian art. One of these "yellow-faced" coffins only measures some four and one-half feet in length, suggesting that it was made for a young boy or girl. Even more poignant was the tiny coffin (originally covered in gold leaf) measuring less than two feet in length that must have been made for an infant. Stored inside the coffins were various objects, including finely made and elaborate collars with actual flowers still attached to their papyrus backings, eight feather-filled pillows and cushions, and various pottery vessels. Gathered around the coffins were twenty-eight largely intact storage jars that contained a variety of interesting objects, including cloth, bandages, shells, resin, seeds, nuts, reeds, amazonite (a semiprecious stone), twine, beads, and bones from fish and birds.

The style of the coffins and the other artifacts found in the chamber dates them to the Eighteenth Dynasty and the time of Tutankhamen, but where they came from, and who they were made for, remains a more difficult question to answer. However, given their location (close to the young king's tomb) and their date, it could be that they were made for Tutankhamen himself.

## DEIR EL-MEDINA: VILLAGE OF THE ROYAL TOMB BUILDERS

Many of the skilled workforce who labored to construct and decorate the royal tombs in the Valley of the Kings[50] would have lived in the village of Deir el-Medina, which lies in a hot and dusty bay about midway between the Ramesseum and Medinet Habu[51] on the west bank at Thebes. This New Kingdom settlement was discovered in the early nineteenth century, around 1815, and the site has since been excavated on several occasions. The most notable archaeological investigation of Deir el-Medina was carried out by Bernard Bruyère of the French Archaeological Institute in Cairo, who directed excavations here from 1922 to 1951.

The construction of the village (which was inhabited c.1550–1070 BC) was begun in the early Eighteenth Dynasty, either in the reign of Amenhotep I or Thutmose I, although the settlement remains seen today date to the Nineteenth Dynasty, when it grew to its maximum size (approximately 5,600 meters squared). It is hard to say for sure how many people lived in the village, but it would probably have been in the low hundreds. Deir el-Medina was gradually abandoned by its community during the reign of Rameses XI in the Twentieth Dynasty, when there was civil unrest in Egypt and incursions by Libyan bandits.

The village is sub-rectangular in plan and is enclosed by a stone wall with a northern entrance giving access onto the main street, and a western one that leads to the village cemetery. Inside the enclosing wall, the closely packed sixty-eight houses of the final phase of the settlement were made from mud-brick, with stone foundations, and their external and internal walls were whitewashed, with the latter featuring colored decoration. The houses had wooden doors, with limestone frames, and in some cases, these were inscribed with the name of the owner and also painted red to ward off evil spirits and demons. Although they vary considerably in size, the houses tended to have four to six rooms and a rear courtyard where cooking and food preparation were carried out, as shown by the round brick ovens and stone millstones and grinders that remain in place. The houses were only one story high, but stairways from the courtyards led to the roof, which would have been used for various activities such as keeping birds, drying and washing crops, and storing produce, and also as a cooler place to sleep during the hot summer months (the roofs of village houses in Egypt today are used in a similar fashion).

An interesting feature of the Deir el-Medina houses are the bed-like platforms found in many of the front rooms that open onto the street.

Deir el-Medina. The ancient village of the workforce (and their families) who built and decorated the tombs of the New Kingdom pharaohs in the Valley of the Kings. Photo courtesy of Lenka and Andy Peacock

Bruyère coined the term *lit clos* ("enclosed beds") for these structures, and suggested that they were used specifically by women giving birth. Alternatively, and perhaps more plausibly, the first rooms of the Deir el-Medina houses were the location of a "household cult, centered around mature females."[52] Support for this theory may be provided by the fact that painted and molded images of the male dwarf god Bes, who was associated with the protection of the family and fertility, have been found in some of the first rooms at Deir el-Medina, sometimes also appearing on the *lit clos* themselves. However, Bes is also strongly linked with sexuality and childbirth and this could suggest that the earlier birthing theory may be the more likely of the two. Whatever the case, nondomestic items such as small ancestor steles, statuettes, and offering tables have been recovered from these front rooms, lending further weight to the idea that they had a mainly cultic purpose.

From these "cultic" front rooms, a step leads up into the main living rooms, which often still have stone bases in place. These probably mark the previous existence of wooden columns that supported a raised section of the roof with clerestory windows, which let in light and air (it is thought that the Deir el-Medina houses had no windows in their walls). Along one wall of the living rooms, people would sit and sleep on low mud-brick divans, and these rooms may have largely been the domain of male members of the Deir el-Medina households. Several houses also had cellars, and the discovery of large numbers of pottery vessels in some reveals that they were used as storage areas for food and drink.

The people of Deir el-Medina were buried in two separate areas to the west and east of the village, with the eastern cemetery dating to the Eighteenth Dynasty and the western one mainly dating to the Nineteenth and Twentieth Dynasties, although it also contains a small number of Eighteenth Dynasty burials such as the famous one of Kha, chief of works in the Valley of the Kings for Amenhotep II, Thutmose IV, and Amenhotep III. Kha was buried alongside his wife, Meryt, and many beautiful artifacts were found in his tomb when it was excavated by the Italian Egyptologist Ernesto Schiaparelli in 1905/1906. Schiaparelli found such objects as a gaily decorated wooden box containing finely made and elaborate glass and stone cosmetic jars, various clothes and foodstuffs, and a small but somewhat haunting wooden statue of Kha.

Unlike the earlier tombs of the eastern cemetery, which are undecorated (but nevertheless contained huge quantities of domestic furniture and many other grave goods), those of the western cemetery feature lively and colorful decoration on their walls that is often well preserved. The western

*Surviving decoration seen in Tomb 291, the burial place of Nakhtmin in the western cemetery at Deir el-Medina. Photo courtesy of Lenka and Andy Peacock*

cemetery tombs are also more complex in plan, with open courtyards leading to chapels topped by small but striking stone pyramids; from the courtyards, a shaft of steps leads down to one or more burial chambers (usually three or four, but sometimes more). The most famous tomb in the western cemetery is that of Sennedjem, which features charming and colorful scenes of Sennedjem and his wife, Iyneferti, in the afterlife, where they are depicted reaping grain, harvesting flax, and plowing the mythical fields of Ialu with a pair of dappled cattle. Along with Sennedjem and his wife, eighteen other family members were interred in the tomb along with numerous grave goods, among which was a set of simple surveying instruments that could quite possibly have belonged to Sennedjem.

As well as fascinating archaeological evidence such as the above, which provides us with important insights into life and death at Deir el-Medina, a huge wealth of textual evidence has also been found at the village. As we will see in chapter six, it is this evidence that really brings alive the people who lived in this ancient Egyptian village some three and a half thousand years ago.

# 3

# FAMOUS FIGURES IN EGYPTOLOGY

**N**apoleon Bonaparte is a towering figure in European history, and he looms large in the history of Egyptology too. Although various interesting individuals before Napoleon had helped Egyptology to take its first tentative steps toward becoming the sophisticated, scientific discipline of today,[1] it is thanks to his invasion of Egypt in July 1798 that "Egyptology took a huge, unintentional leap forward."[2]

Napoleon and his army had invaded Egypt under the pretext of liberating the country from its oppressive Turkish rulers, but in reality, the French wished to cut a canal at Suez that would not only isolate Britain from her colonies in India, but would also give them access to the rich markets of east Africa and the Levant. In the longer term, Napoleon also planned to move on from Egypt to resource-rich India, where he hoped to overthrow his archenemy, Britain, with the help of local rulers.

Within three years, though, the British and their Turkish allies had defeated the French and therefore, from a political perspective, the invasion was a disaster. From an archaeological perspective, however, it was a qualified success, as accompanying the army was the Commission des Sciences et Arts d'Égypte, comprising around 160 scholars or *savants* from various academic disciplines, who had been given the task of investigating and recording Egypt's natural and ancient history.

Heading up the commission was the dashing Baron Dominique Vivant Denon (1747–1825), who, although an aristocrat with strong links to the hated monarchy in France, managed to keep his head on his shoulders during the brutal revolution because he had been in Venice when the infamous guillotine was putting paid to many of its members. As well as being an accomplished diplomat, Denon was also an author and gifted artist, and as he traveled south with the army he planned, recorded, and drew many Egyptian monuments. In 1799, Denon escaped from Egypt with Napoleon (who by then had become a close friend of Denon's) after the famous Battle of the Nile on 2 August 1798[3] had left the French in a precarious position. In 1802, Denon published his *Voyage dans la Basse et la Haute Egypte* (*Journey in Lower and Upper Egypt*), which contained numerous finely drawn and accurate illustrations of Egyptian monuments.

Denon's book became very popular in Europe, but the greatest legacy of the commission was the eventual publication by its surviving members of *Description de l'Égypte* (*Description of Egypt*).[4] This massive, lavishly illustrated work, which is crammed with information on the geography, architecture, natural history, and ancient monuments of Egypt, was published from 1809 to 1830. In its final form, it comprised twenty-four volumes, five of which are concerned with ancient Egypt; these contain numerous maps, plans, and drawings of Egyptian monuments, many of which were produced by Denon. The fact that several of these monuments have now been destroyed[5] means that both Demon's *Voyage dans la Basse et la Haute Egypte* and the *Description* are both valuable sources of information for today's Egyptologists.

After the success of Denon's book, it was inevitable that the *Description* would be even more popular, and it created something of a mania for ancient Egypt in Europe (ancient Egypt also became hugely popular in North America), which has never really gone away. More importantly, the *Description* also helped to lay the foundations for the science of Egyptology, which, some two hundred years later, continues to shed much light on the ancient civilization that most captivates people around the world.

## JEAN-FRANÇOIS CHAMPOLLION

The decipherer of the hieroglyphs on the Rosetta Stone, Jean-François Champollion, was born on 23 December 1790 in the small town of Figeac, near Grenoble in southwestern France. Although the world's most famous "code-breaker" was not a particularly healthy child, it was soon evident that Jean-François was blessed with intelligence far greater than his years. In 1799, Jean-François, who was a difficult and unruly pupil at primary school, was sent to Grenoble, where he was to live his brother, Jacques-Joseph, who generously put up the money to pay for his private education. It was clear that like his older brother, Jean-François was linguistically gifted, and he studied many ancient languages, including Hebrew, Arabic, Chaldean, Syriac, Persian, and Sanskrit (he also learned Italian, English, and German). Here, he met Jean-Baptiste Fourier, one of the members of the Napoleonic Commission in Egypt who was deeply interested in ancient Egypt. Remarkably, Fourier employed the eleven-year-old Champollion to help research the preface for the *Description*, and it was in this work that the very young scholar probably first encountered the mysterious Egyptian hieroglyphs.

On 1 September 1807, the sixteen-year-old boldly told the Grenoble Society of Sciences "that he intended to decipher Egyptian and reconstruct the entire history of the Pharaohs."[6] To achieve this great academic feat, however, Champollion had realized that he would have to learn Coptic, the language of the early Christian church in Egypt, which had developed out of the earlier hieroglyphs. He thus enrolled at the School of Oriental Languages in Paris and supplemented his learning with visits to the National Library and an Egyptian Coptic priest. Two years later, Champollion was offered a joint professorship with Jacques-Joseph at Grenoble University, where he would teach ancient history; his older brother, Greek literature.

Champollion, however, was not the only scholar who wanted to unravel the hieroglyphic riddle, as "closeted in their libraries, hunched over their books, the intellectuals of Europe were engaged in a discreet but determined battle to be the first to solve the riddle."[7] Champollion would eventually win this battle, but Dr. Thomas Young, a professor of natural philosophy at the Royal Institute in London, and a skilled astronomer and physician, undoubtedly helped him in his academic victory.

Like Champollion, Young was a child prodigy (he was reading fluently by the age of two) and was a master of languages, fluent in Latin, Greek, Italian, French, Hebrew, Persian, and Arabic by his early forties. Young had recognized early on that the Rosetta Stone's demotic script was derived from the hieroglyphic one, and that as the former "appeared to contain phonetic elements as well as other signs and groups of signs which were more problematic, there was a chance that [the latter] would also turn out to be a complex script."[8] He also wondered whether the Coptic language would provide the key to understanding that of ancient Egypt.

Young's initial interest in the ancient Egyptian language began in 1814 when Sir William Broughton, a wealthy collector of Egyptian antiquities, brought the remnants of a papyrus scroll back to England from an Egyptian tomb. The bandaged mummy also found in the tomb accompanied the scroll on the long sea voyage back to England, just one of the many that ended up here and in other countries. Young was soon at work deciphering the Rosetta Stone, painstakingly analyzing its hieroglyphic text word for word, finding correspondences between these and the accompanying words and phrases of the Greek text. Young managed to not only tease out words such as "King," "Egypt," and the conjunction "and," he also identified the name Ptolemaios (Ptolemy). Because of his identification of the name Ptolemaios, Young was also able to recognize the name of Cleopatra on an obelisk brought back to England from the Temple of Philae by his friend William Bankes, since it contained six of the same letters found in the former epithet.

In 1831, Young's *Rudiments of an Egyptian Dictionary in the Ancient Enchorial Character* was posthumously published, and it contained an entire translation of a demotic text as well as a translation of a large part of the one featured on the Rosetta Stone. Although Young's interest had always leaned more heavily toward understanding demotic, he did correctly identify some forty signs of the hieroglyphic text on the Rosetta Stone. Therefore, he deserves more credit than he sometimes receives, for although he was not the decipherer of hieroglyphs, his work on the ancient script did "shed indispensable light on what was to come."[9]

Following on from the foundations laid by Young, Champollion continued with his quest to decipher the hieroglyphic script on the Rosetta Stone. Although it took him several years to complete his quest, eventually he was rewarded for his long hours of academic struggle. On 27 September 1822, Champollion presented his paper *Letter to M. Dacier Relating to the Phonetic Hieroglyphic Alphabet Used by the Egyptians* at a meeting of the Academy of Inscriptions in Paris, which, somewhat ironically perhaps, Thomas Young also attended in his capacity of foreign secretary of the Royal Society. Fearing that his rivals would steal a march on him if he presented them with too many clues, Champollion had not felt ready to reveal too much about his hieroglyphic research in *Letter*. However, two years later, he felt confident enough to publish his *Précis du système hiéroglyphique des anciens égyptiens* (*A Summary of the Hieroglyphic System of the Ancient Egyptians*). Here, he summed up the hieroglyphic alphabet: "Hieroglyphic writing is a complex system, a script at the same time figurative, symbolic and phonetic, in one and the same text, in one and the same sentence, and, if I may put it, almost in one and the same word."[10] For his great scholarly efforts, Champollion was offered the distinguished post of curator of the Egyptian collection in the Louvre Museum.

In 1830, after spending sixteenth months investigating the ancient monuments of Egypt on his one and only visit to the country, he returned to his native France, where he was appointed professor of archaeology at the Collège de France. His life's great work, *Grammaire égyptienne*, was published in 1836, but he was not around to witness its publication, as he sadly died on 4 March 1832, from a stroke or heart attack, age just forty-one.

Not everyone was prepared to accept that Champollion was right in his conclusions (particularly the academic rivals who were jealous of him) and there was still much work to do in regard to a thorough understanding of the hieroglyphic script.[11] However, Champollion had nevertheless made giant strides in this direction and as a result, "the door to the ancient Egyptian mind now stood ajar. Further progress would be but a matter of time."[12]

## THE GREAT BELZONI

The publication of the *Description* left the public of early nineteenth-century Europe clamoring for more from the land of the pharaohs, and it also turned the covetous gaze of Europe's great museums firmly toward this land. A new breed of Egyptological adventurers and collectors thus emerged to satisfy this demand for Egyptian antiquities, and the most famous of these Egyptological opportunists is the famous Giovanni Battista Belzoni.

Belzoni was born in Padua, Italy, on 5 November 1778, and the route that led him from here to ancient Egypt was rather circuitous to say the least. At age sixteen, he moved from Padua (where he had been a barber) to Rome, but subsequently moved from Rome after it fell to Napoleon's forces in 1797. His next stop was Paris; from there, he traveled to Holland to learn hydraulic engineering, but subsequently ended up in England in 1803, where he embarked on a new career as circus strongman, subsequently traveling to fairs throughout the length and breadth of the British Isles, amazing the crowds with his remarkable shows of strength.[13] The *Gentleman's Magazine* claimed that Belzoni could "bear on his colossal frame, not fewer, if we mistake not, than 20 or 22 persons."[14] This is very probably an exaggeration, and the real number is likely to be more like twelve persons, but even to lift this number would still have required exceptional strength.

After leaving Britain, accompanied by his wife, Sarah, and their teenage servant, James Curtin, Belzoni traveled through Portugal, Spain, and Sicily before finally arriving in Egypt in 1815. A year later, he was unsuccessful in his attempt to sell to Pasha Mohammed Ali (the governor general of Egypt) an innovative water-lifting device he had designed. Belzoni's luck had not totally deserted him, however, as he was subsequently introduced to Sir Henry Salt (the British consul general in Egypt) by his friend, the Swiss explorer Johann Ludwig Burckhardt.[15] Salt had a genuine interest in ancient Egypt, and the pasha, who seems to have been more interested in ancient Egyptian monuments as a useful source of income or building stone, had given him authority to collect Egyptian antiquities for the British Museum in London. Belzoni, with his considerable strength and engineering skills, thus seemed to be the perfect man for the job.

Henry Salt, though, came to regret his decision to employ Belzoni, as the charismatic Italian pleased himself in his new role as Salt's agent in Egypt, happy to collect antiquities for the British Museum, but not Salt, whom he had never really considered his employer. The upshot was that Belzoni was out to make his name and did not want Salt getting the credit for any new discoveries that he might make. It is therefore hardly surprising that the relationship between Salt and Belzoni ended in bitter acrimony (at least on Salt's part), as after he returned to England in 1819, Belzoni not only displayed his Egyptian finds in a hugely successful exhibition in London, but he also denied ever having known Salt in his subsequent autobiography published in 1820.[16]

Whatever his faults, Belzoni led a daring and somewhat dangerous life as he roamed Egypt looking for antiquities (we should not forget that Sarah and James also accompanied him on his many adventures). He was rewarded for his troubles with many remarkable discoveries, and his achievements were truly impressive. One of the most notable took place in Nubia, at Abu Simbel, where he dug out the Great Temple of Rameses II from the windblown sands that had all but hidden it for many millennia. In doing so, he restored to the world one of its greatest ancient monuments.

Another of Belzoni's great feats was his removal of the "Younger Memnon" from the Ramesseum on Luxor's west bank, which as previously mentioned was Rameses II's mortuary temple. The Younger Memnon was actually the top half of a colossal and beautifully made statue of Rameses II that had been shattered because of an earthquake, but it was still nine feet tall and weighed about eight tons. Today, this statue resides in the British Museum, but the beautifully sculpted head of its counterpart can still be seen lying on the ground in the second court of the Ramesseum.

Through a combination of Belzoni's engineering skills and the sheer effort of his eighty-strong team of native workmen, the massive bust was dragged some two miles down to the banks of the Nile. From there, the statue was transported to Alexandria via Cairo, and then onward to the Brit-

*Superbly carved head from a destroyed colossal statue of Rameses II in the second court of his mortuary temple, the Ramesseum. The statue was one of a pair, and today, the other can be seen in the British Museum, London.*

ish Museum, where it still stands today, its imposing presence reminding the museum's countless visitors of the power of Egypt's greatest pharaoh.

Belzoni transported the colossal head of Rameses II from the Rameseum while he was still on good terms with Salt, who also asked him to search for a sarcophagus in the tomb of Rameses III, which had been noted by the Scottish explorer James Bruce during his explorations of the Valley of the Kings in the eighteenth century. Belzoni found the sarcophagus, which was subsequently moved to the Nile for transportation (today, it can be seen in the Louvre), but unknown to Salt, he also discovered its lid, which he kept for himself (it is now part of the collection of the Fitzwilliam Museum in Cambridge, England). After his discovery, Belzoni decided to strike out on his own and make a search of the Valley of the Kings for the lost tombs of the New Kingdom pharaohs. Thanks to his almost uncanny ability to read the landscape, he found eight tombs with little real difficulty, including the tomb of the Ay, Tutankhamen's successor, and the magnificently decorated tomb of Prince Mentuherkhepshef, a son of Rameses IX.

However, Belzoni's star finds were the New Kingdom tombs of Rameses I and Sety I, with the former still containing the king's red granite sarcophagus and two life-size wooden guardian statues. At the time of its discovery, Sety's tomb was the finest yet found in the Valley of the Kings. Architecturally, it is the most impressive tomb in the valley, and when Belzoni entered, the colors on its beautifully decorated walls still shone vividly, as though the tomb artists had only just left. Sadly, this decoration was badly ruined by a flash flood that hit the tomb soon after its discovery, and the wax impressions that Belzoni and later tourists took of the tomb reliefs led to further damage, as did the soot left on the walls by the oil lamps and candles of the tourists. It was later scholars, however, who caused the most serious damage, as they removed entire sections of decoration from the tomb walls. Champollion, of all people, was one of these scholars, but like his counterparts, it could be said in his defense that he felt that this was a necessity in a time plagued by unscrupulous treasure hunters.

Belzoni found several items of funerary equipment in Sety's tomb, including numerous wooden and faience *shabti* figures[17] and some large wooden statues, but his most significant discovery was undoubtedly the finely decorated stone coffin of the king, carved from a single block of honey-colored alabaster. This superb example of ancient Egyptian craftsmanship was acquired from Belzoni by the architect Sir John Soane in 1824, who gave it pride of place in his "crypt" of antiquities at his house in Lincoln's Inn Fields, London, where it can still be seen today.

*The severely damaged, but still magnificent, Colossi of Memnon. Virtually all that remains of Amenhotep III's mortuary temple on the west bank at Luxor.*

Belzoni made many more notable discoveries, including the upper entrance of King Khafre's pyramid at Giza, a cache of superb statues from Karnak Temple depicting the lion-headed goddess, Sekhmet, and a black granite statue of Amenhotep III and further Sekhmet statues from the area behind the Colossi of Memnon.[18] After a long search, Belzoni also made the significant discovery of the lost Greco-Roman port of Berenice on the Ras Banas Peninsula on Egypt's Red Sea coast. He did not undertake excavations at the port, as by the time his party found the site, both their food and water supplies were dangerously low (the site was finally excavated in the 1990s). They thus had to turn back, and Belzoni never returned, dying of dysentery (at the age of forty-five) in Benin on 3 December 1823, while looking for the legendary city of Timbuktu in west Africa.

## MARIETTE AND MASPERO

Belzoni and his fellow adventurers had been given free rein to wander throughout Egypt and collect her antiquities at will, but their days were numbered. As the nineteenth century progressed, some scholars began to voice serious concerns that this unchecked collecting (some might say plundering) of Egypt's ancient past could not continue, as this past was fragile and finite. The most notable voice raised in protest was Champollion's, whose pleading had led the French government to establish the "Service for the Conservation of Antiquities" in 1835. It was not until 1850, though, and the arrival in Cairo of Auguste Mariette, that it could be said that the writing was finally on the wall for the great collectors of the earlier nineteenth century. Although a few individuals, such as John Gardner Wilkinson and James Burton,[19] had stood out from the collecting crowd because of their scholarly approach to Egypt's antiquities, and Mariette was certainly no Egyptological saint, the Frenchman nevertheless "put Egyptian archaeology and Egyptology on a firm and permanent footing."[20]

Auguste Mariette was born in Boulogne-sur-Mer (northern France) on 11 February 1821. When he was eighteen, Mariette went to England, where he briefly taught French at a private school in the birthplace of William Shakespeare, Stratford-upon-Avon, and then, rather oddly, he spent an even shorter time designing ribbons. On his return to Boulogne, he took up a teaching position at a local college, and it was here that his passion for Egyptology was born, after meeting the father of the recently deceased Nestor L'Hôte, who had been a draftsman with Champollion's solitary Egyptian expedition. Nestor's father, who was a relative of the Mariettes, had been transferred to Boulogne in his capacity as a customs official and had brought with him his son's voluminous archive of notes and drawings from Egypt. These badly needed sorting for publication and he asked Mariette if he would be interested in this task. Mariette was, and he soon found himself fascinated by the mysterious land of the pharaohs.

Subsequently, Mariette compiled a catalog of the Egyptian artifacts in Boulogne Museum, and then he moved to Paris, where he landed a position as a junior curator at the Louvre in 1849. While there, he cataloged the museum's growing collection of Egyptian papyri, and in his spare time, he threw himself into learning everything he could about ancient Egypt and taught himself to read hieroglyphs to a high standard.

As we saw in the previous chapter, a year later, Mariette was in Egypt and he discovered the remarkable Serapeum at Saqqara, and he went on to make many other notable discoveries. Included amongst these were the richly furnished burials of King Kamose[21] and Queen Ahhotep (who may have been Kamose's mother) at the huge necropolis of Dra Abu'l-Naga on the Theban west bank. Exquisitely made weaponry and jewelry were recovered from the two burials, although most impressive of all was Queen Ahhotep's beautiful coffin lid, which was completely covered in gold leaf.

Mariette also found many remarkable sculptures, including two undoubted masterpieces of Egyptian art: a granite statue from Tanis, which depicts King Amenemhat III of the Twelfth Dynasty as a brooding and powerful sphinx, and a diorite gneiss statue of King Khafre and the falcon-god Horus that was found underneath the valley temple of his Giza pyramid.

Seen through the eyes of today's Egyptologists, Mariette's excavation methods leave a lot to be desired: he often had several excavations running at the same time (at one stage he had thirty-seven running simultaneously throughout Egypt),[22] and he was not averse to using the odd stick of dynamite or two to recover the spectacular artifacts that were his main goal. Like many early Egyptologists, though, Mariette was a man of his time and Egyptology was a science still in its infancy. He was genuinely concerned with the preservation of Egypt's ancient past, and this led to Khedive Said Pasha appointing Mariette as the first director of the Egyptian Antiquities Service in 1858, which allowed him to create the first Egyptian museum in 1863 at Bulaq, Cairo.

Mariette died in 1881 and was succeeded as director of the Antiquities Service by his compatriot, Gaston Maspero, who was born in Paris in 1846 to parents of Italian descent. By the age of nineteen, Maspero was an expert in Egyptian hieroglyphs, and when he was twenty-three he was appointed professor of Egyptology at the prestigious École des hautes études (School of Higher Studies), the graduate school of Paris University. Four years later, his star rose even further in the world of Egyptology when he was chosen to fill the chair of Egyptology at the renowned Collège de France in Paris.

However, Maspero was thirty-one before he first set foot in Egypt, where he was asked by the French government to set up the Institut français de l'archéologie orientale in Cairo. He also served as the director of the Antiquities Service and the head of the Bulaq Museum from 1881 to 1886, before he returned home to Paris, where he devoted much of his time to teaching Egyptology.

In 1899, he was called back to Egypt to take up his old post as director of the Antiquities Service, only resigning some fifteen years later when his health began to fail. Maspero returned home to Paris in August, at the outbreak of World War I, and after having suffered a heart attack he was dealt an even more terrible blow, as his son (a superb scholar who was showing strong signs of following in his father's footsteps), who was serving in the French army, was killed in battle in 1915. Maspero died suddenly a year later, a heartbroken man.

Nevertheless, despite this sad end, Maspero had led a very full and active life, and published many important works on Egyptology. One of his greatest achievements was his copying and translation of the pyramid texts found in the later Old Kingdom pyramids at Saqqara. When uttered (either by the funerary parties or by the dead king himself), it was believed that these spells would ensure the king's successful resurrection, protect him from harm, and provide him with sustenance in the afterlife. Today, Egyptologists are still engaged in the study and restoration of the Pyramid Texts.

## THE FATHER OF POTS

Many notable names are associated with the early days of Egyptology and its subsequent development into the modern and sophisticated science of today, but that of Flinders Petrie perhaps stands out above all others. Petrie had a long and distinguished career in archaeology that lasted a remarkable seventy years, and he spent some forty of these improving the standards of excavation and publication in Egyptology and training a new generation of Egyptologists.

William Matthew Flinders Petrie was born in Kent in 1853, and although he had a somewhat unconventional home education, it clearly did him no harm. By his late teens he had already surveyed and planned many of the prehistoric earthworks of southern England, and in 1877, with his father, William (who was something of a Victorian polymath), he produced the most accurate plan of Stonehenge to date. Three years later, Petrie made his first visit to Egypt, the purpose of which was to measure the Great Pyramid of Khufu at Giza and to disprove the outlandish theory put forward by Piazzi Smyth in his book *Our Inheritance in the Great Pyramid*. Smyth's theory was that under divine guidance, God's chosen few had built the Great Pyramid, not the Egyptians, and furthermore, they had done so using a system of measurement based on the "pyramid inch" (which he claimed equated to 1.001 of a British inch).

Petrie's home during the two arduous seasons he spent surveying the Great Pyramid was an empty tomb in the Giza necropolis. Although he had to share his Spartan new home with rats and fleas, and was often kept awake by local dogs barking or fighting outside the tomb, it is evident that Petrie was happy nonetheless: "Life here is really comfortable, without many of the encumbrances of regular hours: bells, collars and cuffs, blacking, tablecloths or many of the other unnecessaries of Civilisation."[23] Two years later, Petrie had finished his survey, proving that Piazzi Smyth had been way off the mark and that his "pyramid inch" was nothing short of a fantasy. The survey was also so accurate that Egyptologists still turn to it today.

Petrie's pyramid survey was published in 1883 in *The Pyramids and Temples of Giza*, alerting Egyptian scholars to the potential of the young Englishman, and the newly formed Egypt Exploration Fund (EEF) thus dispatched Petrie to begin excavations in the Nile Delta later that year. The EEF was founded by another of the many interesting characters that fill the early pages of the story of Egyptology—Miss Amelia Ann Blanford Edwards, a popular Victorian author and journalist, whose enchanting travel book, *A Thousand Miles Up the Nile* (1877), is still required reading for any "Egyptophile." Edwards was spellbound by the wonders of ancient Egypt, but her trip also made her painfully aware that much still needed to be done to protect its sites and monuments.[24] Therefore, in 1882, she set up the EEF with Dr. Reginald Poole of the British Museum and the respected surgeon Sir Erasmus Wilson, with the aim of financing proper scientific excavations in Egypt. It is still going strong today, although it has since changed its name to the Egypt Exploration Society. Edwards became a close friend of Petrie's. He corresponded regularly with her while he was working in Egypt, and it was thanks to Edwards that he became the first professor of Egyptology at University College London. In 1892, Edwards unfortunately died, but she left money in her will to fund a chair of Egyptology at the college, stipulating that its new professor should be under forty and should not be employed by the British Museum. Although Edwards had not officially stated his name in her will, it was clear from her stipulation that she wanted Petrie to be offered the professorship.

In the Delta, Petrie excavated first at San el-Hagar (ancient Tanis), uncovering such things as the remains of Roman and Greek houses, numerous domestic artifacts, and an important collection of papyri featuring demotic texts, and on his next mission, he made the major discovery of the ancient Greek trading center at Naukratis. During his Delta explorations, Petrie was given the nickname "Father of Pots" by his Arab workers (whom he treated with respect, and genuinely liked), as he believed that pottery and the other more mundane items of everyday life found at ancient Egyptian sites were just as interesting (if not even more so) than the more spectacular ones. As we will see later, this interest led him to develop an ingenious dating technique that still plays a vital role in archaeology today.

Petrie made many more important discoveries in Egypt during his long career, and he continued to excavate in Egypt until 1926, when he was abruptly forced to transfer his attention to the ancient sites of Palestine. This was because new and strict regulations had been put in place that severely restricted the remit of foreign excavations in Egypt, limiting the scope of their excavations and keeping a tight rein on the artifacts they discovered. By this time, however, "Petrie's work was done. Forty years of excavation, training, and publication had improved standards of field archaeology and brought forward a whole new generation of Egyptologists."[25]

## HOWARD CARTER AND LORD CARNARVON

Among this new generation was Howard Carter, who secured a kind of immortality with his discovery of the tomb of King Tutankhamen. However, as amazing as this discovery was, it actually marks the final chapter in the fascinating story of Howard Carter, which, as with all of the other personalities covered here, can only be looked at briefly.

Carter was born in Brompton, London, on 9 May 1874, although because he was a rather sickly child, it was thought better that he be sent to live with his two aunts in the village of Swaffham in Norfolk (the original home of the Carter family), where he would be educated privately at home. Howard's father, Samuel Carter, was a fine draftsman and animal painter who was a member of the Royal Academy, and it soon became clear that his son had inherited his artistic talents (four of the other seven Carter children also grew up to be professional artists).

Carter's father had produced a number of commissions for Lord and Lady Amherst, whose country estate lay just outside Swaffham, and whose family seat, Didlington Hall, contained one of the most important collections of Egyptian antiquities in Britain. The Amhersts were friends with the English Egyptologist Percy Newberry (later professor of Egyptology at Liverpool University and professor of ancient history and archaeology at Cairo University) and he had mentioned to them while visiting Didlington Hall that he was looking for a young, talented draftsman to help him on his excavations in Egypt. The Amhersts were well aware that the young Carter was a talented artist and they had no hesitation in recommending him to Newberry. Thus in October 1891, the seventeen-year-old Carter found himself setting sail for Egypt, where his first job was tracing the beautiful and extensive scenes found in the tombs of Eleventh and Twelfth Dynasty officials at Beni Hasan in Middle Egypt.

Carter excelled in his work at Beni Hasan, but his next job presented him with even more of a challenge, as in 1892 he was sent to work as an assistant excavator at el-Amarna with the famous Flinders Petrie. Petrie was not particularly happy with Carter's appointment, as he wanted an excavator, not an artist—no matter how talented. However, there was not much Petrie could do about it, as Lord Amherst was financing his excavations (hoping to obtain some antiquities from the site for his collection) and Carter came as part of the deal. They were also rather contrasting personalities, as Petrie famously eschewed unnecessary comforts and was careful with his money, while Carter was fond of the good life.[26] However, Petrie soon overcame his reservations, realizing that Carter was an intelligent individual who was quick to learn the skills and techniques of archaeological excavation.

The experience Carter gained under Petrie was invaluable and after working at el-Amarna, he found his services in demand, working at various sites in Egypt over the next six years. His most notable work was carried out at Queen Hatshepsut's temple at Deir el-Bahri, under the French Egyptologist Édouard Naville, where he produced an extremely accurate record of the temple scenes as well as assisting in its architectural restoration.

In 1899, thanks to Gaston Maspero, Carter landed the plum job of chief inspector of antiquities for Upper Egypt, with much of his work involving recording and conservation in the Valley of the Kings, although he also made several interesting discoveries. One of the first things he did in his new role was to fit somewhat ugly, but necessary, iron gates and grilles on the royal tombs in the valley. Carter was well aware of the serious threat posed by tomb robbers, as he had to deal with the notorious Rassul family, who had robbed the tomb of Amenhotep II, either directly or by bribing its guards. Footprints belonging to Mohammed Abd el-Rassul were found at the scene of the crime and led to his brother Ahmed's house in the nearby village of Qurna (something of a tomb robber's den), although he was never convicted. During his work in the Valley of the Kings, Carter also cleared great amounts of debris from inside the tombs and equipped some of them with electric lighting for the first time.

Three years later, in February 1902, Carter was scouring the valley looking for the lost tomb of the New Kingdom pharaoh Thutmose IV when he came across a small hollow above the tomb of Maiherpri (a half-Nubian prince who was connected in some way to Eighteenth Dynasty royalty), which had been discovered by Victor Loret in 1899. In the hollow, Carter discovered a concealed yellow wooden box bearing the name of Maiherpri, inside which were two finely made and remarkably well preserved leather loincloths. The box and one of the loincloths now reside in Boston Museum, while the other has since been stolen from the Field Museum of Natural History in Chicago, where before its theft it had been displayed as an early example of a freemason's apron.

Carter was finally rewarded in his search for the tomb of Thutmose IV, discovering the royal sepulcher in January 1903. Although the king's mummy had already been found by Loret in the remarkable mummy cache from the tomb of Amenhotep II, the king's fine quartzite sarcophagus was still intact in the burial chamber. Rather grotesquely propped up against a wall of one of the side chambers, there was also a mummy with its stomach ripped open, and although it is not certain, it is quite possible that this upright cadaver was the king's son, Webensenu. As was the norm, the tomb had been plundered in antiquity, and we can only guess as to what valuable and beautiful treasures were taken. Nevertheless, many impressive artifacts had been left behind by the thieves, including the king's war chariot, a calcite Canopic chest, various faience vessels, boxes, chests, statuettes, leather gloves and armlets, a game board, mummified geese, and jars still filled with wheat.

In 1904, Carter, who by then was a highly respected figure, swapped places with the inspector of Lower Egypt, James Quibell, and was transferred to his new base at Saqqara. He relished the new challenges that working in the north offered him, but his move was to lead to the end of his career as an inspector of antiquities. He was involved in a brawl with a group of drunken French tourists at Saqqara and they subsequently complained of the rough treatment meted out to them by the Egyptian guards, which led the French consul to demand an apology from Carter. However, Carter was a proud and stubborn man and he flatly refused to apologize, demanding that the French tourists be tried in a court of law. Maspero, feeling he had no other choice, moved Carter farther north to the Delta city of Tanta, where he would be out of harm's way. Carter, however, was unhappy with his new home, and disgusted with the way he had been treated during the Saqqara incident, he resigned from the inspectorate in 1905. He spent the next few years of his life living a somewhat impoverished existence in Luxor, where he sold watercolor paintings to tourists and sometimes worked as a draftsman for excavators in the Valley of the Kings, such as the wealthy American Theodore Davis, who had funded much of Carter's work in the valley during his time as inspector of Upper Egypt.

Carter's life took a turn for the better in 1907, as Maspero recommended him to George Herbert, the fifth Earl of Carnarvon, who was looking for a man of skill, intelligence, and experience to help him with his new hobby of Egyptology; Carter fit the bill nicely. Carter was from a vastly different social background from the aristocratic and very wealthy Lord Carnarvon, whose family home was the grand Highclere Castle in the English county of Berkshire. Lord Carnarvon was almost a caricature of the English country gentleman, and could have stepped straight out of the pages of a P. G. Wodehouse novel, or perhaps more aptly, out of Kenneth Grahame's *The Wind in the Willows*. Like the famous Toad of Toad Hall, Carnarvon had a penchant for speed and loved his motor cars, and like his amphibious counterpart, he found himself hauled before the magistrates for speeding. Carnarvon was a pioneer of motoring in England, as he imported the second car ever seen there, while his good friend John Moore-Brabazon imported the first. His love of motoring, though, led to his being seriously injured in a car accident while racing in Germany, and although he recovered from his injuries (which included punctured lungs), he was left in generally poor health and prone to chest infections. Subsequently, his doctors recommended that he spend more time in a warmer country during the cold, wet English winters, and Egypt was his preferred choice.

Although Carter and Carnarvon came from different sides of the tracks, they became close friends and colleagues; little did they realize, however, that their partnership would eventually lead them to the splendor and glory of King Tutankhamen's tomb in the Valley of the Kings. They are justifiably famous for the discovery of this tomb, but Carter and Carnavon made several important finds before this, such as the two wooden tablets found in a tomb near the Deir el-Bahri valley, on which hieratic texts recorded the conflict between King Kamose and the Hyksos. Carter and Carnavon also excavated several tombs underneath Queen Hatshepsut's temple at Deir el-Bahri, recovering numerous objects from these sepulchers, including an ivory gaming board, a fine bronze and gold mirror, and a beautiful electrum statuette of a boy named Amenemheb. Their most significant discovery at Deir el-Bahri was a cache of sixty-four finely decorated coffins dating from various periods of ancient Egyptian history. These coffins provided important and striking evidence of the developments that took place in Egyptian coffin design and decoration.

Carter was also something of a daredevil, who would go to rather extreme lengths in his quest for Egyptian antiquities. In October 1916, he decided to investigate a tomb above Deir el-Bahri that had attracted the attention of local tomb robbers. It was located at the end of a small valley about halfway down a sheer cliff face that was over one hundred meters in height, and Carter recorded his dangerous visit to the tomb:

> It was midnight when we arrived on the scene, and the guide pointed out to me the end of a rope which dangled sheer down the face of a cliff. Listening, we could hear the robbers actually at work . . . [W]hen I reached the bottom there was an awkward moment or two. I gave them the option of clearing out by means of my rope, or else of staying where they were without a rope at all, and eventually they saw reason and departed.[27]

Inside the cliff-tomb Carter discovered few artifacts, but he did find a yellow-sandstone sarcophagus that had been prepared for the famous

Hatshepsut before she became queen and was still only a princess. The tomb, however, had clearly been abandoned at an early stage of its preparation, presumably because Hatshepsut had ascended to the throne, and she was instead later laid to rest in a tomb more befitting of her status in the Valley of the Kings.

## AMERICANS IN EGYPT

The Americans arrived relatively late on the burgeoning Egyptological scene in comparison to their European counterparts, but we likewise find a number of individuals amongst the American contingent who stand out as key figures in the development of Egyptology. One of these figures was Theodore Davis, whom we have already met briefly above as the wealthy patron of Howard Carter's excavations in the Valley of the Kings.

Theodore Monroe Davis was an extremely wealthy financier from Newport, Rhode Island, who had been taking winter holidays in Egypt since 1889, sailing along the Nile in his Egyptian *dahabiya* with his mistress, Mrs. Emma B. Andrews. Apparently, "Mr Davis was a very charming American gentleman who in his old age, used to spend his winters on a dahabiyeh [traditional Egyptian boat] at Luxor, and there became interested in Egyptology."[28] Davis' huge wealth meant that he could indulge this interest, and after Howard Carter had been sent north by Maspero, he continued to fund the excavations carried out in the Valley of the Kings by Carter's replacement, James Quibell.

It must have galled Carter to learn of Quibell's discovery of the tomb of Yuya and Tjuyu, who were the father and mother of the principal wife of Amenhotep III, Queen Tiye. Although small, the tomb was packed with the coffins of Yuya and Tjuyu, exquisite furniture, and many other fine pieces of burial equipment, including a war chariot, which would enable the military officer Yuya to continue his role in the afterlife. Although tomb robbers in antiquity had rifled through the beautifully decorated coffins looking for jewels, their occupants still lay inside, their faces covered with magnificent cartonnage burial masks covered in gold leaf. Yuya's outer coffin was also huge in size and when stood on end, reached about ten feet in height. Arthur Weigall, the English Egyptologist who succeeded Quibell shortly after the discovery of Yuya and Tjuyu's tomb, provides us with an eloquent and evocative description of his first entrance into their final resting place:

> Imagine entering a town house which had been closed for the summer: imagine the stuffy room, the stiff, silent appearance of the furniture, the feeling

that some ghostly occupants of the vacant chairs have just been disturbed, the desire to throw open the windows to let life into the room once more. That was perhaps the first sensation as we stood, really dumbfounded, and stared around at the relics of the life of over three thousand years ago.[29]

Weigall, though, was having too much of his precious time taken up with the somewhat frantic pace set by Davis in the Valley of the Kings, and in 1905, he handed the excavator's reins to a young Englishman, Edward Russell Ayrton. During his first season working for Davis, as well as finding the previously undiscovered tomb of King Siptah of the Nineteenth Dynasty, which featured high-quality decoration in its outer passages, Ayrton also found several interesting tombs belonging to high-ranking officials as well as Tomb KV55. We will look at this intriguing tomb in more detail in the next chapter.

Ayrton's most significant find was made during clearance work in the western part of the valley, where he found a number of small antiquities including a small faience cup inscribed with the name of Tutankhamen. This was the first evidence of the existence of the boy-king that had been found in the Valley of the Kings. In 1907, Ayrton also found a small chamber (KV54) containing the embalming materials used on Tutankhamen's mummy, and smashed pots probably left over from the meal held at the king's funeral. Davis was never to know how close he came to finding the jewel in the crown of great Egyptological discoveries, as when he finally gave up his search for royal tombs in the Valley of the Kings in 1912, his excavator at the time, Harry Burton, had only been some two meters from the tomb of Tutankhamen.

Although Theodore Davis made a great contribution to the archaeological exploration of the Valley of the Kings, he was, in truth, more of a treasure hunter than his compatriots, George Reisner (1867–1942) and James Breasted (1865–1935), two of American Egyptology's greatest scholars. Reisner, who is known as the "American Petrie," was funded by Phoebe Hearst, the mother of William Randolph Hearst and the founder of the Lowie Museum of Anthropology at the University of California (now renamed the Phoebe A. Hearst Museum). Reisner was the director of the Hearst Egyptian expedition from 1897 to 1899, carrying out notable excavations at the site of Deir el-Ballas in Upper Egypt. Here he uncovered the remains of a large, early New Kingdom town or royal city that appears to have been associated with King Kamose and Ahmose I, the two pharaohs responsible for the expulsion of the Hyksos from Egypt.

Reisner was somewhat unusual amongst his contemporaries in that he also excavated at Nubian sites in the Sudan, among them a remarkable royal cemetery at the royal city of Kerma, the capital of the Kushite kingdom. Here, Kushite rulers had been buried under large burial mounds along with hundreds of servants who had been sacrificed to serve their masters in the afterlife. Reisner's meticulous excavation of the burial mounds revealed that horrifically, many had been buried alive, and in some cases, skeletons were discovered in the spaces under funerary beds, revealing how people had tried in vain to ward off death. They must have been utterly terrified as they lay in the darkness listening to the earth of the burial mounds being piled high above them, dying slowly as the air pockets trapped underneath the beds slowly dissipated.

Reisner also worked on the Giza Plateau, investigating the Old Kingdom tombs in the necropolis near the pyramids, and while working at the pyramid of King Menkaure he found a cache of some of the most stunning royal statues from ancient Egypt. While working at Giza he also discovered the tomb of Queen Hetepheres, the wife of King Sneferu and the mother of King Khufu. Reisner's colleague, Dows Dunham, was largely responsible for carrying out the excavation of the small burial chamber, which was packed with many items of funerary equipment, such as several extremely fragile pieces of furniture covered in gold leaf (these were later reconstructed using new wood thanks to the painstaking recording of the tomb's contents). Unfortunately, the queen's alabaster sarcophagus was empty, having probably been later been removed by her son for reburial elsewhere. However, the queen's Canopic chest was found hidden in a secret niche, and inside lay her organs, preserved in the natron (a type of salt) solution that had been used to embalm them thousands of years ago.

It has been said of Reisner's contemporary, James Henry Breasted, that he "was effectively the founder of American Egyptology,"[30] although in contrast to Reisner, who was a talented excavator who did much to advance the science of archaeology, his real area of expertise was the ancient Egyptian language. From 1905 to 1909 he published his important five-volume work, *Ancient Records of Egypt*, and in 1905 he also published *A History of Egypt*, which remains "one of the best accounts of ancient Egyptian history ever written."[31] In 1905, Breasted became the first professor of Egyptology in the United States, at Chicago University, and he subsequently spent much of his career helping to develop and establish Egyptology in the country.

Breasted also had the support of a wealthy benefactor in the form of the famous American philanthropist John D. Rockefeller Jr., whose money helped Breasted in his greatest achievements—the founding of the Oriental Institute at the University of Chicago in 1919, and its sister establishment, Chicago House, in Luxor in 1924. Many high-quality academic publications have since been published by Chicago House, with its most notable being the huge and comprehensive account of the Medinet Habu (the mortuary temple of Rameses III) that was published in several volumes from 1930 to 1970. Chicago House continues to set high standards today, an institution that is of undoubted importance in the wider world of Egyptology, and the same can be said for the Oriental Institute in Chicago.

# 4

# CONTROVERSIES AND
# SCANDALS IN EGYPTOLOGY

On 6 January 1907, Theodore Davis' excavator in the Valley of the Kings, Edward Ayrton, uncovered the entrance to a new tomb while he was working close to the tomb of Rameses IX. After breaking through the limestone walling that blocked the entrance, Ayrton found a simple tomb consisting of a flight of steps and a sloping corridor leading to a single, square burial chamber. It has been said that this tomb (KV55) "represents perhaps the most controversial archaeological discovery made in Egypt."[1]

Ayrton found that KV55 was in something of a state, with building debris, various broken funerary items, and workers' tools scattered across the floor of the burial chamber. Stacked against one of its walls were the components of a dismantled decorated wooden shrine gilded with gold leaf, fragments of which were everywhere inside the tomb. Hieroglyphic texts on the shrine recorded that Akhenaten had provided it for the burial of his mother, Queen Tiye, the wife of Amenhotep III. In a niche in the southern wall (probably an unfinished second chamber), there was a set of four alabaster Canopic jars with stoppers in the form of finely carved female heads wearing the distinctive Nubian-style bobbed wigs worn by Akhenaten's daughters and wives. Egyptologists now believe that these jars were originally made for Akhenaten's secondary wife, Kiya. Lying amidst the mess on the floor, on the southern side of the chamber there was also a decaying wooden *rishi* coffin[2] that would originally have featured a beautiful sheet-gold face mask. Unfortunately, the thieves who had plundered the tomb in antiquity had brutally ripped this off, leaving just one eyebrow and an eye remaining. Lying in the coffin's gold-plated interior was a mummy that had been badly damaged by water steadily dripping into the burial chamber over the centuries from a crack in its roof. Wrapped around the head of the mummy was a beautiful sheet-gold vulture that had originally been designed to be worn as a pectoral or collar. It is quite probable that the person who ripped off the outer face mask also stole the golden mummy mask that would originally have covered the face of the deceased, although why they left the collar behind is something of a mystery.

Given that the burial chamber contained her shrine, as well as Canopic jars made for female royalty, Theodore Davis came to the reasonable conclusion that the mummy must be that of Queen Tiye. Looking for further support to prove his theory, he asked a local physician, Dr. Pollock, and an American obstetrician who was overwintering in Luxor, to examine the mummy. Davis reported that both men confirmed that the body was that of a female. Interestingly, though, Arthur Weigall, who was chief inspector of antiquities at the time of the discovery of KV55, wrote, "I saw Dr Pollock in Luxor the other day, who denies that he ever thought that it was a woman, and he says the other doctor could not be so sure."[3] However, even though it appears that the two physicians had given Davis reason to doubt his theory about the body from KV55, he stood by his belief that it was Queen Tiye's and in 1910, he published *The Tomb of Queen Tiyi*.

In 1912, however, "the anatomist Grafton Elliot Smith emphatically announced that the skeleton was male [and] [e]very expert who has since examined the bones has agreed with this reassessment."[4] However, although Egyptologists widely agree that the occupant of KV55 was male, the same cannot be said when it comes to his actual identity. At the time of the discovery, Arthur Weigall believed that the body in the tomb was that of Akhenaten himself, and others since have agreed with him. Support for this theory may be provided by the fact that Akhenaten's name appears on the "magical bricks"[5] found in the tomb:

> In view of their cheap nature and ready manufacture it is exceedingly improbable that one king's bricks would have been utilized for the burial of another, or would have been regarded as effective for that purpose without a change of name. We have no option, therefore, but to conclude that [KV55] served as the burial chamber of Akhenaten, and his was the body within the coffin.[6]

Weigall also reported that Akhenaten's tiles were inscribed both on the thin gold ribbons (probably the remains of gold foil bracelets) found on the mummy (unfortunately, these were stolen soon after the discovery of KV55) and on the coffin. Furthermore, the coffin, which had originally been made for Kiya, was subsequently adapted for reuse by a royal male with the secondary addition of a false beard and *uraeus*.[7] In addition to this evidence, royal seals bearing the name of Tutankhamen were found in the entrance debris, strongly suggesting that he had transferred the burials of both Tiye and Akhenaten (and perhaps even Kiya) to KV55 from their original tombs at Amarna. Several Egyptologists believe that it is very likely that Tutankhamen was Akhenaten's son, probably by his secondary wife, Kiya.

The evidence then seems to be quite compelling that KV55 was indeed the final resting place of Akhenaten, but the waters have been rather muddied in this regard by the various anatomical studies that have since been undertaken on the royal male found in KV55. Grafton Elliot Smith had originally estimated that he had been around twenty-five years old when he died (he subsequently revised his estimate to about thirty). Dr. Douglas Derry and Professor Ronald Harrison of Liverpool University, who examined the skeleton in the 1920s and 1963, respectively, came to a similar conclusion, putting the age of death between twenty and twenty-five. In 2000, the Egyptologist and anthropologist Joyce Filer also examined the bones from KV55 and concurred with Derry and Harrison, agreeing that they belonged to an individual who probably died in his early twenties.

These scientific conclusions present something of a problem with the theory that it was Akhenaten who was buried in KV55, as most Egyptologists are of the opinion that he was closer to forty when he died. However, after their analysis of the human remains from KV55, E. F. Wente and J. E. Harris concluded that the age of death was between thirty and thirty-five. A team from Egypt's Supreme Council of Antiquities, who are responsible for the most recent analysis of the skeleton, came up with an even higher age range, estimating that the male from KV55 died between thirty-five and forty-five years of age. They have even suggested that he may have been around sixty when he died, but this is very unlikely.

Although the various analyses carried out over the years on the male from KV55 present us with a very contrasting picture regarding his age at death, it does seem very likely that he was closely related to Tutankhamen. This is strongly suggested by the fact that not only do he and Tutankhamen share the same, rather rare blood group, but their skulls are also very similar in appearance, being platycephalic (broad and flat-topped). Dr. James Harris has recently studied computerized tracings of the two skulls and "suggested that Tutankhamen and the KV55 body were first-degree relatives, either a father and son or full brothers."[8] Tutankhamen never had a son, so "the body must therefore be that of his father, almost certainly Akhenaten, or his brother the ephemeral Smenkhkare."[9] Not much is known about Smenkhkare, but he mysteriously disappeared just before Tutankhamen became king. Whether it was his body rather than Akhenaten's that was recovered from KV55 is obviously open to question, but it has been pointed out that "increasingly scholars are reverting to the original assessment that this is the corpse of Akhenaten."[10]

## IMAGES OF AKHENATEN

Whether or not it was the damaged mummy of Akhenaten that Ayrton found in KV55, there can be little doubt that he is the most intriguing and controversial of Egypt's pharaohs, and he continues to be the subject of much heated Egyptological debate. Much of this debate is centered on the royal iconography or "art" that was produced during the reign of Akhenaten, or the Amarna Period, as it is also known.

At the beginning of his reign, Akhenaten stuck to tradition and his early portraits show nothing out of the ordinary; we see "a conventional new kingdom monarch performing typical kingly deeds."[11] However, within a few years, Akhenaten had turned his back on the long-established gods and goddesses of the complex Egyptian pantheon in favor of the faceless solar deity, the Aten (the sun-disc), and subsequently moved the royal capital to Amarna. This religious revolution went hand in hand with the emergence of a remarkable new artistic style (Amarna art) that depicted Akhenaten in a startling or even shocking way:

[Akhenaten's] head, perched atop a long, thin neck, was now elongated, its length deliberately emphasized by his preference for tall head-dresses plus the traditional pharaoh's false beard. His face, in spite of its narrow almond-shaped eyes, fleshy earlobes, pendulous jaw, long nose, hollow cheeks, pronounced cheek-bones and thick lips, had a curious sensuality in its knowing and secretive smile. His body had become the exact opposite of the king's traditional manly physique. His shoulders, chest, arms and lower legs were weedy and underdeveloped and his collar bone excessively prominent, and yet he had wide hips, heavy thighs, pronounced breasts, a narrow waist and a bloated stomach which bulged over his tight-fitting kilt. The colossal statues [of the king] . . . must be classed amongst the most effective and disturbing pieces of dynastic art. Even today . . . they retain a haunting power to disturb.[12]

*Colossal statue of Akhenaten from Karnak Temple in the Egyptian Museum, Cairo. Egyptological opinion is divided as to whether the king's unusual features reflect reality or royal ideology.* © Rutherford Press Limited

Egyptological opinion is highly polarized concerning the meaning of these hugely intriguing images of Akhenaten, with some arguing that although undeniably unusual, they are nevertheless still symbolic and related to his new ideology. Other Egyptologists beg to differ: "There can be little doubt that the extraordinary manner in which Akhenaten portrayed himself, his family (and to a lesser extent, all other human beings) on his monuments somehow reflects the king's actual physical appearance."[13]

Some of those who favor the latter theory believe that Akhenaten may well have had some kind of genetic disorder or disease, such as Fröhlich's syndrome (dystrophia adiposo-genitalis), a feminizing disease that causes men to develop female-like breasts, hips, and thighs. However, it seems unlikely that Fröhlich's syndrome affected Akhenaten, as its sufferers are nearly always sterile and Akhenaten fathered several children. If some type of illness does indeed explain Akhenaten's strange, androgynous appearance, perhaps the best candidate is Marfan's syndrome. The sufferer of this rare hereditary disease "grows very tall and thin, with elongated limbs, a wide pelvic girdle, an abnormally elongated skull and an unusual distribution of subcutaneous fat."[14] Recently, it has been suggested that rather than having Marfan's syndrome, Akhenaten and his bloodline "were riddled with the aromatase excess syndrome, which might have contributed to or simply reinforced Akhenaten's belief that he was the incarnation of the father and mother of all mankind."[15]

Most Egyptologists are perhaps of the opinion that Akhenaten's strange appearance "represents a bold attempt to portray kingship as a force with characteristics that place it outside the normal plane of human experience."[16] In other words, Akhenaten was simply doing what other Egyptian rulers had done, and would continue to do after him—albeit in an exaggerated and highly stylized way—using art to portray himself as a semi-divine being in order to reinforce his ultimate position of power in society.

These Egyptologists may well be right, as a recent reexamination of the body from KV55, which formed part of the multidisciplinary research program recently carried out on Tutankhamen and other members of his family, claimed to have found no clear signs of Marfan's syndrome, or any of the other diseases that Akhenaten is purported to have had.[17] Of course, as we have seen, the KV55 body may not actually be that of Akhenaten, and so the jury remains out on Egypt's "Heretic Pharaoh" and the reason for his strange appearance.[18]

## THE YOUNGER LADY: NEFERTITI?

In 1898, the French archaeologist Victor Loret discovered the remarkable Tomb KV35 in the Valley of the Kings. As we have seen, this was the final resting place not only of the renowned pharaoh Amenhotep II, but also several other notable Egyptian rulers who had been cached in the tomb by necropolis officials after their original tombs (and mummies) had been plundered. In a side room off the burial chamber, Loret also discovered the bodies of an older woman and a younger woman lying on either side of a young boy. Their mummy wrappings had been stripped away, revealing their somewhat pitiful corpses; the older woman still had long flowing hair attached to her wizened head and the young boy still had a sidelock on his shaven head, denoting his royal status. However, it was the countenance of the young woman—whom Loret initially believed to be a young man—that most affected the Frenchman:

> The last corpse nearest the wall seemed to be that of a man. His head was shaved but a wig lay on the ground not far from him. The face of this person displayed something horrible and something droll at the same time. The mouth, running obliquely from one side nearly to the middle of the cheek, bit a pad of linen whose two ends hung from the corner of the lips. The half-closed eyes had a strange expression; he could have died choking on a gag but he looked like a young, playful cat with a piece of cloth. Death, which had respected the severe beauty of the woman and the impish grace of the boy, had turned in derision and amused itself with the countenance of the man.[19]

The two women have since been labeled the "Elder Lady" and the "Younger Lady," and it is possible, although debated, that the former is Akhenaten's mother, Queen Tiye, and the latter, Prince Thutmose, eldest son of Amenhotep III. However, the Younger Lady has been the subject of far greater controversy as some scholars have identified her as Nefertiti, Akhenaten's legendarily beautiful queen. The first to propose this theory was Marianne Luban,[20] who argued that the unusual shape of the Younger Lady's skull (which she suggests was caused either by the same illness that Akhenaten may have had or by artificial shaping) indicated that she was a member of the Amarna royal family. Luban also believes the fine bone structure of her face mirrors that of the famous painted limestone bust of Nefertiti found at Amarna. Furthermore, she feels that the severed, flexed right arm that was found near the Younger Lady could also be of some significance, as pharaohs were buried with their right arms raised and a royal scepter clasped in their right hands. Although this discovery does not provide firm evidence to support the idea that Nefertiti ruled as pharaoh, some Egyptologists have argued that Nefertiti may have ruled alongside Akhenaten as co-regent, succeeding him as pharaoh when he died. Furthermore, Luban points out that the double piercing seen on the surviving ear of the Younger Lady is also evident on this bust and other portraits of the queen, and that Nefertiti would have needed to shave her head in order to wear her striking blue crown.

*A masterpiece of ancient Egyptian art. The painted bust of Nefertiti found at Amarna in the workshop of the royal sculptor Tuthmosis by Ludwig Borchardt, who may have illegally removed the bust from Egypt to Berlin, where it can be seen today in the Neues Museum. Photo, taken 6 December 2010, courtesy of Philip Pikart*

Luban was not only the Egyptologist to identify the Younger Lady as Nefertiti: a few years later the media broke the story that the English Egyptologist Joann Fletcher had found the famous queen.[21] This claim and the subsequent publication of Fletcher's controversial book, *The Search for Nefertiti*, were not greeted with enthusiasm by many Egyptologists, including Luban, who was angry not to have been given the credit that she felt she deserved, although it is quite possible that Fletcher was unaware of Luban's theory. Whatever the case, Fletcher, who had the rare privilege of entering the tomb and being able to closely examine the Younger Lady and take X-rays of her body, followed a similar line of reasoning to Luban:

> The evidence shows that a woman ruled as pharaoh in the late 18th dynasty at the end of the Amarna Period, and the Younger Lady appears to have been buried with her right arm arranged in the pose of a pharaoh. She was also buried with a short wig most likely set in the Nubian style [and] Amarna-era double ear piercings and gold beads of the type found in the Amarna Period tomb KV55. Having suffered malicious damage[22] at the time when all traces of Amarna underwent similar treatment, her mummy was then reburied with two individuals who seem to have been members of the Amarna royal family.[23]

One of Fletcher's colleagues, Professor Earl Ertman of the University of Akron, Ohio, who has made a study of Amarna royal crowns, suggested that a noticeable impression on the Younger Lady's forehead "had been caused by a gold browband, a piece of regalia only worn by reigning kings and their chief wife."[24]

The above evidence is intriguing but it does not provide proof that we have indeed found the famous Nefertiti, and there are other possibilities to consider. For example, it has been suggested that the Younger Lady is too young to be Nefertiti and therefore could either be Meritaten, the eldest daughter of Nefertiti and Akhenaten, or Ankhesenamen, their third daughter, who later became Tutankhamen's queen.[25] To be fair to Fletcher, though, she has never claimed that she has definitely found Nefertiti, only that she believes that it is likely that the Younger Lady is Nefertiti.

## THE MYSTERIOUS DEATH OF TUTANKHAMEN

Ever since Howard Carter discovered the body of Tutankhamen in his stunning tomb in the Valley of the Kings, people have wondered about how the so-called boy-king came to die a premature death. Dr. Douglas Derry conducted the first autopsy on Tutankhamen in 1925 and although he was able to ascertain that he had been between eighteen and twenty years old when he died, to the disappointment of Carter, he was not able to provide any reasons for his death. However, in 1923, Arthur Mace had suggested that Tutankhamen might have been murdered by the man who succeeded him on the throne of Egypt—his elderly vizier Ay.

We have reason to believe that he was little more than a boy when he died, and that it was his successor, Eye [Ay], who supported his candidature to the throne and acted as his advisor during his brief reign. It was Eye moreover, who arranged his funeral ceremonies, and it may even be that he arranged his death, judging that the time was now ripe for him to assume the reins of government himself.[26]

The murder theory, though, did not find many supporters, with most people believing that he may have died from tuberculosis, inflammation of the arteries, or even a brain tumor. However, in 1968, Professor Ronald Harrison of Liverpool University performed the first-ever X-rays on Tutankhamen's body and he found possible proof to support Mace's earlier suggestion in the form of a bone fragment lodged inside the king's skull. At first, Harrison thought this may have been dislodged from the nasal cavity by the ancient embalmers, as they extracted Tutankhamen's brain during the mummification process using a long metal probe. On closer inspection of the X-rays, he changed his mind and subsequently suggested that something somewhat darker could account for the bone fragment: "On the other hand, the X-rays also suggest that this piece of bone is fused with the overlying skull and this could be consistent with a depressed fracture, which had healed. This could mean that Tutankhamen died from a brain hemorrhage caused by a blow to his skull from a blunt instrument."[27]

Professor Harrison also noticed a dark spot at the base of the skull and it has been suggested that this could be a calcified membrane that formed over a blood clot that occurred after Tutankhamen "was struck from behind, perhaps while he was sleeping or on his back."[28]

However, recent scientific analysis of Tutankhamen's body suggests that it is very unlikely that Tutankhamen lost his life to a club-wielding assassin. In 2003, Harrison's X-ray plates were reexamined, and it was concluded that the bone "fragment" (there were actually two fragments) were related to the mummification process: "If these had been dislodged . . . by a blow causing a skull fracture before death, the fragments would have been embedded in the [embalming] resin, which was instilled after death, and hence the fragments would not be visible in the radiographs."[29] This same examination also concluded that the blood clot theory does not hold up to scrutiny and that there is "no calcified membrane . . . only normal posterior fossa [base of the skull] anatomy."[30]

In 2005, Dr. Zahi Hawass and a team of experts drawn from both Egypt and Europe gave Tutankhamen's body a CT scan (1,700 images were produced) and they agreed that there was no evidence of a blow to the back of his head, or indeed any other evidence of a murderous act. Nevertheless, although there seems to be no real evidence to support the blow-to-the-back-of-the-head theory, we should perhaps be a little cautious in accepting that Tutankhamen was not murdered. Not all causes of death—violent or otherwise—show up on skeletons, and with this in mind, it could perhaps even be possible that Tutankhamen may have been poisoned. If Tutankhamen was indeed murdered, then perhaps the most likely perpetrator of this heinous crime was indeed Ay, as Arthur Mace originally suggested. As vizier (effectively the prime minister), Ay was the most powerful man in Egypt and with the king "removed" he would thus be in a position to marry Tutankhamen's wife, Queen Ankhesenamen.

Interestingly, cuneiform letters found at the ancient Hittite capital of Bogazköy in Turkey reveal that the queen was none too keen on marrying an unnamed "servant" and that she asked the Hittite king, Suppiluliuma, to send one of his sons to Egypt to become her new husband and king. We also know from the Bogazköy cuneiform archive that Suppiluliuma agreed to Ankhesenamen's request. However, the Hittite prince never got the chance to become the new pharaoh, as he was murdered somewhere near Egypt's border en route to meet his new queen.[31]

However, although it is possible that Ay did murder Tutankhamen, perhaps the biggest stumbling block to this theory is that "those closest to the king—the people most likely to kill him—had the opportunity to block his elevation to the throne when he inherited as a child. Why wait until the child became a man?"[32]

The most plausible theory—or at least the one that seems to be now favored by several Egyptologists—is that Tutankhamen died as the result of a very violent accident. During his examination of the first X-rays of the king's corpse, Harrison had noted something very odd—a large part of the rib cage and the king's heart were missing. In regard to this mystery, it has been said:

> Since one does not reach his teenage years with such a congenital deformity, it has to be assumed that these bones and cartilage were removed after Tutankhamen's death, during the embalming process. Why would this be done, however, unless they were severely damaged (and thus imperfect)? And how would they be damaged, unless the young king's chest had been crushed, presumably accidentally. . . . If crushed accidentally, under what circumstances?[33]

The CT scan of Tutankhamen's body also uncovered further possible evidence to support the death-by-accident theory. A serious, apparently unhealed fracture could be seen on the lower end of his left femur (thighbone) and as this contained embalming material it must have occurred around the time of Tutankhamen's death and not during the rough treatment meted out to his body during the first autopsy.[34] It may be possible that this fracture became seriously infected and Tutankhamen subsequently died of septicemia as a result, but most scholars feel that this is unlikely. Carter's team had also noticed that the king's left patella (kneecap) was also loose, lending further support to the accident theory, and the CT scan confirmed this (in fact it had completely separated from the leg at some point since), as well as revealing further fractures on the right kneecap and lower right leg.

Tutankhamen's mummy underwent further scientific scrutiny during a two-year investigation (2008–2009) conducted by Zawass and his colleagues into the royal mummies of the late Eighteenth Dynasty.[35] They subsequently suggested that the king was a somewhat sickly individual who may have died after contracting malaria and, furthermore, that he had bone necrosis of his left foot: in other words, he had a "clubfoot" that would have impeded his movement. Although it is probable (but not certain) that the king would have been immune to malaria, in light of the idea that he may have had problems walking, it is interesting to note that around 130 walking sticks and canes were recovered from his tomb. It is quite possible, though, that Tutankhamen's "clubfoot" was simply caused by the bandages being wrapped too tightly during the final part of the mummification process.

Returning to the idea that Tutankhamen was probably killed in a terrible accident, how might this have occurred? One scenario certainly worth considering is that Tutankhamen was killed in a chariot accident while out hunting in the desert and that he was hunting ostriches when he met his untimely and violent end. A fine golden fan that has a scene depicting Tutankhamen hunting ostriches and that once held ostrich feathers was found close to the king's body between the walls of the inner shrine in his burial chamber. It has therefore been asked in regard to this fan, "Could it have a particular relevance to his death?"[36]

The death-by-chariot theory has been questioned, however, on the grounds that Tutankhamen's injuries are not consistent with this idea, and instead, "death by hippo" has been proposed.[37] This may seem somewhat improbable, but there are depictions in New Kingdom tombs of hippo hunts, and this practice dates back at least as far as the Old Kingdom, if not earlier. Furthermore, hippos have been known to attack boats and then savage anyone unlucky enough to topple into the water. It could be possible, then, that this could explain the severe damage done to Tutankhamen's chest and ribs, as hippos have fearsome jaws that contain huge, tusk-like teeth (which can reach over fifty centimeters in length). It is hardly surprising, therefore, that their victims often die because of massive injuries to their abdomen or chest area. The following horrific scenario has thus been proposed:

> Tutankhamen was in a small boat in the Nile. His boat was attacked by a hippo and the king was thrown into the water. The hippo gored him with one of its lower tusks, at a point in the lower abdomen just below the lower end of the sternum. As the animal's powerful jaws snapped shut, the tusk drove upward, deep into the king's chest and ripped out the heart and front of the chest wall. Parts of one or both lungs might have been punctured or removed.[38]

We should also consider the intriguing possibility that none of the above theories account for Tutankhamen's apparently fatal injuries and that, rather, they were received in battle. Recently, the Epigraphic Survey of the Oriental Institute at the University of Chicago (which has been working at Luxor Temple for over twenty years) discovered reused limestone blocks, probably from Tutankhamen's previously unknown mortuary temple, and interestingly, these feature carvings depicting the king engaged in military activities. For example, in one scene, Tutankhamen is seen in his chariot valiantly leading his forces against a Syrian-style fortress and in another, the king is depicted receiving prisoners, booty, and severed enemy hands, which have been impaled on spears like gruesome shish kebabs. In addition to these scenes, there is also a depiction of a Syrian prisoner hanging in a cage attached to the sail yard of Tutankhamen's barge as it progresses up the Nile in a royal flotilla, and in the tomb of Horemheb at Saqqara, Syrian and Nubian prisoners are seen being brought to the king.

Of course, these scenes could simply be royal propaganda rather than a reflection of reality but it is quite possible—if not probable—that during Tutankhamen's reign military campaigns were undertaken against some of Egypt's traditional enemies: the Nubians, Hittites, Libyans, and Syrians.

Whether Tutankhamen was actually an active participant of the battle-field, however, is open to question, as some Egyptologists feel that kings are more likely to have been "protected at the back of their armies."[39] This may well have been the case, but we should perhaps consider a recent tentative theory put forward in regard to the mystery of Tutankhamen's missing chest, ribs, and heart:

> [Perhaps] the king went into battle and became isolated from his troops long enough to be killed. Perhaps an arrow struck him in the heart, and his enemies promptly cut open his chest and took his heart. Ultimately the Egyptian army under Horemheb rallied to recover his ravaged body and returned it for embalming without those tissues.[40]

This exciting and imaginative theory undoubtedly takes us some way down the road of speculation, but the mummy of Seqenenra Taa perhaps may lend it some support. Seqenenra was a ruler of the Theban Seventeenth Dynasty and he set in motion the military campaigns that, under his son Ahmose, eventually drove the Palestinian Hyksos from Egypt. So far, his tomb has not been located, but his mummy (and his son Ahmose's) was recovered from the famous Deir el-Bahri cache. The savage wounds that are clearly evident on Seqenenra's mummy strongly suggest that he either died on the battlefield in actual combat or, alternatively, that he was brutally executed by the Hyksos king or his vassal after he was captured following the defeat of his army:

> The examination of the mummy of Seqenenra shows that he died by violence. His forehead bears a horizontal axe cut; his cheek bone is shattered and the back of his neck carries the mark of a dagger thrust. It has been argued that the shape of the forehead wound is consistent only with the use of an axe of Middle Bronze Age type, similar to those found at Tell el-Dab´a [the Hyksos capital]. Egyptian axes . . . took a different form. . . . The angle of the dagger thrust suggests that the king was already prone when it was inflicted.[41]

While I was writing this book in 2013, a fascinating program entitled *Tutankhamun: Mystery of the Burnt Mummy* aired on Channel 4 in the UK, presented by Dr. Chris Naunton, director of the Egypt Exploration Society. As well as conducting an experiment that suggested that Howard Carter had been right in his belief that the king's mummy bandages had spontaneously combusted as the embalming fluids that covered his body slowly decomposed, Naunton also put forward an interesting new theory in regard to the king's death. He proposed that Tutankhamen did indeed die in battle, but rather than having his heart savagely ripped out by an enemy soldier, he was killed by a speeding chariot that crashed into him while he was on his knees on the battlefield (perhaps having fallen out of his own chariot). As Naunton pointed out, nobody has ever really been concerned with the fact that all Tutankhamen's injuries are on the left side of his body, and he thus argued that they are consistent with the king's having been run over by a heavy chariot wheel.

## BORCHARDT AND THE NEFERTITI BUST

The painted limestone bust that Ludwig Borchardt recovered from the workshop of Thutmose at Amarna is one of the most captivating artifacts to have survived from the ancient world. Today, it takes pride of place in the German Neues Museum in Berlin, where it was put on display for the first time in 1924, and ever since, countless visitors have come to gaze on the haunting countenance of Akhenaten's queen. What many visitors may be unaware of, however, is that there is more than just a whiff of scandal attached to this famous masterpiece of ancient Egyptian art, as it is unclear how it arrived in Berlin and some suspect foul play on Borchardt's part.

It is known that after its discovery the bust was placed in a storage magazine with the many other objects that Borchardt and his team found during their excavations at Amarna, which at the end of the digging season would be examined by an inspector from the Egyptian Department of Antiquities. At the time of the bust's discovery, concessions were granted to foreign excavations on the proviso that they agree to split all finds fifty-fifty with the Department of Antiquities. The inspector appointed to the task of looking over the Amarna finds was a junior official named Gustave Lefebvre, but for some reason, he appears to have handed over this superb four-thousand-year-old sculpture to Borchardt as part of the German team's equal share of the spoils.

It seems incredible that Lefebvre would have given the Germans such a wonderful and obviously significant artifact. However, perhaps the inspector, whose main area of expertise was the ancient Egyptian language, was hoodwinked by Borchardt, who concealed its true value by not cleaning off the ancient dirt that encrusted it. Alternatively, he may have given the inspector a poor-quality photograph of the bust, or maybe even a crude copy of it. It may even be possible that Borchardt simply hid the bust from the inspector and then removed it to his house in Cairo for further concealment before it was shipped to Germany in secret. Of course, it may simply be that Borchardt was indeed given the Nefertiti bust in good faith by a rather naïve inspector who did not grasp its true significance, and the German, scarcely able to believe his luck, quickly sent it on its way to Germany. Whatever the truth, it is clear that Borchardt was well aware that the Nefertiti bust was a major piece of Egyptian art, as is revealed by a brief entry that he made in his diary shortly after its discovery: "You cannot describe it in words. You must see it."[42]

The bust caused something of a sensation when it was first revealed to the world, and it is therefore not surprising that the Egyptian authorities soon got wind of this remarkable artifact. Therefore, in 1925, they made an informal request to Germany that it be repatriated. This first request was ignored, as were the others that followed it in 1929 and in the 1950s. It was not until the appointment of Zahi Hawass as the head of the Egyptian

Supreme Council of Antiquities in 2002 that the Egyptians renewed their efforts to get back the Nefertiti bust from Berlin, putting forward a strong case that Borchardt had hidden its true identity and smuggled it out of Egypt.

Hawass undoubtedly reignited the debate on the repatriation of the Nefertiti bust and brought it to the attention of the international community, among whom he found many sympathetic ears, but he has since been fired from office because of his alleged close connections to the deposed president Mubarak. Hawass' sacking, combined with the troubled current political situation in Egypt, probably means that those who feel that the Nefertiti bust should be returned to its rightful home because it was taken illegally from the country will be waiting some time before their wish is granted. However, it is very likely that at some point, the Egyptian plea for the return of this stunning reminder of the Amarna Age will once again be heard.

## THE AMARNA PRINCESS

Over the years, the world of archaeology has been rocked by several high-profile scandals. For example, there is the "Piltdown Hoax" involving Charles Dawson, who, in 1912, claimed to have found pieces of a skull and the jawbone of a previously unknown, early human species in a gravel pit at Piltdown in East Sussex, England. This was later found to comprise skull fragments from a modern human and the jawbone from an orangutan. There is also the "Dorak Affair" in Turkey, which involved the well-known Dutch archaeologist James Mellart, who may or may not have been guilty of being involved in a plot to smuggle out of the country a fabulous hoard of stunning gold and silver artifacts that had probably been looted from various sites around Turkey.

England—or more precisely, the unassuming market town of Bolton in North West England—has also recently been the setting of an archaeological scandal. Although it is probably not as well known amongst the wider archaeological community as the two famous examples just mentioned, it has certainly become somewhat famous amongst the Egyptological one, and at its center is a small stone statue known as the Amarna Princess.

The beginning of the story of the Amarna Princess can be traced back to the purchase of an 1892 auction catalog listing the contents of the stately home of Silverton Park in Devon, the residence of the fourth Earl of Egremont, George Wyndham, until his death in 1845. The catalog was bought by the Greenhalgh family, a gang of master forgers from South Turton on the outskirts of Bolton, who produced an incredible range of fake artworks.[43] Some of these were sold on the international market and also to museums and private buyers, with the family amassing nearly a million pounds as a result. It has been estimated that if the family had sold all of the forged items that were found in their family home by the police, then they could have made as much as ten million pounds (c.$16.5 million).

Shaun Greenhalgh was the talented "artist" responsible for the forgeries and he worked out of a garden shed in the house he shared with his parents, Olive and George, who made contact with possible clients, while George Jr., the youngest son, handled the money made from successful sales of their fake artifacts. Somewhat predictably, the family was named the "Garden Shed Gang" by the British media.

Among the items listed in the 1892 auction catalog previously mentioned were "eight Egyptian figures" and this ambiguous description presented the Greenhalghs with the perfect opportunity to perpetrate yet another hoax. Shaun was thus soon back in his shed, manufacturing a superbly made stone statue measuring about fifty centimeters in height, which he "aged" not only by coating it in a mixture of tea and clay but also by cleverly leaving it incomplete, with its head, arms, and lower legs missing. The statue was so convincing that Bolton Museum bought it in 2003 for over four hundred thousand pounds, and it was seen as a hugely important find by the international Egyptological community. The following quote is taken from a short article written on the Amarna Princess after she had been "discovered" following George Greenhalgh's approach to Bolton Museum, which was told that the statue had been bought by his grandfather at the Silverton auction:

> The sculpture is carved in translucent Egyptian alabaster (calcite), is 52 centimeters high and represents a royal female of the Amarna Period (c.1350–1334 BC), with head, arms and lower legs not surviving. The body wears an elegant, pleated robe with fringes and side streamers and is that of a princess with the remains of the side lock of youth on the shoulder. . . . She is one of the daughters of the Pharaoh Akhenaten and his chief queen, Nefertiti. . . . Although various sculptures survive from Akhenaten's reign, pieces like this are rare and of great significance.[44]

The Amarna Princess remained on display in the museum for three years and would probably have gone on fooling visitors and Egyptologists[45] for many years more, were it not for an uncharacteristic slipup made by Shaun Greenhalgh, when, in 2005, he tried to sell three fake Assyrian reliefs supposedly made around 700 BC to the British Museum. Unfortunately for

*The Amarna Princess. The small but superbly made fake Egyptian statue, which had many scholars in the international Egyptological community fooled. Photo courtesy of Bolton News*

Greenhalgh, suspicions were raised about these reliefs not only by spelling mistakes seen in the cuneiform script but also by his atypical depictions of the horse's reins. The Greenhalghs' house was subsequently raided by the police and the game was finally up for this family of master forgers, with the police discovering a remarkable collection of forgeries, among which were two more Amarna Princesses in a wardrobe.

The brief tenure that the Amarna Princess held as a rare and beautiful artifact of the Amarna Period thus came to a somewhat ignominious end, but she remains a striking reminder of the devious talents of a family from Bolton who came very close to completely fooling Egyptologists around the world.

# 5

# HARMING EGYPT'S PAST

## The Antiquities Market

It would be hard to disagree that "since the 1960s, the antiquities market has been escalating at an alarming rate to become a billion-dollar-a-year business involving archaeological artifacts and works of art from all over the world."[1] Whether the money pulled in by the worldwide antiquities trade actually runs into billions of dollars is disputed (unsurprisingly, most vehemently by those involved in the antiquities trade) and estimates presented by museum professionals, archaeologists, and law enforcement agencies vary considerably, with figures ranging from three hundred million to six billion dollars per year. However, the evidence from specific case studies suggests that a figure toward the higher end of the scale is probably more likely, and massive sums of money are clearly changing hands in the world's famous auction houses. For example, in the summer of 1990, Sotheby's in New York sold the Nelson Bunker Hunt collection of sixteen Greek vases and the William Herbert Hunt collection of classical bronzes for a combined total of $11,398,200. One vase alone sold for a staggering $1,760,000, which set a new world record for the sale of an ancient Greek vase. These figures pale in comparison with the $57.2 million that was paid for the "Guennol Lioness" at Sotheby's, New York, in December 2007. Measuring only around eight centimeters high, this three-thousand-year-old limestone figurine of a lioness-goddess or feline demon, which probably originated in Iran, easily beat the $28.6 million paid for the two-thousand-year-old bronze figurine known as "Artemis and the Stag" (Artemis was a Greek god-dess associated with hunting), also sold at the Sotheby's New York auction room, earlier in 2007.

Whatever the true figure for the annual turnover of the worldwide antiq-uities trade, as the antiquities market continues to grow it creates an ever-increasing demand for antiquities. Worryingly, this demand is more often than not met by the illicit looting of archaeological sites, with the looters having little concern for the damage and destruction they are doing:

> When artifacts are ripped from the ground without proper documentation, their context is irretrievably lost without ever being known. Unlike archae-ologists, looters are not interested in the context of artifacts, nor are they concerned with all artifacts from a site. They are interested only in those few, such as intact vessels, sculptures, and textiles, for which a market exists or can be created. All other material is ruthlessly broken and tossed aside, and in the process the site itself may very well be destroyed.[2]

The looted artifacts that surface on the antiquities market can thus be seen as "cultural orphans, [which] torn from their contexts, remain for ever dumb, and virtually useless for scholarly purposes."[3] It would be unfair to claim that all of the "unprovenanced" artifacts that surface on the antiqui-ties market are such "orphans," but it would be naïve to believe that for the most part, they have been acquired honestly. As has been pointed out, "unprovenanced objects is a shorthand of sorts. When these objects come to market, someone knows where they originated, but isn't saying."[4]

In fact, the sad truth is that archaeological sites are being looted in coun-tries all over the world, with thousands of artifacts ripped from sites on a frequent basis. This is borne out by a recent survey involving 2,350 archae-ologists worldwide, with 70 percent of the archaeologists reporting actual evidence of looting on sites and 98 percent reporting looting taking place at some level in the areas where they carried out their research; 24 percent had actually come face-to-face with looters at work and also discovered stashes of stolen artifacts.[5]

The handful of examples of worldwide looting cited here are thus just a few among many, though they clearly show how the world's ancient heritage is suffering as a result. It is well known that Iraq has suffered par-ticularly badly at the hands of looters because of the two Gulf Wars, with ancient Assyrian palaces being targeted as well as several museums and nu-merous sites that have gone unrecorded. At the end of the last Gulf War in May 2003, the National Museum in Baghdad was ransacked by thieves and it was estimated by an official US investigation that at least 13,500 objects were stolen.[6] Although a fair percentage of these artifacts have since been recovered (with the American military playing a major part in the recovery of stolen objects), many objects from the museum found their way onto the international antiquities market and looting continues to be a very serious problem in Iraq.

Another country whose archaeological sites are under serious threat from looting is Italy, and between 1969 and 1999, the Italian police recovered around 330,000 objects from illegal excavations; in 1997, they arrested a dealer who was in possession of between ten thousand and thirty thousand illegal antiquities. In the same year, Swiss police discovered a further ten thousand Italian antiquities in four warehouses in a Geneva free port.[7]

In Greece, huge damage has been done to Early Bronze Age cemeteries in the Cycladic Islands by looters searching for stone Cycladic figures, which are greatly desired by antiquities collectors for their simple aesthetic beauty. In fact, it has been estimated that "some 85 percent of the funerary record of the Early Bronze Age Cyclades may have been lost through this unscientific search for figurines."[8]

Illicit excavation is also a big problem in the Maya region of Central America, and looted Maya ceramics alone fetch around $120 million on the antiquities market every year.[9] In China, at least 220,000 ancient tombs have been looted for antiquities in recent years, and these are probably China's biggest illegal export.[10]

Looting of archaeological sites in the United Kingdom is also not uncommon, and Roman sites in particular are favored, with many being dug at night by looters who have thus earned themselves the less-than-flattering sobriquet of "Nighthawks."

Aside from damaging or destroying the valuable information on past human societies that is found at archaeological sites, "a further detrimental effect of looting is in the loss to a country of its cultural assets as they travel to overseas markets."[11] I am not proud to report that my own country, the United Kingdom, is heavily involved in this illegal trade. As has been noted, the UK "is home to one of the largest market centers, in terms of volume of trade, for the sale of antiquities. Antiquities looted from source countries routinely travel here to be sold by international dealers and auction houses to other dealers, private collectors and museums."[12]

Unfortunately, much the same could be said for the United States, with New York clearly an international center of the antiquities trade, and "the United States has been credited with being the largest single buyers' market for stolen or illegally exported cultural property."[13] Other rich "market nations," such as France, Brussels, Switzerland, Germany, and Japan, also have a significant part to play in the purchase of illegal antiquities. The exact percentage of illicit antiquities that come to market is hard to ascertain for sure but it has been suggested that it could be as high as 80 percent[14] and that measured in dollars, the illegal antiquities market is second only to international gun and drugs crime in terms of the revenue it produces.[15] It is also interesting to note that illegal antiquities revenues are used to finance the terrorist activities of Hezbollah, the Taliban, and Al-Qaeda; it is known that Mohammed Atta, who flew American Airlines Flight 11 into the north tower of the World Trade Center, had been trying to sell Afghan antiquities before he perpetrated this crime against humanity.

Another "detrimental consequence of looting is the corruption of the historical record through the introduction of artifacts that may be forgeries."[16] Furthermore, "the willingness of buyers to accept undocumented antiquities permits the proliferation of forged artifacts on the market."[17] An example of this is very probably provided by the Cycladic figures mentioned above, as it is very likely that many of the high-quality examples that appeared on the antiquities market in the later twentieth century are fakes produced by modern workshops in Greece and elsewhere in Europe.[18]

It would also be very naïve to believe that many of the people involved in the antiquities trade are oblivious to the fact that the numerous ancient objects that pass through their hands have been acquired illegally. In fact, an investigation into the famous Sotheby's auction house in London, in 1997, uncovered clear proof of this. Documents leaked by a former employee revealed that many of the unprovenanced artifacts sold by Sotheby's were illegally excavated and smuggled from Italy to Switzerland by an Italian dealer named Giacomo Medici. The same documents also revealed that in some cases, Sotheby's staff were not only all too aware of the murky background of these artifacts, but had also helped get them to Britain.[19]

It would be wrong to tar everyone involved in the antiquities trade with the same illegal brush, but further evidence of the many dishonest dealings that go on in the antiquities market has been provided by the antiquities dealers themselves:

> There are always collectors that have insisted on provenance. There are collectors that thrive on no provenance. I can think of two major collectors in the US that are absolutely thrilled to find a piece that's just come out of the ground illegally. It's something exciting. They're cheating. . . . And they're known for it.[20]

> There is an awful lot of illicit stuff . . . and you know, the answer is one doesn't know, one can only suspect. And being involved in the marketplace I know

a vast swathe of people, and I think off the top of my head I have or will do business with less than 10 percent of them. Purely because I regard the rest as untrustworthy, to put it mildly.[21]

## THE EGYPTIAN SITUATION

Unsurprisingly, given the vast wealth of its archaeological record, Egypt is one of the richest source nations for antiquities and the country has undoubtedly "suffered grievously from the illegal antiquities trade and illicit excavation."[22] This suffering can be traced back to the formative years of Egyptology when numerous antiquities were leaving Egypt in the hands of foreign government agents, excavators, and tourists, all too easily. This was largely due to the indifference of its Turkish rulers to Egypt's ancient history, who often gave away antiquities as diplomatic gifts. Several official acts were therefore passed throughout the nineteenth century (the first was passed in 1835)[23] and these sought to stop the severe hemorrhaging of antiquities from Egypt by banning their export without a proper permit or license, and by requiring that foreign missions obtain permission from the Egyptian Antiquities Service before they began excavating sites. Gradually, the official Egyptian stance on illegal antiquities became stricter, but it was not until the current Antiquities Act passed in 1983 that the Egyptian government began to take a more hard-line stance against the illicit trade in antiquities, which had been going on in their country for some two hundred years. This act states that

> all monuments and artifacts uncovered in Egypt are the property of the Egyptian government. In addition, any object that has been duly registered as the property of Egypt, regardless of when it was discovered, should continue to be regarded as such unless a clear record exists that it was legally sold or given to another owner.[24]

It is perhaps also rather surprising that it was not until this act was passed that the system of "partage"—whereby foreign missions were allowed to take a share of the objects they had recovered during their excavations back to their own countries—was finally revoked. In February 2010, the Antiquities Act of 1983 was further strengthened by the passing of new legislation that levies a possible fifteen-year jail sentence and a twenty-thousand-dollar fine on anyone caught smuggling cultural property. An amendment to this act is currently awaiting implementation and this will impose even harsher penalties for those involved in the illegal antiquities trade, with sentences of twenty-five years to life in prison and fines ranging from $50,000 to $250,000 Egyptian dollars.

As well as trying to protect its antiquities by passing domestic laws, Egypt is also party to the 1970 UNESCO[25] Convention on the Means of Prohibiting and Preventing the Illicit Import, Export and Transfer of Ownership of Cultural Property. Furthermore, the Supreme Council of Antiquities, or SCA, which until recently was led by the powerful and divisive figure Zahi Hawass,[26] does its best to keep illegal excavations in check (a tough ask in a country as large and antiquities-rich as Egypt) and generally monitors the welfare of Egypt's considerable cultural heritage.

Unfortunately, as in other rich source nations, neither domestic nor international law can ever fully protect Egypt's cultural heritage, and the truth is this heritage has long been—and will continue to be—seriously threatened by the illicit looting and export of antiquities for sale on the international market:

> The destruction in countries like Egypt is catastrophic. As I know from my own experience of working in the field there and talking to my colleagues in Egypt, Egypt is not alone but it is probably uniquely rich in antiquities. Massive destruction is being done to archaeological sites in Egypt on a daily basis. Objects are finding their way out through various laundering systems.[27]

Staggeringly, 56,000 of these objects were recovered from one of the largest hauls of illicit antiquities ever made (113,000 in total), which was impounded at Heathrow in April 2002. The shipment was found to belong to Mamdouh Michael, who was living in Zurich (one of the world's major centers of the antiquities trade) at the time, and who claimed that he inherited this huge collection of antiquities from his father. This claim was treated with the suspicion it deserved and it is no surprise that the joint investigation subsequently carried out by the SCA and Egyptian State Security discovered the objects had previously been registered by the SCA, revealing that they had been stolen from various government storehouses in Egypt.

Less extreme than the above example of illicit trading in antiquities, but more well known, is the case involving Frederick Schultz, an antiquities dealer from New York and former president of the National Association of Dealers in Ancient, Oriental and Primitive Art. Schultz worked in partnership with the former British cavalryman Jonathan Tokeley-Parry, and together, they concocted a devious plan to sell illegal Egyptian antiquities in the United States.[28] The antiquities that they brought to the States were supposedly from a collection legally acquired in the 1920s by the English

Egyptologist Thomas Alcock and the great-uncle of Tokeley-Parry. In reality, Alcock was a fictitious character invented by Schultz and Tokeley-Parry, and Tokeley-Parry—with the aid of the Egyptian brothers Ali and Toutori Faraq—had been smuggling antiquities out of Cairo since the early 1990s. Using his skills as an antiquities restorer, Tokeley-Parry disguised the antiquities as cheap tourist souvenirs by covering them in plastic, plaster, and paint, and then smuggled them out of Egypt to Switzerland. These coverings were then removed and "original" labels (artificially aged with tea bags) attributing the antiquities to the "Thomas Alcock Collection" were attached, making them ready for sale on the antiquities market. One such antiquity was a sculpted head of the Eighteenth Dynasty pharaoh Amenhotep III that Schultz sold to a private collector in 1993 for $1.2 million.

However, Tokeley-Parry's days as a dealer in illicit antiquities ended in 1994 after his assistant (somewhat brazenly) took twenty-seven papyrus texts stolen from a storeroom in Egypt to the British Museum, with the aim of authenticating them for a potential buyer. Unfortunately for Tokeley-Parry, a curator at the museum recognized them as coming from an Egyptian site where a legitimate excavation had previously been carried out. The curator informed the relevant authorities (i.e., Scotland Yard, the Egyptian embassy, the SCA, and the Egyptian Tourism and Antiquities Police) and after further illegal Egyptian antiquities were found along with incriminating papers and photographs at a country estate in Devon, Tokeley-Parry was sent to trial in 1997. He subsequently received a six-year prison sentence in England (of which he served three years) and fifteen years of hard labor in absentia by the Egyptian courts.

Journals later seized from Tokeley-Parry clearly implicated Schultz and other accomplices in Tokeley-Parry's smuggling ring, and in fact, they revealed that the American had financed many of the Englishman's illegal activities in Egypt. In 2001, Schultz was "charged with conspiring to receive, possess, and sell antiquities stolen from archaeological sites in Egypt."[29] Although there was much legal wrangling by his defense team as they sought to prove his "innocence," it was to no avail, as Schultz was eventually sentenced to thirty-three months in an American jail.

It is not just in the hands of private collectors that looted Egyptian antiquities have ended up, but also in notable museums, and we have seen a probable (but unproven) example of this with the famous Nefertiti bust in Berlin's Neues Museum. More recently, the renowned Louvre Museum in Paris has been embroiled in a scandal involving illicit Egyptian antiquities.

In 2008, Dr. Eva Hoffman and her team from Heidelberg University were investigating the tomb of the Eighteenth Dynasty noble Tetiky on

Luxor's west bank and realized that several pieces of the beautiful wall paintings in the tomb had been hacked away (an earlier photo showed them to be intact). Hoffman subsequently discovered that five painted wall fragments held by the Louvre matched those missing from the tomb. Quite rightly, the SCA demanded them back from the Louvre and also suspended their excavations at Saqqara until the missing wall fragments were returned to Egypt.

The Louvre acquired the wall paintings from private collections and denied having any knowledge that they were stolen, but they do not seem to have been particularly concerned about properly researching the provenance of these pieces. However, it would be wrong to cast the Louvre as a major villain, as it is certainly not the only international museum to adopt this laissez-faire attitude to buying antiquities with a somewhat murky background.

It is also extremely likely that many illicit Egyptian antiquities found their way onto the antiquities market as a result of the so-called Arab Spring that removed President Hosni Mubarak from power. As the first protests to oust Mubarak began in early January 2011, so did the damage and looting. Inevitably, it was not long before looters made their way to the Cairo Museum, from which they stole forty ancient artifacts and damaged many others. An archaeological storage magazine at Qantara was also attacked by an armed gang and although the robbers did not steal anything of particular note, they still managed to get away with a statue and various pottery vessels. More serious is the looting that took place at the site of Lisht, with tombs being broken into and illegal excavations taking place under cover of darkness; similar problems were encountered at the famous sites of Dashur and Saqqara.[30] In fact, in May 2012, Egypt's Ministry of Interior reported a staggering "5697 illegal digs, 1467 cases of illicit trading in antiquities, 130 attempts to smuggle antiquities abroad and [that] at least 35 people have been killed in incidents connected to illegal digs."[31]

Unsurprisingly, as Egypt's political troubles have continued, so too have the looting and destruction of its archaeological heritage. In August 2013, for example, the Mallawi National Museum in central Egypt was ransacked during the riots that erupted in the city following the clashes in Cairo between supporters of the former president Mohammed Morsi and the army, which resulted in hundreds of protesters being killed. Many hundreds of artifacts were stolen (and many of those left behind by the thieves were badly damaged). Although some of these ancient objects have since been recovered, there are still hundreds missing, with the most grievous loss being the beautiful limestone statuette of one of Akhenaten's daughters.

Several experts believe that the raid on the museum represents more than just opportunistic looting by criminals and that an organized gang of antiquities smugglers deliberately targeted the statue, knowing it would fetch a very high price on the illegal antiquities market because of its connection to the famous Amarna era. Unfortunately, looting and cultural vandalism continue to be a serious problem in Egypt, and the authorities fight a daily battle to keep it in check, although they are having a very tough time winning this battle.

To end this chapter on a more optimistic note, as we have seen above with the Schultz and Tokeley-Parry cases, not all of the dishonest dealers are getting away with the illegal trading of antiquities. In 2003, the government of the United Kingdom also passed the Dealing in Cultural Objects (Offences) Act. Under this act, anyone found guilty of dishonestly acquiring and trafficking cultural objects is subject "to imprisonment for up to seven years and/or an unlimited fine or conviction in the Magistrate's Court to a maximum of six months imprisonment and/or a fine up to £5000." Furthermore, the Vienna-based United Nations Office on Drugs and Crime "has now recognized that the actions of illicit traffickers in art and antiquities have many similarities to those engaged in other organized transnational criminal activities, including drugs and arms trafficking."[32]

Life has become much harder for dishonest dealers in Egyptian antiquities in the United States too, as thanks largely to the famous Schultz case they now face the knotty problem of having to provide a very firm provenance for any looted ancient artifacts they are trying to sell. In 2009, the Metropolitan Museum of Art in New York repatriated to Egypt a fragment of a red granite naos[33] of the Twelfth Dynasty king Amenemhat I, a piece the Met had previously purchased from a private New York collector with this specific purpose in mind.[34] The well-known antiquities dealer Phoenix Ancient Art, which has galleries in both New York and Geneva, has also returned to Egypt two inscribed funerary steles that were illegally excavated from the ancient town-site of Akhmim in northern Upper Egypt. A larger stele from the same site had already been seized in New York the previous year from the collector who had purchased it, and subsequently returned to Egypt. It is interesting to note that Frederick Schultz was involved in the smuggling of these artifacts from Egypt.

The more stringent legal barriers and harsher convictions now facing dishonest antiquities dealers and the return of the above looted artifacts are welcome developments, as is the recent formation of the organizations SAFE (Saving Antiquities for Everyone) and the Lawyers' Committee for Cultural Heritage Preservation. Of course, given the scale of the problem and the fact that there will always be those who are willing to trade in illegal antiquities, it would be unrealistic to believe that this worldwide trade can ever be completely eradicated. Nonetheless, organizations such as the above, and the continuing efforts of the many individuals who strive to protect the world's ancient heritage, can only help in the fight against those who plunder humanity's past in the name of greed.

# 6

# CONTRIBUTIONS TO
# KNOWLEDGE OF THE PAST

**S**ince Egyptology took its first faltering steps in the earlier nineteenth century thanks to the great achievement of Jean-François Champollion, Egyptologists have slowly but surely revealed the compelling story of ancient Egypt. In the process, they have made significant contributions to furthering our knowledge of the past, and one person who definitely stands out in this regard is Flinders Petrie. As has been said of this famous scholar, who played a major part in Egyptology's formative years, and in those of the wider world of archaeology in general:

> In a long and illustrious career, he excavated many of the most important ancient Egyptian sites. . . . His energetic fieldwork was matched by his excellent publication record. . . . Petrie's techniques of excavation were vastly superior to those employed by most of his contemporaries. Above all, he was determined to preserve and record as much of the evidence as possible, rather than concentrating purely on the kinds of objects that would command a good price on the art market.[1]

Perhaps the most important aspect of Petrie's archaeological work was his development of "sequence dating," which he devised so that he could place the thousands of Predynastic graves he excavated at Naqada into a relative chronological order. Generally, archaeologists before Petrie had shown little interest in pottery, but he realized that careful study of the various pottery vessels found in the graves would allow him to order them into a relative sequence approximately dating from the early to late fourth millennium BC. Petrie's recognition of distinctive types of pottery (e.g., the "black-topped" and "wavy-handed" classes) allowed him to divide the Predynastic Period into its various cultural stages, which, we as saw in chapter one, were the Amratian, Gerzean, and Semainean. Although this Predynastic chronology was subsequently "fine-tuned," firstly by Walter Federn of the Brooklyn Museum and then by the German Egyptologist Werner Kaiser, to this day, Egyptologists still broadly follow it. More importantly, Petrie's sequence dating (or "seriation dating" as it is now more commonly known) is a dating technique still used by archaeologists on sites throughout the world.

Petrie also seems to have been "the first archaeologist in Egypt to exploit the importance of stratigraphy, the principle that through time archaeological remains are deposited in layers or strata of soil."[2] Although stratigraphic excavation can be complicated by such factors as later intrusive deposits dug into earlier layers, burrowing animals, or even earthquakes, it generally follows that "the latest artifacts and other remains are in layers closest to the present surface, while the earliest ones are lower in the ground, just above bedrock or sterile soil."[3]

However, although Petrie was undoubtedly a careful and meticulous archaeologist way ahead of many of his contemporaries, and the first person to stratigraphically excavate a *tell* in Palestine (Tell Hesy in 1890), he was not a great advocate of stratigraphic excavation in Egypt. This was because he did not dig many settlement sites, which was where stratigraphic deposits (i.e., buildups of different phases of occupation) would be more likely. As he wrote in his *Methods and Aims in Archaeology* (1904): "The two objects of excavations are (1) to obtain plans and topographical information, and (2) to obtain portable antiquities."[4]

In fact, it was George Reisner (the so-called American Petrie) who was the greater advocate of the use of stratigraphic excavation and from 1900, when Reisner began working at the site of Deir el-Ballas[5] in Upper Egypt, onward he ensured it was a routine part of the extensive fieldwork he carried out in Egypt and the Sudan. Reisner also sought out and recorded the archaeological sites in northern Nubia that were threatened by the heightening of the first High Dam at Aswan. As a result, he developed the concept of "rescue archaeology," which was to become so important in the later twentieth century as urban and agricultural development increasingly encroached on archaeological sites. It could be argued, then, that Reisner was an even more influential figure than Petrie and it has been said of this American archaeological pioneer:

No excavator anywhere in the world has equaled the care in digging and the completeness in recording exhibited by Reisner in his best work. . . . In his archaeological work it may be said that no phase is neglected, whether the technique of fieldwork, the recording of details, or the treatment of surveying, architecture, photography and drawing. . . . Reisner has created the most important contemporary school of excavators. His methods have been copied by British archaeologists . . . and have powerfully influenced German and French excavators.[6]

During his time teaching at Harvard in the early twentieth century, Reisner established the important course "Theory and Practice of Archaeological Field-Work as a Branch of Historical Research." He put his words into practice during his long years in Egypt (he worked there for over forty years and died in the Harvard-Boston expedition camp at Giza), and was proud of his Harvard-Boston expeditions, which had championed "the development and improvements of methods of excavation and recording, with the idea of making archaeological field-work a scientific method of historical research."[7]

Ultimately, it is of little import who is the more famous of these two early Egyptological scholars from either side of the Atlantic, as both Petrie and Reisner were undoubtedly hugely influential figures who employed innovative archaeological techniques that are now established as fundamental principles underlying the modern archaeology of today.

## SPACE ARCHAEOLOGY

Egyptologists today continue to make valuable contributions to the study of the past, and of particular note in this respect is Sarah Parcak, an associate professor of anthropology at the University of Alabama at Birmingham, who has been a leading figure in the establishment of satellite or "space" archaeology (the more technical term is "remote sensing"). Space archaeology has undoubtedly "contributed much to archaeology and has great potential for Egyptian archaeology and archaeology across the globe."[8] It is an exciting prospect in regard to the new discovery of sites and monuments in Egypt (and elsewhere) and it also provides archaeologists with a broad-scale surveying tool.

In 2012, CNN's "The Next List" said of Parcak: "Her work is mind boggling and is literally transforming the field of archaeology. . . . Sarah literally wrote the book on satellite technology, publishing the first methods guide for the field."[9]

As its name suggests, satellite or space archaeology uses infrared satellite imagery to locate previously undiscovered or lost archaeological sites, and although still somewhat in its infancy, its popularity has been steadily growing, with archaeologists elsewhere using it in their own work. For example, in 2005–2006, Ghent University (Belgium) completed a thorough archaeological survey of Iron Age, Bronze Age, and Turkish monuments in the Altai Mountains (south Siberia), which had previously not been possible because the topographic and military maps that were already available were not detailed enough.[10]

The images used by the Ghent team in their survey were taken by CO-RONA, a well-known American spy satellite that was operational between 1960 and 1972, during which time over eight hundred thousand high-resolution images were taken by one hundred spacecraft. As well as using images gathered by CORONA, archaeologists also use images taken by the Landsat, Quickbird, and ASTER (Advanced Spaceborne Thermal Emission and Reflection Radiometer) satellites, with the latter being NASA's flagship satellite on board its Earth Observing System (EOS). Of course, many satellite images can be seen on the well-known Google Earth program, and although its coverage of the globe is patchy in terms of both the areas covered and the quality of the images, the usefulness of Google Earth in regard to the study and discovery of archaeological sites is undoubted.

Parcak has uncovered numerous new sites in Egypt through her analysis of satellite imagery, with perhaps her most notable discovery being the remains of the pyramid of Queen Sesheshet (the mother of King Teti, founder of the Sixth Dynasty) at Saqqara. In addition to discovering the remains of the queen's pyramid, she also rediscovered the remains of three more pyramids at Saqqara that were lost after being excavated in the nineteenth century by the French Egyptologist Gustave Jéquier.

Also notable is Parcak's analysis of the satellite imagery that she has gathered of the remains of the ancient city of Tanis in the Delta. Her examination of the crop markings seen in the modern cultivation that borders the city has led her to suggest—probably quite rightly—"that the site likely extended up to twice its current size."[11] Furthermore, Parcak's satellite data for Tanis revealed a remarkable maze-like plan of streets and buildings, showing the true complexity of the site. Some of the buildings were of a substantial size, suggesting that they had been elite residences, and a French team that excavated the site found that the satellite imagery closely matched what was actually found on the ground.

Parcak has also made less "spectacular" finds in more remote corners of ancient Egypt. For example, on the El-Markha Plain in South Sinai, where there is a late Old Kingdom fortress (Ras Budran) that protected the Egyptian copper and turquoise mining expeditions heading to the mines at Wadi Maghara, she identified several circular features along the coast (located about two miles to the south of the fort). These are about half the size of Ras Budran and could quite possibly be ancient Egyptian copper smelting sites or perhaps even a chain of smaller forts. Although excavation of these features is still needed, it is interesting to note that "they lie within a large wadi system that could have provided them with seasonal water [and] appear to be within fire/smoke signaling distance . . . of the northern fortress."[12]

It has been widely reported in the press that Parcak has found a total of seventeen new pyramids and thousands of new Egyptian tombs and settlements.[13] Such reports should be treated with caution as many of the sites have not been subjected to "ground-truthing" (a ground survey or excavation of a site by archaeologists), and what they actually are cannot be verified until this has been carried out. However, it still seems very likely that many of the new sites identified are indeed remnants of ancient Egyptian life.

## VOICES FROM DEIR EL-MEDINA

As has been pointed out, "The key to understanding the hieroglyphs has given us insights into Egypt's past which are completely absent from other parts of the world."[14] This has allowed us to come that much closer to the actual people and personalities of ancient Egypt who left behind such a staggering wealth of archaeology. For instance, from the tomb of the vizier Rekhmire, we can read the advice given him on his appointment by the king some three and a half thousand years ago: "Bear in mind what was said about the vizier Akhtoy. Whenever his friends or family petitioned him about a matter, he always found against them, for fear of people saying, 'He favors his own.' That is excess of justice."[15] Or we can read a rather hectoring letter sent by Sennufer, mayor of Thebes (c.1425 BC) to one of his employees:

> The mayor of the southern capital Sennufer speaks to the tenant farmer Baki son of Kyson, to the following effect. This letter is brought to you to tell you that I am coming to see you when we moor at Hu in three days' time. Do not let me find fault with you in your duties. Do not fail to have things in perfect order. Also, pick for me numerous plants, lotuses and flowers, and others

worth offering. Further, you are to cut 5,000 boards and 200 timbers; then the boat which will bring me can carry them, since you have not cut any wood this year—understood? On no account be slack. If you are not able to cut them you should approach Woser, the mayor of Hu. Pay attention: the herdsman of Cusae and the cowherds who are under my authority, fetch them for yourself in order to cut the wood, along with the workmen who are with you. Also, you are to order the herdsmen to prepare milk in new jars in anticipation of my arrival—understood? You are not to slack, because I know that you are a wiwi[16] and fond of eating in bed.[17]

Luckily for Baki, the papyrus on which Sennufer had written his letter never reached him, as it was found near Sennufer's tomb, rolled up and still sealed, with the Egyptologist who translated it the first person to read the letter since the day it was written some three and a half thousand years ago.

However, as fascinating as such snippets of ancient Egyptian life are, they cannot compare to the extraordinary wealth of textual evidence recovered from the village of the royal tomb builders at Deir el-Medina. This stands head and shoulders above all other such evidence from Egypt, and indeed, from anywhere in the world. This is because this evidence not only reveals in considerable detail the lives of the people who lived here, but it also provides us with an unrivalled picture of life in an ancient settlement— Egyptian or otherwise. As has been said, "The community of the ancient world about which we know the most is the village of Deir el-Medina."[18] Although the remains of the village and its associated cemeteries have obviously helped in this respect, it is the many thousands of documents found here that have really brought back to life its people, providing us with intimate details of their lives that the silent remains of the village cannot.[19]

The nature of the work carried out in the Valley of the Kings by the villagers of Deir el-Medina meant that they possessed an unusually high level of literacy in comparison to other non-royal ancient Egyptian communities, and this allowed them to leave us their unique archive. For the most part, the villagers wrote in ink on smooth flakes of local white limestone or potsherds (i.e., ostraca), which provided them with convenient note pads. However, a limited number of papyri have also been recovered from a private archive belonging to the scribe Quenherkhepeshef (also known as "Kenhirkhopeshef") and his descendants, which was unfortunately stolen after it was found during the French excavations at the village in 1928. There are also many papyri that are likely to have come from Deir el-Medina in the Egyptian Museum in Turin.

The many thousands of texts from Deir el-Medina are wide-ranging in their subject matter and we can read things such as laundry lists, magical spells, doctors' prescriptions, legal disputes, records of water deliveries, hieroglyphic exercises written by student scribes, economic transactions, and love songs. There are also hundreds of letters, many between family and friends. It is these letters that provide us with our most personal glimpses of the people of Deir el-Medina; for example, we have this intimate and informative snapshot of domestic life in the village:

> To inform you of the items left behind me in the village: three khar [sack]-measures of barley, one and a half khar-measures of barley of emmer [wheat], twenty-six bundles of papyrus, two beds, a clothes hamper (?), two couches for a man, two folding stools, one chest, one inlaid (?) box, a stool, two griddle stones, one box (?), two footstools, two folding stools of wood, one basket of lubya-beans (amounting to) three oipe-measures, twelve bricks of natron [salt], two pieces of iker-furniture, one door, two seteri-pieces of sawn wood, two offering tables (?), one small offering table (?), one mortar, and two medjay containers. They are with Pashed and the woman Sheritre, all recorded. A further matter for Sheritre: Please let Amenemwia dwell in my house so that he may keep an eye on it. Please write me about your condition.[20]

On a more emotional level, there is the moving letter sent by the draftsman Pay, who has gone blind, and who writes to his son asking him to send a cure. In this letter, we can sense the helplessness that Pay feels because of his blindness, which was obviously the worst thing that could happen to a draftsman, although it would have been a terrible burden for anyone in the village, regardless of their role:

> Do not turn your back on me—I am not well. Do not c[ease] weeping for me, because I am in the [darkness? since] my lord Amen [has turned] his back on me.
>     May you bring me some honey for my eyes, and also ochre which is made into bricks again, and real black eye-paint. [Hurry!] Look to it! Am I not your father? Now, I am wretched; I am searching for my sight but it is gone.[21]

We also know from the texts that the Deir el-Medina workforce was split into a "left" and a "right" gang, with each gang responsible for the construction of one side of whichever royal tomb they were constructing in the Valley of the Kings. Their work was overseen by a chief workman or foreman and his deputy (the deputy was often the foreman's son and he would usually inherit his father's position when he retired or died), and a scribe would document all the comings and goings of the construction work. The extensive lists they left us record such things as work rosters, absentee workmen, and the delivery of equipment and supplies to the tomb. The scribes also recorded the rations of food, water, and other supplies sent to the village from the royal warehouses or by the retainers who worked for the villagers at Deir el-Medina. One such scribe was Ramose, who recorded his new appointment (he had previously worked in one of the royal temples, where he seems to have held various positions such as "Scribe of the Temple Treasury") on a limestone ostracon, writing in his neat hand: "Made Scribe in the Place of Truth[22] in year five, third month of the season of inundation, day ten [13 September 1275 BC] of the King of Upper and Lower Egypt, Usermaatre Setepenre, Son of Re, Ramesses Beloved of Amun."[23]

Ramose stands out in the texts as a hardworking and well-respected member of the Deir el-Medina community, but the same can hardly be said for the "bad boy" of the village—the notorious Paneb. It is thanks to the famous document known as Papyrus Salt 124 that we know about the various crimes of this notorious individual, who was given the position of chief workman after the death of his adoptive father, the chief workman Neferhotep. It is Neferhotep's younger brother Amennakht who records the crimes of Paneb in the papyrus, and although we should be wary of accepting everything that is written in this scathing document at face value, on account of the fact that Paneb had been promoted to an important position that Amennakht felt was rightfully his, it is likely that it "contains rather more than a grain of truth."[24]

The most serious of the various accusations leveled at Paneb by Amennakht are that he broke into the tomb of Sety II with his accomplices and stole part of the king's chariot, wine, and incense, and also cut stone from the area of the tomb, which he had the temerity to use for pillars in his own tomb in the village cemetery. Amennakht also records that Paneb's criminal activities were not confined to the Valley of the Kings, as he tells us that Paneb also broke into the tomb of Henutmire in the Valley of the Queens and stole a goose (presumably a valuable statue, not a real goose), and that he even robbed some of the tombs of his neighbors in the village cemetery. We also learn from Amennakht that Paneb "debauched" several married women from the village (and also a daughter of one of these women), and he has left us this intriguing snapshot of an unsavory incident that Paneb was at the center of: "Charge concerning him running after the chief-workman, Neferhotep, my brother, although it was he who reared him. And [Neferhotep] closed his doors before him and [Paneb] took a stone and broke his doors. And they caused men to watch Neferhotep because [Paneb] said: I will kill him in the night, and he beat nine men in that night."[25]

It is not clear why Paned threatened to kill the man who had taken him in and raised him, nor exactly how his story ends. However, the fact that he disappears from the village records shortly after King Siptah succeeded Sety II perhaps suggests that Paneb was finally brought to book, and was either banished from the village or maybe even executed.[26]

The Deir el-Medina texts also make it clear that, as in the modern world, relations between the Deir el-Medina workmen and the state were not always smooth, and this is revealed by the famous "Turin Strike Papyrus." This document (written by a scribe named Amennakht) is actually a journal that records the incidents and events that took place as a result of shortfalls in the workmen's grain rations in year twenty-nine of the reign of Rameses III. The papyrus records that Amennakht personally delivered a letter of complaint to the authorities at the temple complex of Rameses III at Medinet Habu. As a result, some grain was subsequently delivered to the men, but the situation did not really improve, as the ration deliveries remained irregular and inadequate. This led to both the left and the right gangs downing their tools and marching to the Temple of Merneptah, where they staged a "sit-in," in the process attracting the attention of the mayor of Thebes, who was passing by. The texts also record that the men further expressed their anger by holding torchlight protests at night: "(Year 2, third month of summer), day 28. Nefer-her. . . . The gang carried torches on account of their rations for the third month of summer and the fourth month of summer."[27] Although the situation was eventually resolved and the men received the rations they were due, it would not be the last time that the workmen of Deir el-Medina went on strike during the reign of Rameses III because of shortfalls in their rations.

## THE AMARNA LETTERS

As we have seen, the Amarna Letters were found in the House of Correspondence of Pharaoh at Amarna, the capital city of King Akhenaten. These documents represent one of the largest archives of diplomatic correspondence from the Late Bronze Age world of the Near East and "they provide a remarkable insight into [Egyptian] civilization in general and diplomacy in particular of the Ancient Near East."[28]

The majority of the letters are written in the Akkadian language of ancient Mesopotamia, which was the lingua franca of the ancient Near East in the Bronze Age, although a smattering are written in the Hurrian and Hittite languages of Anatolia (ancient Turkey). The letters date from approximately 1355 to 1330 BC and span the reigns of Amenhotep III, Akhenaten (Amenhotep's son), and his probable son, Tutankhamen.

Although we cannot look at the contents of the letters in great detail here,[29] scholars have divided them into two main groups. The first documents the correspondence between pharaoh and his equals in countries such as Assyria, Babylonia, and Alashiya (ancient Cyprus), who sought to maintain the status quo or establish relations by sending each other fine gifts:

> Say to the king of Egypt: Thus Ashur-uballit, the king of Assyria. For you, your household, for your country, for your chariots and your troops, may all go well. I send my messenger to you to visit you and visit your country. Up to now, my predecessors have not written; today I write to you. I send you a beautiful chariot, 2 horses, and 1 date-stone of genuine lapis lazuli, as your greeting gift.[30]

The second—and largest—group of letters records the correspondence that took place between the Egyptian king and the lesser rulers of Egypt's vassal states in Syria and Palestine, who were expected to be loyal to the Egyptian throne and provide tribute "in the form of useful goods like raw glass and beautiful girls."[31] The unequal relationship between pharaoh and these Levantine rulers is well reflected in the following letter:

> To the king, my lord, my god, my sun, the sun from the sky. This is a message from Shur-Ashar, the ruler of Akhtishana, who is your servant, the dirt at your feet, the groom of your horse. I prostrate myself at the feet of the king, my lord, my god, my sun, the sun from the sky, seven times on the stomach and on the back. I have listened carefully to the orders of the commissioner of my king, my lord, very carefully. Who is the dog that would not obey the orders of the king, his lord, the sun from the sky, the son of the sun?[32]

The letters are not all about gift giving and maintaining the status quo, however, and in one notable example we learn of a peace treaty proposed by the famous Hurrian king Tushratta, of Mittani (northern Mesopotamia), who was seeking a defensive pact with Egypt that would be of mutual benefit to both parties in the unstable world of the ancient Near East. Such treaties between Egypt and Mittani had taken place before and they were probably prompted, for the most part, by the considerable threat posed to both countries by the other superpower of the ancient Near East—the Hittites of Anatolia. It has been said of this proposed treaty between Mittani and Egypt that it "is not so very different from Article V of the North Atlantic Treaty of 1949,"[33] which was originally created to protect the United States and western Europe from the threat of a nuclear strike by the Soviet Union.

It is also obvious from the letters that envoys were an important part of the nascent diplomacy that was taking place between Amarna and its neighbors, and the Egyptian envoy, Mane, and his Hurrian counterpart, Keliya or Gilia, are often mentioned. This stands in contrast to other envoys such as Niu and Hanni (Egyptians), Akia and Ilimilku (Canaanites), or Etilluna and Kunēa from Alashiya (ancient Cyprus), whose names are only mentioned once. The fact that Mane and Gilia are mentioned many times marks them out as being well respected and trusted individuals and this is confirmed by the following letter sent by Tushratta to Amenhotep III:

> If I should desire to send a word to my brother, concerning my land, then let my brother not listen to rumors (?) but let Mane say (it). If Mane and Gilia speak anything concerning me, concerning my land, then my brother may listen to it as authentic. . . . If Mane and Gilia say anything about my brother, about his land, I will accept it as authentic.[34]

Mane and Gilia thus probably knew each other quite well and perhaps they were even friends, as the envoys of Egypt and her neighbors often traveled together between their respective countries (with both given diplomatic immunity). The envoys of both sides were clearly more than mere "messenger boys" carrying cuneiform letters to kings and would have been skilled and literate individuals capable of dealing with the massive egos and complex machinations of the royal courts of the ancient Near East.

The above is just a brief snapshot of the fascinating contents of the Amarna Letters, but even from this it can be seen that they "preserve a body of material that permits us to observe in detail a constitutive phase in the development of a central feature of Western civilization, [as the] diplomatic forms and practices that appear here . . . anticipate the structures of the modern world."[35]

## PALEOPATHOLOGY: LOOKING AT MUMMIES

In 1973, the Manchester Egyptian Mummy Research Project was established at the University of Manchester in North West England by Dr. (now Professor) Rosalie David, and this project "has since become an acknowledged pioneer and leader in the field of paleopathology, and its development of non-destructive techniques for investigating mummified (both human and animal) remains has been adopted for use in many other research programmes."[36] The team members of the project (who were—and still are—drawn from several scientific disciplines) used a wide range of techniques and skills to make a detailed study of the mummies in Manchester Museum, and in 1975, in order to further develop their new methodology they decided to carry out an autopsy on one of the mummies from the collection. This was the first one to be carried out in Britain since 1908, when Dr. Margaret Murray and her colleagues unwrapped and autopsied the mummies of the so-called Two Brothers, whom we will meet again shortly.

The subject of the 1975 autopsy was Mummy 1770, which appears to have come from Flinders Petrie's excavations at Hawara in the late nineteenth century. Previous X-rays taken some years earlier had shown the mummy to be that of a girl about thirteen years of age, who was missing her lower legs, and who was believed to have been buried in the Greek or Roman Period (the decorated mummy wrappings were characteristically Greco-Roman). Interestingly, the autopsy suggested that it was not carelessness on the part of the ancient embalmers that accounts for the girl's missing legs, but rather that she may have lost them (and her life) in a tragic accident: "The irregular line of the amputations are more like those of accidental trauma such as might occur in a body damaged by falling masonry or even a road traffic accident."[37] Carbon dating studies of the girl's bones also revealed, somewhat remarkably, that she had died c.1000 BC, meaning that her mummy was rewrapped over a thousand years later. This rewrapping perhaps hints at a possible royal role for the young girl, but whatever the truth, it does suggest that those responsible knew that she had been someone important in the past.

More recently, the remains of the "Two Brothers" have been subjected to an extensive reevaluation by the project, some one hundred years after the autopsies carried out by Margaret Murray and her multidisciplinary team. These two individuals, whose finely decorated coffins can still be seen in Manchester Museum, lived during the Middle Kingdom. They were actually half brothers (they had different fathers) named Nakht-Ankh and Khnum-Nakht, whose rock-cut tombs were discovered high in the desert cliffs above the village of Rifeh in Upper Egypt, by an expedition led by Flinders Petrie in the early twentieth century.

This recent scientific scrutiny of the Two Brothers provided new and interesting insights into their ancient lives. For instance, it was discovered that Nakht-Ankh's lungs had been damaged and scarred by breathing in fine sand particles, and that he had also suffered from both pleurisy (inflammation of the lungs) and pericarditis (inflammation of the surface of the heart). It is possible that Nakht-Ankh died because of his lung conditions, or alternatively, he died from a heart attack brought on by the strain put on his heart by his damaged lungs. Furthermore, it was discovered that the unfortunate Nakht-Ankh had also suffered from both Schistosoma mansoni and Schistosoma haematobium, parasitic diseases of the gut and bladder,

The Tomb of the 'Two Brothers'

The finely decorated Middle Kingdom coffins of the "Two Brothers," Nakht-Ankh and Khnum-Nakht, which today can be seen in Manchester Museum, North West England. Photo courtesy of Paul Cliff and Manchester Museum

respectively. These diseases may have caused him considerable discomfort, as in serious cases they lead to such things as abdominal pains, frequent urination, and diarrhea.

Khnum-Nakht's remains are less well preserved than his brother's, although the researchers were able to identify evidence of kyphoscoliosis (abnormal curvature) in his spine and a healed rib fracture. Also, his left "clubfoot," which had been identified during Murray's original investigation, was found to be the result of excessively tight bandaging of the body during the mummification process, rather than a congenital deformity.

Using digital data that allowed a sophisticated milling machine to produce solid, three-dimensional replicas in polystyrene, the Manchester Egyptian Mummy Project built reconstructions of the heads and faces of the Two Brothers in order to emphasize the striking anatomical differences noticed in the original investigation of the two men's skeletons. Dr. John Cameron, a medical member of Murray's team, examined their skulls and wrote: "These differences are so pronounced that it is almost impossible to convince oneself that they belong to the same race, far less the same family."[38] The reconstructed heads not only lent support to Cameron's statement but their appearance also tallied nicely with the earlier clay busts made in 1979 by Dr. Richard Neave (an expert in ancient facial reconstruction). As with these original busts, the new, polystyrene ones depicted Khnum-Nakht as "a man with strong features somewhat Negroid in appearance [while] Nakht-Ankh . . . is less prepossessing than that of his half brother, with a much weaker face and less well defined features."[39] The marked differences seen in the two men's physiognomies can no doubt be explained by the fact that they had different fathers, with Khnum-Nakht's probably of Nubian origin and Nakht-Ankh's, Egyptian. The head and face of Mummy 1770 was also reconstructed by Neave and "the results . . . were most unexpected and show a young girl, perhaps slightly adenoidal [in other words—she had a big nose] but not unattractive."[40]

Dr. Campbell Price (curator of ancient Egypt and Sudan at Manchester Museum) and his team have been reexamining a total of twenty-four mummies from the museum's collection. They have used CT scanning technology and as a result, some fascinating and previously unknown details have been revealed about these mummies. For example, the scans revealed severe arthritis on the neck of the mummy of Asru, a woman who had been employed as a chantress at the Temple of Karnak during the Twenty-Fifth and Twenty-Sixth Dynasties. It could be that this arthritis was caused by the wearing of large ceremonial headdresses, or alternatively, maybe Asru often had to carry heavy jars or other objects on her head during temple ceremonies and rituals.

Another female mummy of similar date examined by Price and his team is that of a temple singer from Thebes named Perenbast. The CT scans carried out on her mummy have revealed that she wears a series of protective amulets on her body along with a plate decorated with a *wedjat* eye, which covers the incision through which her internal organs would have been removed by the ancient embalmers.

In 1987, the Manchester Mummy Project also set up the International Egyptian Mummy Databank to record information on the numerous Egyptian mummies found in museums and other collections worldwide. In 1997, this was enhanced by the establishment of the Ancient Egyptian Mummy Tissue Databank at Manchester Museum. The tissue bank now has over two thousand tissue, bone, and hair samples from mummies spanning the whole of ancient Egyptian history, and these have provided the Manchester team and other researchers with valuable insights into such things as diet, disease, cause of death, and mummification techniques. Future technological advances can only help to make biomedical Egyptology more sophisticated, and undoubtedly, "this type of research has the potential to make a major contribution not only to Egyptology but also the universal history of disease and medical treatment."[41]

# 7

# CURRENT DIGS

**E**gypt remains a sharply divided country because of its ongoing political troubles, and because of this, Egyptology now faces an uncertain future. However, it can only be hoped that at some point, the opposing factions in Egypt can put aside their differences and that in the meantime, the many archaeological projects currently underway in the country (some of which have been running for several decades) will not be badly affected.

One of the most notable of these is the Giza Plateau Mapping Project, which since 1988 has been undertaking excavations in order to "find evidence of the social and economic structures that supported the building and maintenance of the Giza famous pyramids and their surrounding tombs and temples."[1] This project has certainly gone some way toward achieving its aims as it has steadily been uncovering a large urban center that was home to the builders of the Giza pyramids and their associated monuments. Amongst the discoveries made within this fascinating "pyramid city" by Dr. Mark Lehner (of the Oriental Institute, Chicago) and his international team is the central Gallery Complex where some of the pyramid builders lived, with open-air bakeries and facilities for food storage attached to the complex. The Gallery Complex also features a small hypostyle hall, which was more usually an essential part of Egyptian temples.[2] The one at the Gallery Complex seems to have served a practical rather than a ceremonial function and may have been a fish or grain processing center, or alternatively, a communal dining hall. The excavations in the complex have uncovered thick, ashy deposits containing numerous pottery shards, animal bones (mostly sheep, goat, and cattle), and discarded pottery molds used for baking bread.

In contrast to the Gallery Complex, the nearby Eastern Town area appears to have been a more informally planned place of habitation, with a dense concentration of small houses with attached courtyards. Unlike the Gallery Complex, which probably housed the workers who were drafted in from the various parts of Egypt to take their turn in the building of the pyramids at Giza, the Eastern Town was probably home to a more permanent village-like community.

In addition to the above settlement areas, Lehner and his team have also investigated the Khentkawes Town, which abuts the large mastaba tomb of Queen Khentkawes (who may have ruled as a pharaoh at the end of the Fourth Dynasty), and the Western Town, where there are large house compounds that may have been the homes of high officials. Artifacts such as flint knives, weaving tools, and thousands of shards from beer jars were found at the two sites, but most notable was the discovery of a cache of over two thousand clay seals dumped in a large mound of pottery shards. Many of these were inscribed with the names of the kings Menkaure and Khafre, and a large number of them preserve impressions of wood or string on their reverse sides, indicating they had once sealed boxes and perhaps also rolled-up papyrus documents.

Many other interesting features have been uncovered during the excavations and include a large building that, amongst other things (e.g., evidence of copper production and the dressing of the huge stone blocks used in the pyramids), has yielded many more inscribed clay seals. These seals strongly suggest that this building was very probably an administrative center in the pyramid workers' settlement. The bases of large mud-brick silos that were used for storing grain, or perhaps some other commodity, were also found in an enclosed sunken court in the southeastern corner of the site.

Important excavations are being carried out at the city of Amarna by the Amarna Project, which has been working at the ancient city under the directorship of Professor Barry Kemp since 1979. Relatively little remains today of the huge temples, palaces, and other royal buildings at Amarna, as these were demolished by later pharaohs who wanted to erase Akhenaten from the pages of Egyptian history, with the stone from these buildings often being recycled for use in their own building projects. However, extensive archaeological material relating to the general populace of Amarna—both rich and poor—still survives, providing the Amarna Project with a huge wealth of archaeological material that will keep them busy for many years to come.

One of their most significant recent discoveries in recent years is a major cemetery where many of the ordinary members of Amarna's population were buried: the South Tombs Cemetery, which lies in a wadi in the escarpment[3] marking the eastern edge of the Amarna plain. Over two hundred simple, oblong graves (topped by pointed grave slabs and cairns or small tower-like constructions) have so far been excavated in the cemetery, which is likely to contain many thousands of burials. People were buried in both simple mats and coffins and although the burials are not particularly richly furnished, many small items, such as cosmetic jars, various pendants and beads from necklaces, rings, amulets, mirrors, and a bronze woodworker's tool, have been recovered from the graves.

The degenerative joint disease, spinal arthritis, and fractures that have been identified in a large percentage of the skeletons (both teenagers and adults) reveal that many of the people (most of whom did not reach thirty-five years of age) from the South Tombs were involved in work that was not only physically hard but also dangerous. Many of the excavated skeletons also have very well-preserved hair, revealing that braiding and hair extensions were popular amongst the living.

The research undertaken by the Amarna Project has also involved the reexamination of some of the wealth of archaeological material found by earlier archaeologists, which in many cases has not been thoroughly studied. For example, there has been a project to record and interpret the preserved leather objects (shoes are most common) found at Amarna. Flint tool technology at Amarna, which is a little-understood aspect of New Kingdom society, has also been examined.

Another important aspect of the project's work is the restoration and repairs that are being undertaken on various royal buildings at Amarna, such as Meretaten's[4] bathroom, the North Palace, and the Great Aten Temple (or "House of the Aten"), with the latter the current focus of a long-term project that aims to reinvestigate this building. The project is also surveying the desert plain, which is revealing hitherto unknown features of Amarna and indicating possible areas for excavation in future seasons.

At the famous site of Abydos,[5] which was the main cult center for Osiris, the ancient Egyptian god of death and rebirth, the Abydos Votive Zone Project (comprising the Universities of Yale, New York, and Pennsylvania) has been carrying out archaeological investigations since 1996. A huge wealth of material has already been unearthed by the project, which is seeking to understand how both royal and non-royal individuals contributed to the development of the ceremonial landscape at Abydos. They have made many exciting discoveries, such as the small but finely decorated temple built by King Thutmose III, a remarkable royal wooden statue (which is perhaps a representation of the famous female pharaoh Hatshepsut) that may originally have come from this temple, and a rare wooden sculpture of the head of the hawk-god, Horus. Other finds include the rather extraordinary mummified head of a young man from the Roman Period still partly gilded with the gold leaf that had covered the man's face, a substantial mud-brick offering chapel dating to the Middle Kingdom, and about eighty mummified dogs from the Ptolemaic Period.

A joint mission between the Metropolitan Museum of Art in New York and Emory University, Atlanta, has recently returned to Malqata, a royal residential site and associated urban center from the time of Amenhotep III. Lying on the west bank of the Nile opposite Luxor, the site was first excavated by the Met and the Egyptian Antiquities Service, who carried out six seasons of work here from 1910 to 1920.[6] Further work at Malqata was carried out by Barry Kemp and David O'Connor in the 1970s. The Met and Emory University have undertaken excavations in both religious and urban zones of the palace city, and also carried out magnetometer surveys to assess possible targets for excavation that may lie buried below the desert.

The Met also has a mission working at the pyramid complex of the Middle Kingdom pharaoh Senwosret III, which was first excavated by the French Egyptologist Jacques de Morgan in 1894 and 1895. He found a beautiful red granite sarcophagus (but no body) in the burial chambers beneath the collapsed mud-brick core of the pyramid, which was originally faced with fine limestone blocks. Finds from the new excavations include thousands of beautifully decorated limestone fragments from the destroyed temples and chapels, and a small but superb collection of jewelry made for Queen Weret (principal wife of the Middle Kingdom pharaoh Senwosret III).

The Egypt Exploration Society (EES, based in London) has been funding and supporting archaeological expeditions in Egypt since it was founded in 1882 (originally as the Egypt Exploration Fund), and has several important projects currently ongoing in various parts of Egypt. Much of their work is being carried out in the Delta, where they are investigating numerous sites, with perhaps the most significant being Tell Basta.

Tell Basta is located in the eastern Delta and is the site of the famous ancient city of Bubastis, the center of the cult of the cat-goddess, Bastet. Unlike most Egyptian sites in the Delta, Tell Basta features substantial remains of monumental buildings, and the EES is currently supporting the Tell Basta Project, which is being undertaken by a joint mission of the University of Potsdam, Germany, and the Supreme Council of Antiquities, who have been investigating the site since 1991. In 2001, in the Great Temple of Bastet, they made a spectacular discovery in the form of a colossal pink statue measuring some eleven meters in height, which probably represents Meritamen, the daughter and queen of Rameses II.

Other major projects funded by the EES are the Survey of Memphis, which since the early 1980s has been investigating Egypt's northern capital, looking at both its archaeology and changes in the course of the Nile in antiquity. In a similar vein, the Theban Harbors and Waterscapes Survey, begun by the EES in 2011 under the directorship of Dr. Angus Graham, "aims to advance our understanding of the past locations and migrations of the Nile in the Theban region over the last five millennia."[7] The survey also aims to locate any ancient basins and canals that may have connected the palaces and temples of the Theban west bank to the Nile.

We have already come across the superb artifacts uncovered at Hierakonpolis by J. E. Quibell and F. W. Green in the late nineteenth century, but these two men only really scratched the surface of this huge and important early urban center with their discoveries, and it was not until the initiation of the Hierakonpolis Research Project that the true archaeological potential of Hierakonpolis finally began to be realized. The project began in 1967 under the directorship of Walter Fairservice and is now led by Renée Friedman, curator of the Department of Ancient Egypt and the Sudan at the British Museum.

A huge wealth of diverse archaeological material has already been recovered from Hierakonpolis by the project, but the site undoubtedly has many more ancient secrets to give up in future excavations. Included amongst this material are the remains of a large area of early Predynastic settlement and a large administrative/ceremonial center (in use for some five hundred years) where nearly forty thousand bones from a wide range of animals (e.g., sheep, cattle, fish, crocodile, gazelle, and hippopotami) were found in trash pits around its edges, revealing that animals were sacrificed and consumed in large feasts.

Numerous Predynastic/Early Dynastic cemeteries have also been identified in the locality of Hierakonpolis; a major cemetery for the non-elite population has been excavated by the project, and excavations are ongoing at an elite cemetery. In the former, over five hundred graves of Naqada II date (c.3650–3500 BC) were excavated with various pottery vessels the main grave goods, although smaller items such as stone cosmetic palettes, stone pendants, and bone and flint tools were also buried with the dead. The hot desert sand had superbly preserved organic materials such as the reed grave mats, loaves of bread, and various fruits (e.g., dates and melons) placed in the graves, and also hair, with one woman discovered with dyed hair (henna), and another sporting a Mohawk-type hairstyle.[8] Disturbingly, examination of the skeletons revealed that several people in the cemetery had cut marks on their vertebrae, revealing that their throats had been slit and also that some had been decapitated. These people may well have been criminals who paid the ultimate price for their crimes.

The excavations in the elite cemetery have produced significant results, which include the discovery of the largest tombs yet known from the Naqada II Period, funerary temples and chapels, and an extensive animal necropolis. Many remarkable artifacts have been recovered from the various tombs and ceremonial structures in the cemetery, including the remains of the earliest known human statue (made of limestone) from Egypt, an ivory wand decorated with images of hippopotami, superb flint arrowheads, animal figurines made from flint, somewhat spooky pottery face masks, and beautifully decorated pottery. Graves containing both animal and human burials flank some of the tombs, and it is probable that like the animals, which include an African elephant, a crocodile, hippopotami, and baboons, the young men found in the graves were sacrificed.

Renée Friedman and her colleagues have also excavated graves belonging to people of the Nubian Pan Grave and C-Group cultures,[9] from which they recovered artifacts such as distinctive decorated pottery and the remains of fine leather garments and textiles. They have also found a significant concentration of petroglyphs (carved rock art) on an isolated sandstone outcrop in the desert to the north of Hierakonpolis. This rock art dates from the Predynastic to the New Kingdom, with the ancient artists carving such things as animal and human figures, and also painting a boat on the rocks at this presumably sacred site.

Far to the west of the Nile Valley, there is the intriguing site of Zawiyet Umm-el Rakham, a fortress-town that was founded during the reign of Rameses II and then somewhat mysteriously abandoned at the end of his reign. Since 1994, a team from Liverpool University led by Dr. Steven Snape has been excavating this remote but important site, which is located about two hundred miles west of Alexandria on the narrow coastal strip between the Western Desert and the Mediterranean Sea.

This substantial fortified settlement (it was surrounded by a massive mud-brick wall some eight to ten meters high, enclosing an area of approximately two thousand square meters) is likely to have been garrisoned by over five hundred soldiers. It was probably the most westerly of a chain of forts located along the Mediterranean coast west of the Delta that may have been primarily built to stop or dissuade the aggressive incursions of Libyan groups into Egypt. However, it is perhaps more likely that Zawiyet Umm-el

Rakham and the other probable fortresses (these have not been definitively identified but their presence seems likely) that ran along the coast from the Delta were built in order to guard the important east Mediterranean ancient trading circuit from Libyan tribes and other aggressive opportunists. The significant collection of imported pottery (some of which originally contained products such as olive oil and wine) from the Aegean, Cyprus, and the Levant that has been recovered during the excavations lends some support to this idea. Whatever the true role of the fortress, we know that its commander was a rather shadowy individual named Neb-Re, as inscriptions found in various parts of the site (e.g., on door lintels) name him and give him the titles of "Overseer of Troops" and "Overseer of Foreign Lands."

Along with the large amounts of both Egyptian and imported pottery, a wide range of artifacts attesting to daily life at Zawiyet Umm el-Rakham has been recovered by the Liverpool team from domestic areas. There are objects such as small but finely made rectangular and circular limestone tables, quern-stones for grinding grain into flour, loom weights, spindle whorls, bone needles, and flint sickle blades for harvesting grain.

The most notable finds from the site, however, are the superb group of limestone monuments found during the 2000 excavations, which were crammed into a small room (probably a sanctuary) in the remnants of a largely destroyed small temple. This group comprises three large, limestone

*In situ pottery vessels in a storage magazine at the Ramesside fortress at Zawiyet Umm el-Rakham on Egypt's Mediterranean coast: 1. Canaanite amphora; 2. Greek or Cypriot "stirrup jars"; 3. Egyptian storage vessel. Photo courtesy of Steven Snape*

The superb two-thirds life-size statue of Neb-Re, the commander of the Ramesside fortress at Zawiyet Umm el-Rakham. What happened to Neb-Re and the soldiers he commanded is something of a mystery. Photo courtesy of Steven Snape

steles, a naos containing images of the god and goddess Ptah and Sekhmet, and a superb two-thirds life-size statue depicting Neb-Re, who carries an unusual Sekhmet standard. Ptah and Sekhmet were the chief deities of the city of Memphis, and as they seem to have been favored by the garrison (their names were also found on the surviving doorjambs of the temple) at Zawiyet Umm el-Rakham, it may be that its soldiers originally hailed from here.

Interestingly, it was discovered that someone had taken a chisel and partially erased Neb-Re's name and titles from the statue and the temple, and also damaged images of him that appear on the naos and one of the steles. Why this vandalism was carried out remains unknown but it does perhaps indicate "an assumption of royal prerogatives by an official, who, stationed over a week's march from the Nile Delta at the unfashionable and little-visited end of Egypt's empire may well, rather unwisely, have regarded this area as his own personal fiefdom."[10] Furthermore, the fact that the monuments in the sanctuary were not destroyed and were found tightly packed into this small room "suggests that they had been deliberately stored there [and were] awaiting re-inscription by a new 'owner' who never arrived."[11]

On the opposite edge of Egypt's New Kingdom empire, a joint Polish-Slovak mission from the University of Warsaw has been investigating another fortress built during the time of Rameses II at Tell el-Retaba on the edge of the eastern Delta. The role of the fortress was to control the important route between the eastern Delta and the Sinai Peninsula and the joint Polish-Slovak mission has been undertaking surveys and excavations at the site since 2007.

On the western edge of the Delta, Dr. Susannah Thomas (University of Liverpool) and her team have been investigating the site of Tell Abqa'in since 1994. This fortified settlement also dates to the reign of Rameses II and points to the growing threat posed by the Libyan tribes to the west.

Since 2002, another expedition from Liverpool University[12] has been re-investigating[13] the intriguing tomb of the First Intermediate Period warlord Ankhtifi. This rock-cut tomb is located in Upper Egypt on the east bank of the Nile near the modern village of Mo'alla in a spectacular, pyramid-shaped *gebel* or hill[14] that overlooks the River Nile, and perhaps also Ankhtifi's ancient capital Hefat, which may lie under the modern cultivation on the opposite side of the river.

Ankhtifi's tomb is well known for its autobiographical texts[15] that provide unique insights into the troubled times of Egypt's First Intermediate Period, and initially, the Liverpool expedition focused on studying and recording these inscriptions.[16] These are found on the roughly shaped columns

The spectacular pyramid-shaped hill at Mo'alla in which the First Dynasty warlord Ankhtifi is buried in a rock-cut tomb, which faces the Nile and perhaps also the location of his lost capital, Hefat. Note the other tomb entrances running around the side of the hill. Photo courtesy of Bill Manley/University of Liverpool Expedition to Mo'alla

surrounding the shaft leading to Ankhtifi's burial pit, which lies to the rear and in the center of the columned hall (there are thirty-one columns in total, all of which were originally decorated).

Walking surveys by the Liverpool expedition have made it clear that there is still much previously unknown archaeology to be revealed at Ankhtifi's tomb, and in 2003, the Supreme Council of Antiquities gave the Liverpool team the go-ahead to begin excavations in its forecourt area. Subsequently, the original roughly carved facade of the tomb (today it is covered by a modern concrete facade with a wooden roof) was unearthed from beneath the scree that had slipped down into the forecourt of the tomb. Recovered from this were artifacts such as mummified fish, smashed pottery and coffin fragments (probably dragged out of the tomb by grave robbers), crude offering pots, a wooden fire-stick, the probable end of a bow, and most notably, the collapsed remains of a mud-brick obelisk, which may be one of a series that fronted the tomb's facade. The Liverpool expedition plans to return to the tomb of Ankhtifi to continue their excavation of the forecourt area and to investigate the probable remains of a Valley temple that appears to be linked to the tomb by a stone causeway.

The Gurob Harem Palace Project, which comprises Egyptologists from Liverpool University, University College London, and the University of Copenhagen,[17] has been investigating the urban and funerary remains found at the site of Gurob in the Faiyum region since 2005. This settlement, which was established by Thutmose III,[18] primarily dates to the New Kingdom and was first excavated by Flinders Petrie in the late nineteenth century.

The work of the project has included the mapping of Gurob and also surface surveys that have yielded many thousands of pottery shards (some of which come from vessels imported from Mycenae and Canaan), and an interesting and varied collection of other artifacts. Amongst the latter are a faience figurine of the god Bes, a red faience, a *wedjat*[19] eye amulet, calcite earrings, a small decorated tile with an image of a fish, a loom weight, fragments of a "woman on a bed" clay figurine, stone tools, a comb fragment, a Thoth baboon amulet, and architectural stone fragments from an elite building of some sort. In 2010, the work at Gurob included the excavation of the remains of a New Kingdom mud-brick kiln that was used for making pottery, or alternatively, perhaps, glass vessels.

Since 2001, a team from the British Museum (led by Egyptologist Vivian Davies) have been planning, documenting, and conserving the many hundreds of rock-cut tombs found in the cemeteries near the ancient Egyptian town of Elkab[20] and the nearby site of Hagr Edfu. These finely decorated tombs range in date from the Middle Kingdom to the Greco-Roman Period and were built for elite members of the Elkab community. Although some of the tombs are in a poor state of preservation, many still contain carved and painted imagery of a high quality. For example, in the tomb of Senwosret (a governor of the early Twelfth Dynasty), there are faded but particularly fine paintings depicting birds trapped in a net, and a scene showing hunters (armed with bows) and their dogs returning from a hunting trip. The tombs also contain numerous inscriptions, with one of the most notable being the example found in the tomb of another governor, Sobeknakht. This biographical text records a previously unknown invasion of Egypt by a Kushite army from Nubia, and the subsequent counterattack the Egyptians launched in retaliation.

Belgian archaeologists have been the main excavators at Elkab ever since an archaeological mission was established by the Belgian Fondation Reine Elisabeth in 1937. During the early years of the mission, before and after World War II, the famous Belgian Egyptologist Jean Capart and his successor, Pierre Gilbert, directed excavations within the temples of Thoth (the god of writing and knowledge) and the vulture-goddess, Nekhbet. Included amongst the many discoveries they made were a bust of Amenhotep III and a royal sphinx statue probably dating to the reign of Nectanebo I, the first king of the Thirtieth Dynasty.

During the later twentieth-century excavations at Elkab, Pierre Vermeersch made the significant discovery of the campsites of Epipaleolithic hunter-fishers who had used a previously unknown lithic (stone tool) industry that today is commonly known by Egyptologists as the Elkabian. Stan

Hendrickx also investigated a large cemetery dating to Naqada III, which yielded typical Naqada cultural artifacts such as stone cosmetic palettes from its simple pit graves.

Another important discovery at Elkab was the Greco-Roman village that archaeologists excavated over a ten-year period, uncovering a regularly laid out network of streets and houses. Huge amounts of pottery were recovered from the houses, as well as numerous bronze coins dating from the first through fourth centuries AD and ostraca bearing Greek texts, which include bills, receipts, and lists of names and religious festivals. Somewhat mysteriously, the village was evidently demolished and abruptly abandoned around 380 AD.

Outside the huge mud-brick enclosure walls (around eleven meters in height) of the town, archaeologists have discovered many Old Kingdom burials in the necropolis located in the huge rocky hill nearby. Included amongst these are the tomb of Sawikai, who had been an "overseer" of priests in the Sixth Dynasty, and one belonging to a lady named Irtenakhty, who was a priestess in the Temple of Hathor. The tomb of Irtenakhty consists of two intact burial chambers lying at the bottom of a steep shaft. From the first chamber, in which Irtenakhty's skeleton lay (the wooden coffin had virtually disintegrated), archaeologists recovered pottery, stone vessels, horn bracelets, a faience necklace, and a stunning oval mirror made from bronze, bearing a hieroglyphic inscription naming Irtenakhty. In the second chamber (which contained the probable body of her husband) another fine but uninscribed bronze mirror was found along with a fine copper handbasin containing a copper ewer with a long spout and a collar made of faience beads and semiprecious stones.

Archaeologists found an undisturbed Eighteenth Dynasty tomb in the necropolis, which still contained many fine funerary goods and four badly preserved coffins with their occupants still in place. A unique Third Dynasty mastaba tomb built for a very high-status individual of unknown identity was also found on the summit of the hill. Remarkably, the burial chamber of this tomb is reached by a shaft that is sunk twenty-five meters into the hillside and although its original occupant was missing, the remains of two skeletons that have been radiocarbon dated to the New Kingdom were found in the chamber, attesting to the tomb's much later reuse.

In 2009, the Belgian mission found the remains of the Old Kingdom town at Elkab, after their earlier survey of the area that lay to the northwest of the temple zone. Although archaeologists had long suspected that this area marked the location of the Old Kingdom town, its discovery is one of the most important ever made at Elkab and a significant Egyptological discovery in general.

After an initial magnetometer survey of the site, the excavations began in earnest, and well-preserved archaeological remains comprising the remains of mud-brick buildings and an abundant quantity of pottery dating back to the early Old Kingdom were discovered. In 2010, many new buildings were found, with their mud-brick walls surviving up to more than one meter in some cases. The archaeologists have also identified several separate phases of construction in the town, with the earliest dating to the start of the Old Kingdom. A huge amount of pottery was again found, which included both everyday vessels and luxury wares that would have been brought out on special occasions to impress guests. Large amounts of bread molds and beer jars were also recovered, as well as limited evidence for copper working, suggesting perhaps that this area was an industrial zone with workshops.

The Old Kingdom town at Elkab covers an area of four to five hectares (around forty thousand to fifty thousand square meters) and the excavations carried out here so far have uncovered less than 1 percent of this area. Thus, as has been noted, "the archaeological challenge is enormous and will demand time, money and an exceptional level of logistical management, but the research at Elkab must be encouraged at all costs. Indeed we know of very few archaeological sites in Egypt which offer such important scientific potential."[21]

The British Museum also has archaeological missions currently working at the well-known site of Naukratis in the western Delta and Amara West in the Sudan. As seen earlier, Naukratis was an important Greek trading settlement and has been the subject of various excavations, with the first of these carried out by Flinders Petrie in the late nineteenth century. The famous Greek historian Herodotus, who devotes several paragraphs to Naukratis in his *Histories*, also visited the town, and we may well have a remarkable record of this visit, as a Greek Attic cup bearing an inscription of his name on its base was found in the sacred Hellenion temple complex by D. G. Hogarth in 1903.

The British Museum mission to Naukratis began in 2012, marking the first phase of a program of fieldwork primarily "designed to help fill in the gaps in our understanding of the site's history and to resolve the long-standing controversies surrounding the site, by integrating new fieldwork with critically reassessed old fieldwork."[22] This initial investigation has revealed previously unrecognized features (e.g., a possible harbor area and associated storage magazines) and that the town is not only better preserved than previously thought, but it is also larger, with a great deal of exciting archaeological potential.

Amara West was the site of the Egyptian administrative center of Upper Nubia and was established as a colonial settlement by Sety I of the New Kingdom's Nineteenth Dynasty (the Egyptians had lost control of Nubia by the Twentieth Dynasty). The British Museum mission to the site began in 2008 and excavated a number of burials in Cemetery D, from which artifacts such as ceramic vessels, pottery shabtis, beads, amulets and earrings, and painted coffin fragments were recovered. The ongoing excavations at the site have produced some exciting results, such as the remains of a possible shrine with decorated walls discovered in 2010, which lay underneath two later houses located next to the governor's residence.

Another house was discovered during the 2013 fieldwork season, as was the largest tomb yet discovered at Amara West. Inside the house, the excavators discovered a well-preserved clay floor in its first room, with a circular hearth that still contained ash and charcoal. In the adjoining room, the remains of three bread ovens were found (which were perhaps later in date than the house). In the sand above these ovens, several artifacts were discovered, including a necklace made from faience beads that had as its centerpiece a gold bead flanked by two others made of red carnelian. When found, the necklace was lying on the floor as it had originally been strung (although the string on which the beads had been strung had not survived), almost as though someone had lifted it over their head and casually tossed it aside. Also found in the room were a polished stone dish made from graywacke, a copper chisel, a metal spearhead or blade, and a potsherd bearing a hieratic text (not yet translated at the time of writing). Another interesting discovery from the house was the inscribed (reused) stone doorjamb featuring an inscription naming an official named Horhotep.

The tomb, which is probably late New Kingdom in date, comprises a grave shaft at the bottom of which are a western suite consisting of three burial chambers and an eastern suite consisting of two (a large burial cairn originally covered the shaft, which was a characteristic feature of ancient Nubian burials). Although the burial chambers are yet to be investigated, as they dug down through the sand that filled the deep grave shaft, the excavators came upon a thick layer of debris left behind by the grave robbers who had obviously plundered the tomb. Included in this layer were large pottery vessels, beads from necklaces, faience fragments, large pieces of painted plaster from decorated coffins, and large fragments of wooden funerary furniture. These finds suggest that the burial chambers were originally very well furnished with grave goods, although it unfortunately seems very likely that the more valuable items were whisked away by the tomb robbers.

Since 1990, the Saqqara Geophysical Survey Project, which was established by the late Ian Mathieson of the National Museums of Scotland, has been investigating the Saqqara necropolis using a range of geophysical techniques (e.g., ground-penetrating radar and handheld gradiometers). The project is further helping to elucidate our understanding of this important ancient religious center and is also revealing many previously unknown features and structures. For example, the project has discovered many Early Dynastic and Old Kingdom mastaba tombs (two of which are an impressive approximate seventy meters in length) and that the walls of the Gisr el-Mudir (Great Enclosure), Egypt's earliest monumental stone structure (built sometime in the Second Dynasty), were actually a staggering fifteen to seventeen meters in width. More unexpected was the discovery of two rows of temples near the Serapeum that yielded pottery and amulets dating to the Ptolemaic Period.

The most impressive find made by the project to date is the beautifully decorated limestone stele that had been reused to cover a grave within the Late Period cemetery in the Great Enclosure. The stele features a rare combination of Persian and Egyptian iconography and bears inscriptions naming a man called Djeherbes, who had an Egyptian mother and a high-ranking Persian father. The stele may originally have come from one of the Late Period shaft tombs found on the Saqqara plateau.

The painstaking (and often dangerous) clearance and excavation of Tomb KV5 continues in the Valley of the Kings under the directorship of Kent Weeks and very slowly, but surely, its remarkable story is being uncovered. Recent work at KV5 has concentrated on Chamber 5, which is the third largest of the chambers excavated so far in the tomb. Finds were limited but include a coffin fragment, a shard from a blue faience vessel, a blue faience bead, and fragments of the decorated plaster that would have originally covered the walls and pillars of Chamber 5. Mason's marks on the chamber walls and a graffito (probably dating to the time of Rameses II) found on a limestone block that had detached from the ceiling provide a tenuous but compelling link to the men who worked on the chamber in the ancient past.

Archaeologists from the German Archaeological Institute and the Swiss Institute of Architectural and Archaeological Research in Cairo have been investigating the important settlement site on Elephantine Island since 1969, uncovering the various layers of the town's history and shedding much fascinating light on its occupants. The town has a long history and was occupied from the later fifth millennium BC down to the tenth or eleventh century AD. Unsurprisingly then, numerous and varied architectural remains and many thousands of small finds have also been found across the site. Included amongst the many discoveries of the German/Swiss team are the remains of houses and workshops dating from the Old Kingdom to the First Intermediate Period, with the latter yielding evidence of such activities as baking, grain processing, pottery and stone vessel production, and ivory working. Also discovered are numerous fragments from destroyed temple furniture (e.g., statues and altars) belonging to the temple of the ram-headed god Khnum (Elephantine was the major cult center for Khnum) and over a hundred Old Kingdom burials, most of which belong to adults, although a small number of the graves also contain children. There are also thousands of stone tools dating from the Early Dynastic Period to the Middle Kingdom, hundreds of Greek ostraca featuring trade receipts for items such as date palms and linen, and two nearly complete Egyptian sandals.

Finally, Swiss archaeologists from the University of Basel are currently involved in a re-investigation of the non-royal tombs built for royal courtiers and high officials (often referred to as the Tombs of the Nobles) that are located in the side valley that leads to the tomb of Thutmose III. Although the more valuable objects have been stripped from the tombs, a surprising amount of archaeological material has been recovered by the Swiss team. For example, there are the remains of decorated wooden coffins, many hundreds of pottery vessels, numerous textiles, broken figurines, wigs, ropes, preserved food offerings, and a rare stone sundial from the Ramesside Period. However, the excavations of tombs KV64 and KV40 mark the most notable achievements of the Swiss archaeologists so far. In KV64, a very well-preserved black painted sycamore coffin, featuring yellow inscriptions, and a brightly painted wooden stele were found in the northern half of the chamber, both of which had belonged to a chantress of Amun named Nehmes-bastet.[23] On the stele, Nehmes-Bastet can be seen praying before the god Ra-Herakhte, and her carefully wrapped but blackened mummy was still lying inside the coffin, undisturbed since she was laid to rest in the middle of the Twenty-Second Dynasty.

Tomb KV40 contained a remarkable collection of at least fifty mummified bodies—which had unfortunately been damaged in a fire sparked by tomb robbers. Nevertheless, from inscriptions found on storage jars in the tomb the Egyptologists were able to identify that many of the deceased were members of the families of Thutmose IV and Amenhotep III of the Eighteenth Dynasty.

# EPILOGUE

## Learning More about Ancient Egypt

Listed here are some suggestions for those readers who wish to further explore the remarkable world of ancient Egypt, and an obvious starting point in this respect would be a visit to one of the American museums that have internationally renowned collections of ancient Egyptian artifacts. These are the Museum of Fine Arts Boston (most of the exceptional collection of artifacts that you can see here were excavated by the famous American Egyptologist George Reisner), the Metropolitan Museum of Art, New York (where you can visit an actual Egyptian temple in the Sackler Wing), and the Oriental Institute, Chicago. Smaller but still fairly substantial Egyptian collections can also be seen at museums such as the Rosicrucian Egyptian Museum in San Jose, California, the Field Museum, Chicago, and the Brooklyn Museum. Over the Canadian border, the Royal Ontario Museum also houses a large collection of Egyptian antiquities.

If you are lucky enough to be in Egypt itself, the Egyptian Museum of Cairo is, of course, an absolute must-see. There is a mind-boggling amount of artifacts to be seen in the museum (with those from the tomb of Tutankhamen unsurprisingly the most popular) and personal experience has brought it home to me that much more than a couple of hours, or even a whole day, is needed to fully appreciate the incredible array of ancient Egyptian wonders this building holds. Unsurprisingly, there are many other museums in Egypt that have fine collections of Egyptian artifacts, such as the small but excellent Luxor Museum, in which you can see several masterpieces of ancient Egyptian art, the Malawi National Museum in Al-Minya, and Aswan Museum, which sits in the middle of the River Nile on the beautiful Elephantine Island.

It is not surprising—given the history of Egyptology—that Europe is particularly blessed with museums with major collections of Egyptian antiquities, and of particular note in this regard are the British Museum (home of the Rosetta Stone) and the Petrie Museum at University College London; the Musée du Louvre, Paris; the Neues Museum (home of the Nefertiti bust), Berlin; the Cinquantenaire Museum, Brussels; and the Museo Egizio in Turin. Other European museums with notable collections of Egyptian antiquities include the World Museum in Liverpool, the Manchester and Bolton Museums, located in North West England (a region that has a strong Egyptological heritage), the Fitzwilliam Museum in Cambridge, the Egyptian Museum in Florence, the Kunsthistorisches Museum in Vienna, and the Pushkin Museum of Fine Arts in Moscow.

It is also worth mentioning that you can happily explore the Egyptian collections of many of the museums mentioned here via your computer, as they have digital galleries that allow you to browse through high-resolution images of the many thousands of diverse and beautiful artifacts from ancient Egypt that they have under their care.

There are also numerous websites where "Egyptophiles" can happily while away the hours learning a great deal more about Egyptian archaeology and the famous finds and figures from its formative years. An undoubted star amongst these sites is that of the Griffith Institute, University of Oxford (http://www.griffith.ox.ac.uk), which allows you to examine the complete records from the excavation of Tutankhamen's tomb. Here, you can also look at the wonderful black-and-white photographs taken by Harry Burton of the tomb's numerous artifacts, Carter's meticulous handwritten records and drawings of these objects, and also his excavation and pocket diaries from 1922 to 1930. Other highlights of the site are the galleries that contain Hector Horeau's beautiful watercolors of ancient Egypt monuments and Howard Carter's stunning watercolors of the animals that he saw in the Egyptian countryside. You can also look at some of Petrie's early journals, and a recently discovered sketchbook containing the drawings of Amelia Edwards, the founder of the Egypt Exploration Fund in 1882 (later to become the Egypt Exploration Society) and author of the still highly readable *A Thousand Miles up the Nile* (1877).

Also highly recommended is the Giza Archives (http://www.gizapyra mids.org/) website run by the Museum of Fine Arts Boston. Included amongst the many other features on this superb website are digitized versions of every book or article ever written by George Reisner, twenty-one thousand glass plate photographic negatives, and ten thousand maps and plans, providing us with a huge treasure trove of fascinating information on ancient Egypt.

Another excellent website is *Ancient Egypt Online* (http://www.anciente gyptonline.co.uk), which is undoubtedly a very useful resource for students of ancient Egypt. This is a clear and easy-to-use site that provides a detailed overview of all aspects of ancient Egyptian society, and also numerous photographs and plans.

Sarah Parcak's homepage (http://www.sarahparcak.com) is definitely worth a visit as here you can learn more about the exciting new field of space archaeology, view some impressive satellite images of ancient Egyptian sites, and learn more about Sarah's work in Egypt.

Readers can also look at Otto Schaden's dig diaries and photos of the finds from KV63 online (http://www.kv-63.com), and view a fascinating virtual autopsy of Gebelein Man on the British Museum website (http://www.britishmuseum.org/explore/highlights/highlight_objects/aes/p/ge belein_man.aspx).

The Egyptian Supreme Council of Antiquities has an informative and useful website (http://www.sca-egypt.org/) that allows you to browse through all of the major sites and monuments in Egypt, which are handily arranged in alphabetical order. Also handy is the information provided on the opening times, cost of entry, and directions to these sites, and how safe they are to visit (the Egyptian people are generally very friendly and hospitable, but there are some areas of Egypt that are too dangerous for Westerners to visit).

Many of the expeditions currently working in Egypt also have excellent websites where you can learn about their past and present work, and particularly recommended are those of the Egypt Exploration Society (http://www.ees.ac.uk/publications/egyptian-archaeology.html), the Hierakonpolis Project (http://www.hierakonpolis-online.org/), the Abydos Votive Zone Project (http://individual.utoronto.ca/NACZproject), the Amarna Project (http://www.amarnaproject.com/pages/publications/excavation.shtml), the Gurob Harem Palace Project (http://gurob.org.uk/seasons.php), the Giza Plateau Mapping Project (http://oi.uchicago.edu/research/projects/giz), and the Theban Mapping Project (http://www.thebanmappingproject.com/).

## PUBLICATIONS

For those readers who wish to read in more detail about ancient Egypt I would highly recommend any/all of the following as a good starting point:

Cultural Atlas of Ancient Egypt (John Baines and Jaromir Málek)
The Oxford History of Ancient Egypt (ed. Ian Shaw)
The British Museum Dictionary of Ancient Egypt (Ian Shaw and Paul Nicholson)
An Introduction to the Archaeology of Ancient Egypt (Kathryn Bard)
Ancient Egypt (ed. Donald P. Silverman)
Egypt (Vivian Davies and Renée Friedman)
Ancient Egypt: The Great Discoveries (Nicholas Reeves)
The Complete Tutankhamun (Nicholas Reeves)
The Complete Valley of the Kings: Tombs and Treasures of Egypt's Greatest Pharaohs (Nicholas Reeves and Richard H. Wilkinson)
Egypt: How a Lost Civilization Was Rediscovered (Joyce Tyldesley)
Egyptian Hieroglyphs for Complete Beginners (Bill Manley)

Readers may also like to subscribe to the excellent magazines Ancient Egypt (http://ancientegyptmagazine.co.uk) and Egyptian Archaeology (http://www.ees.ac.uk/publications/egyptian-archaeology.html). Also well worth checking out is Archaeology magazine (http://www.archaeology.org/), which is published by the Archaeological Institute of America and quite often contains good features on Egyptian archaeology, as does another popular magazine—Current World Archaeology (http://www.archaeology.co.uk/join-in/publishers/current-world-archaeology.htm). The British Museum also publishes the online journal British Museum Studies in Ancient Egypt and Sudan (https://www.britishmuseum.org/research/publications/online_journals/bmsaes.aspx), which contains interesting and well-illustrated articles on their various excavations and other ancient Egyptian matters. Readers may also be interested in looking at the Shire Egyptology series in the UK, as this provides slim but informative (and inexpensive) volumes on a wide range of subjects, which are written by well-known Egyptologists.

## WORKING ON EXCAVATIONS IN EGYPT

Getting involved in current archaeological fieldwork in Egypt is not easy even for students who are studying Egyptology at the university level, as places on digs are often limited and the Egyptian Supreme Council of Antiquities is also rather choosy as to whom it allows into the country to work on these excavations. However, there are a few websites listing current excavation opportunities in Egypt, and perseverance and a willingness to part with large sums of cash to pay for airfare, food, and accommodation may lead to being accepted onto one of these excavations. The websites are:

*Survey and Excavation Projects in Egypt* (http://www.deltasinai.com/sepe-00.htm)

*Egyptology Resources* (http://www.fitzmuseum.cam.ac.uk/er/)

It may also be worthwhile to keep an eye on the *Archaeological Fieldwork Opportunities Bulletin* on the website of the Archaeological Institute of America, as they occasionally advertise fieldwork opportunities in Egypt (http://www.archaeological.org/fieldwork/afob).

# NOTES

## CHAPTER 1: INTRODUCING ANCIENT EGYPT

1. The Nile actually receives two tributaries from the Ethiopian Highlands: the Blue Nile and the Atbara; the White Nile also joins the Nile proper from farther south in the Sudan.

2. Truly speaking, the Valley, which is some 660 miles long, is actually more of a deep canyon that is an offshoot of the African Great Rift Valley.

3. Fekri Hassan, "The Nurturing Waters," in *Ancient Egypt*, edited by David P. Silverman (London: Duncan Baird, 2003), 12.

4. Aubrey de Sélincourt, trans., *Herodotus: The Histories* (London: Penguin, 1996), 87–88.

5. This scene is found in the New Kingdom tomb of Senna at Thebes.

6. I should point out that this is not a comprehensive list of the very wide range of minerals that were exploited in ancient Egypt. In this respect, see the excellent *Ancient Egyptian Materials and Technology* by Paul Nicholson and Ian Shaw (Cambridge: Cambridge University Press, 2000).

7. D. Klemm, R. Klemm, and A. Murr, "Gold of the Pharaohs—6000 Years of Gold Mining in Egypt and Nubia," *African Earth Sciences* 33 (2001): 657.

8. Thomas Hikade, "Expeditions to the Wadi Hammamat during the New Kingdom," *Journal of Egyptian Archaeology* 92 (2006): 161.

9. Paul Bahn, pers. comm., 2013.

10. Mary M. A. McDonald, "Early African Pastoralism: View from Dakhleh Oasis (South Central Egypt)," *Journal of Anthropological Archaeology* 17 (1998): 133.

11. Kathryn A. Bard, *An Introduction to the Archaeology of Ancient Egypt* (Oxford: Blackwell, 2008), 85.

12. Dates vary as to the start of the Predynastic Period, with some Egyptologists placing it at the beginning of the Naqada Period c.4000 BC.

13. This view was typical of the times, as earlier archaeologists were fond of attributing previously unrecognized material culture to that of invaders and immigrants.

14. Naqada I and II are still commonly referred to as the Amratian and Gerzean.

15. Beatrix Midant-Reynes, "The Naqada Period (c.4000–3200 BC)," in *The Oxford History of Ancient Egypt*, edited by Ian Shaw (Oxford: Oxford University Press, 2000), 46.

16. Midant-Reynes, "The Naqada Period," 48.

17. Bard, *An Introduction to the Archaeology of Ancient Egypt*, 65.

18. Barry Kemp, *Ancient Egypt: Anatomy of a Civilization* (London: Routledge, 1989), 32.

19. Kemp, *Ancient Egypt*, 32.

20. Stephen H. Savage, "Descent Group Competition and Economic Strategies in Predynastic Egypt," *Journal of Anthropological Archaeology* 16 (1997): 258.

21. However, it is possible that King Narmer actually stands at the head of the First Dynasty, as suggested by a seal impression discovered at Umm el-Qa´ab. This lists the first six rulers of First Dynasty Egypt as Narmer, Aha, Djer, Djet, Den, and Queen Merneith.

22. The Arabic word for "bench"—the superstructures of the mastaba tombs resemble the low mud-brick benches found outside the houses in Egyptian villages.

23. In the earlier part of his reign Peribsen probably held the name Sekhemib, and Khasekhemwy should probably also be identified with Khasekhem, who, like Sekhemib, was originally thought to be a separate ruler.

24. Alternatively, the Meidum Pyramid may actually have been begun by King Huni (last king of the Third Dynasty) but then completed by Sneferu. Today, it is somewhat tower-like in appearance as most of its outer casing has collapsed or been removed.

25. In fact, the pyramids at the Giza necropolis lie almost adjacent to the modern suburbs of southwestern Cairo, and although this spoils the experience of visiting the pyramids somewhat, it cannot take away from the sheer magnificence of these ancient monuments.

26. This evidence takes the form of deliberately destroyed funerary monuments.

27. It is interesting to note that in later times, the Nubians worshipped Senusret III as a god, indicating how strong his grip on Nubia had been.

28. Seqenenra Taa (c.1560 BC) and Kamose (c.1555–1550 BC).

29. Ian Shaw and Paul Nicholson, *The British Museum Dictionary of Ancient Egypt* (London: British Museum Press, 2008), 154.

30. Although the location of Punt is not absolutely certain, it was probably located either in southern Sudan or Eritrea in Ethiopia.

31. Rameses II's most renowned military exploit was the battle of Qadesh (c.1274 BC), fought near the Hittite city of the same name in Syria. However, although the records of the battle that survive on the walls of many of his temples portray him as the outright victor, he was actually forced into a treaty with the Hittite king Muwatallis.

32. Nicholas Reeves and Richard H. Wilkinson, *The Complete Valley of the Kings: Tombs and Treasures of Egypt's Greatest Pharaohs* (Cairo: The American University in Cairo Press, 2000), 8.

33. Some Egyptologists place the beginnings of the Late Period with the foundation of the Twenty-Sixth Saite Dynasty.

34. Named after the city of Sais in the western Delta, which was the capital of the Saite Dynasty.

35. Isis was a female goddess who was one of the major deities of the Egyptian pantheon.

36. This massive lighthouse was probably destroyed by a series of earthquakes. Also lost are the famous Library and Museum of Alexandria, which were burned down—robbing the world of many thousands of irreplaceable ancient texts and artifacts.

37. This dynasty was founded by Ptolemy of Lagos, the former general of Egypt under Alexander IV, the son of Alexander the Great.

## CHAPTER 2: FROM HAND AXES TO MUMMY PORTRAITS

1. The demotic script was a cursive form of the hieroglyphic one and was initially only used for bureaucratic and commercial purposes. However, from the fourth century BC onward, it was also used in religious, scientific, and literary texts.

2. John Ray, *The Rosetta Stone and the Rebirth of Ancient Egypt* (London: Profile, 2007), 1.

3. A. Thoma, "Morphology and Affinities of the Nazlet Khater Man," *Journal of Human Evolution* 13 (1984): 296.

4. Although it is not without its critics, an influential book in this respect is *War before Civilization* by Lawrence H. Keeley, professor of anthropology at the University of Illinois at Chicago.

5. Stan Hendrickx and Pierre Vermeersch, "Prehistory: From the Paleolithic to Badarian Culture," in *The Oxford History of Ancient Egypt*, edited by Ian Shaw, (Oxford: Oxford University Press, 2002), 30.

6. Romuald Schild and Fred Wendorf, "Forty Years of the Combined Prehistoric Expedition," *Archaeologia Polona* 40 (2002): 10.

7. On the eastern hill is a temple of Hathor dating from the Early Dynastic to the Roman Period. Hathor was a major Egyptian goddess often depicted with the ears or horns of a cow and was the sacred mother of the kings of Egypt.

8. Steven Snape, "Making Mummies," in *Tombs, Graves and Mummies*, edited by Paul Bahn (London: Orion, 2000), 182.

9. This nickname is no longer used—at least by the museum—as it is realized that some people may find it offensive in that it shows a lack of respect for the dead.

10. The Belgian mission was able to carry out optically stimulated luminescence (OSL) dating on sand found in a scree slope partly covering one of the rock-art panels, and the results of this dating revealed that the sediments in the base of the slope dated to around sixteen thousand years ago. The rock art must thus be older than this basal level and it is quite possible that it was carved some nineteen thousand years ago.

11. The remaining rock art locations have been dated to the Late Paleolithic (1), the Predynastic (8), and the Dynastic (2) Periods, and there are three locations where the rock art is of uncertain date.

12. Peter A. Clayton, *Chronicle of the Pharaohs* (London: Thames & Hudson), 18.

13. Steven Snape, "The 'Main Deposit' at Hierakonpolis," in *Wonderful Things*, edited by Paul Bahn (London: Seven Dials, 2000), 19.

14. Snape, "The 'Main Deposit' at Hierakonpolis," 19.

15. John Baines and Jaromir Málek, *Atlas of Ancient Egypt* (New York: Facts on File, 1980), 78.

16. Humphrey Case and Joan Crowfoot Payne, "Tomb 100: The Decorated Tomb at Hierakonpolis," *Journal of Egyptian Archaeology* 48 (1962): 18.

17. H. E. Winlock, "The Egyptian Expedition 1925–1927: The Museum's Excavations at Thebes," *The Metropolitan Museum of Art Bulletin* 23, part 2 (1928): 12–13.

18. Quoted in Nicholas Reeves and Richard H. Wilkinson, *The Complete Valley of the Kings: Tombs and Treasures of Egypt's Greatest Pharaohs* (Cairo: The American University in Cairo Press, 2002), 194.

19. Joyce Tyldesley, *Egypt: How a Lost Civilization Was Rediscovered* (London: BBC Books, 2005), 130.

20. Nefertari was the principal wife of Rameses II, whose importance is indicated by her later deification (along with the goddess Hathor, she was worshipped at the smaller temple at Abu Simbel in Nubia) and the fact that her tomb in the Valley of the Queens is the largest and most beautifully decorated.

21. Joyce Tyldesley, "Restoring the Royal Mummies," in *Written in Bones*, edited by Paul Bahn, (Devon: David & Charles, 2002), 178.

22. The events of the coup are recorded in the famous "Turin Judicial Papyrus," which names all those involved and the other chief conspirator, the mother of Prince Pentaware, Queen Tiye, one of Rameses' royal wives, who wanted to supplant the king with her son.

23. Zahi Hawass, et al., "Revisiting the Harem Conspiracy and Death of Ramesses III: Anthropological, Forensic, Radiological, and Genetic Study," *British Medical Journal* 345 (2012): 1–9, doi: 10.1136/bmj.e8268.

24. Apis bulls were not the only animals to be buried at Saqqara, as just to the northeast of the Serapeum is the remarkable Sacred Animal Necropolis, which comprises temples, shrines, and an extensive network of catacombs, in which millions of mummified, ibises, falcons, dogs, baboons, and Barbary macaques were buried.

25. Osiris was one of the major deities of ancient Egypt and was strongly associated with beliefs about death, resurrection, and fertility. The worship of Osiris dates back at least as far as the Old Kingdom.

26. Scarab amulets were common in ancient Egypt from the Old Kingdom onward and were so called as they were made to resemble the sacred scarab or dung beetle, which represented the sun-god Khepri, who was associated with rebirth in the afterlife.

27. Zawi Hawass, *Valley of the Golden Mummies* (New York: Harry N. Abrams, 2000), 53.

28. The portraits were executed in tempera (pigment mixed with egg yolk) or encaustic (pigment mixed with hot wax), although the encaustic paintings tend to be more aesthetically pleasing.

29. Quoted in Margaret S. Drower, *Flinders Petrie: A Life in Archaeology* (Madison: University of Wisconsin Press, 1995), 133.

30. Margaret S. Drower, *Flinders Petrie*, 133.

31. Salima Ikram, "Barbering the Beardless: A Possible Explanation for the Tufted Hairstyle in the 'Fayum' Portrait of a Young Boy (J. P. Getty 78.AP.262)," *Journal of Egyptian Archaeology* 89 (2003): 248.

32. A. J. N. W. Prag, "Proportion and Personality in the Fayum Portraits," *British Museum Studies in Ancient Egypt and Sudan* 3 (2002), 57, http:www.the britishmuseum.ac.uk/egyptian/bmsaes/issue3/prag.html.

33. Howard Carter, *The Tomb of Tutankhamun* (London: Century, 1983), 47.

34. Arthur R. "Pecky" Callender was a former architect and engineer who had recently retired from his job as manager of the Egyptian railways, and several other skilled individuals aided Carter in the clearing, analyzing, and recording of the tomb. Of particular note are the photographer Harry Burton, whose archive of wonderful black-and-white photographs can still be seen today on the website of the Griffith Institute (see epilogue for full details), and the chemist Alfred Lucas, who played a hugely valuable part in conserving most of the king's burial equipment (thanks to him, only some 0.25 percent of this equipment was lost). The American draftsmen Lindsley Foote Hall and Walter Hauser provided invaluable scale drawings of the contents of the antechamber before their removal, and the well-known American Egyptologist James Henry Breasted also assisted Carter.

35. Carter, *The Tomb of Tutankhamun*, 55.

36. There is simply not space here to look in detail at the staggering collection of superb objects found in the antechamber and the other rooms in Tutankhamen's tomb. However, for those readers who wish to do so, *The Tomb of Tutankhamun* by Carter is an obvious starting point, but the best volume in this respect is the excellent *The Complete Tutankhamun* by Nicholas Reeves.

37. Carter, *The Tomb of Tutankhamun*, 71.

38. Carter, *The tomb of Tutankhamun*, 61.

39. The Egyptians loved playing games and a game called senet was particularly popular. The game was played on a thirty- or twenty-squared board and basically, its winner was the person who removed his gaming pieces from the board first. Movement around the board was dictated by throwing casting sticks or knucklebones, which could be made either from the anklebones of goats or sheep or from many other materials such as gold, ivory, glass, copper, wood, stone, and marble.

40. Carter, *The Tomb of Tutankhamun*, 117–118. I should mention here that previous to the "official" opening of the inner sealed doorway, Carter, Carnarvon, and Lady Evelyn had already breached it and entered the burial chamber through the ancient resealed robber's hole. This was done shortly after the discovery of the antechamber and for the record photograph of the antechamber they hid evidence of their visit behind the "Painted Box," a wicker basket lid, and some reeds. It is perhaps possible, as some have argued, that they stole a number of items during this visit, although no firm evidence has been found to prove this.

41. Carter, *The Tomb of Tutankhamun*, 155.

42. John H. Taylor, *Egyptian Coffins* (Princes Risborough: Shire, 1989), 30.

43. Reeves, *The Complete Tutankhamun*, 111.

44. Howard Carter and A. C. Mace, *The Discovery of the Tomb of Tutankhamen* (New York: Dover, 1977), 183–184.

45. Seth, whose mother was the sky-goddess Nut, was the god of chaos and is said to have murdered his brother Osiris.

46. R. G. Harrison and A. B. Abdalla, "A Mummified Foetus from the Tomb of Tutankhamun," *Antiquity* 53 (1979): 20.

47. C. A. Hellier and R. C. Connolly, "A Re-assessment of the Larger Fetus Found in Tutankhamen's Tomb," *Antiquity* 83 (2009).

48. The Theban Mapping Project was initiated by Kent Weeks in 1978 and since then it has been engaged in the mammoth task of recording and documenting the thousands of tombs and temples found on the west bank at Luxor.

49. Kent Weeks, *The Lost Tomb: The Greatest Discovery at the Valley of the Kings since Tutankhamen* (London: Weidenfeld & Nicolson, 1998), 297.

50. As well as working on the royal tombs of the Valley of the Kings, the workforce of Deir el-Medina built and decorated those found in the nearby Valley of the Queens, where the royal wives and sons of the New Kingdom pharaohs were buried. They also worked on the tombs of Theban high officials elsewhere in the extensive west bank necropolis.

51. As we saw in chapter one, the Ramesseum was the mortuary temple of the great Rameses II of the Nineteenth Dynasty; Medinet Habu was the mortuary temple of Rameses III of the Twentieth Dynasty.

52. Lynn Meskell, "An Archaeology of Social Relations in an Egyptian Village," *Journal of Archaeological Method and Theory* 5 (1998): 226.

# CHAPTER 3: FAMOUS FIGURES IN EGYPTOLOGY

1. Notable amongst these early Egyptologists were the astronomer John Greaves (1602–1652), who undertook the first scientific survey of the pyramids at Giza in 1639, subsequently publishing the results in his *Pyramidographia* (1646), and Father Claude Sicard (1677–1726), a Jesuit priest and missionary who was the first European to describe the temples at Kom Ombo, Philae, and Elephantine in Upper Egypt. Another man of the church, the Reverend Richard Pococke (1704–1765), published two volumes on the lands of the eastern Mediterranean, which included detailed (but not accurate) descriptions of several Egyptian monuments, and the Scotsman James Bruce (1730–1794) excavated the tomb of Rameses III in the Valley of the Kings, which is still sometimes called "Bruce's Tomb." It is also known that some members of Egyptian royalty showed an interest in the preservation of their country's ancient past. For example, Prince Khaemwaset (fourth son of Rameses II) restored many temples, tombs, and pyramids, and Prince Thutmose (the youngest son of Amenhotep II, who succeeded his father on the throne as Thutmose IV) made repairs to and repainted the famous Sphinx at Giza. The Middle Kingdom ruler Senusret III appears to have deliberately removed two alabaster sarcophagi from underneath King Djoser's Step Pyramid at Saqqara, which were reburied some eight hundred years later within his pyramid complex at Dashur.

2. Joyce Tyldesley, *Egypt: How a Lost Civilization Was Rediscovered* (London: BBC Books, 2005), 44.

3. The Battle of the Nile actually took place at Aboukir Bay to the east of Alexandria: Napoleon's fleet of warships and frigates were smashed by those of Admiral Nelson and some 1,700 French sailors lost their lives in the battle.

4. The full title of the *Description* is *Description de l'Egypte, ou, Recueil des observations et des recherches qui ont été faites en Égypte pendant l'expédition de l'armée française, publié par les orders de sa Majesté l'Empereur Napoléon le Grand* (*Description of Egypt, or, Anthology of Observations and Researches Conducted in Egypt during the Expedition of the French Army, Published by Order of His Majesty the Emperor Napoleon the Great*).

5. For example, the shrine of Amenhotep III on Elephantine Island near Aswan.

6. John Ray, *The Rosetta Stone and the Rebirth of Ancient Egypt* (London: Profile, 2007), 58.

7. Tyldesley, *Egypt*, 59.

8. Ray, *The Rosetta Stone and the Rebirth of Ancient Egypt*, 44.

9. Ray, *The Rosetta Stone and the Rebirth of Ancient Egypt*, 55.

10. Ray, *The Rosetta Stone and the Rebirth of Ancient Egypt*, 72.

11. The great German scholar Karl Richard Lepsius built on the solid foundations laid by Champollion and proved beyond doubt that the Frenchman's decipherment of the hieroglyph alphabet was essentially correct. Lepsius also published the massive twelve-volume *Denkmäleraus Aegyptenund Aethiopien* (*Monuments of*

*Egypt and Ethiopia*) from 1849 to 1859, which is the definitive nineteenth-century account of ancient Egypt and is still of fundamental importance to Egyptologists today.

12. Nicholas Reeves, *Ancient Egypt: The Great Discoveries* (London: Thames & Hudson, 2000), 16.

13. Belzoni was well over six feet tall, and a very well-built and powerful individual.

14. Brian Fagan, *The Rape of the Nile: Tomb Robbers, Tourists, and Archaeologists in Egypt* (Colorado: Westview Press, 2004), 69.

15. Burckhardt discovered the lost Ramesside temples at Abu Simbel.

16. Its title does not exactly roll off the tongue: *Narrative of the Operations and Recent Discoveries within the Pyramids, Temples, Tombs and Excavations in Egypt and Nubia; and of a Journey to the Coasts of the Red Sea, in Search of the Ancient Berenice; and Another in the Oasis of Jupiter Ammon.*

17. *Shabtis* are small figurines, usually resembling mummies, which were placed in both royal and non-royal tombs as servants who would magically perform various tasks for the deceased in the afterlife, such as working in the fields.

18. These two huge seated statues were badly damaged by an earthquake(s), but they are still awe-inspiring. They stand at the eastern end of Amenhotep III's mortuary temple, of which very little remains today because it was plundered for building stone in later times.

19. Wilkinson devoted much time to copying (very accurately) the inscriptions and scenes found in the non-royal tombs of the Theban necropolis on Luxor's west bank, but he also surveyed tombs in the Valley of the Kings and devised a numbering sequence for them, which is still in use today. James Burton was one of Wilkinson's contemporaries and he carried out a number of excavations in the Valley of the Kings, leaving a valuable archive of this work in the form of sixty-three volumes of plans, notes, and drawings.

20. Chris Humber, "Auguste Mariette, 1821–1881," *Ancient Egypt* 11 (2011): 16.

21. King Kamose made a successful military sortie against the Hyksos rulers of the Delta and set in motion their eventual expulsion from Egypt. When his coffin (which was very poorly made and thus a replacement for the original) was opened, his mummy unfortunately disintegrated upon exposure to the air.

22. Fagan, *The Rape of the Nile*, 185.

23. Quoted in Margaret S. Drower, *Flinders Petrie: A Life in Archaeology* (Madison: University of Wisconsin Press, 1995), 28.

24. On one occasion, Miss Edwards and her traveling companion were offered a papyrus and a mummy taken illegally from a Theban tomb for one hundred pounds. No deal was struck, but they later found out that friends of theirs had bought both papyrus and mummy. The latter, however, ended up being dumped in the Nile because its new owners could not bear its terrible smell.

25. Fagan, *The Rape of the Nile*, 235–236.

26. Petrie famously walked everywhere—often many miles in the fierce Egyptian sun—even though donkeys were an abundant and cheap form of transport. On his excavations, Petrie also expected his colleagues to eat from tins like himself; sometimes, unused tins were even buried as supplies for next year's work. The American Egyptologist Arthur Weigall was a student of Petrie's at the site of Abydos and said of his time there: "You lived on sardines, and when you had eaten the sardines you ate the tin." When Howard Carter arrived at el-Amarna, he had to build his own mud-brick hut to live in and use newspapers as a substitute for bedding.

27. Quoted in Nicholas Reeves and Richard H. Wilkinson, *The Complete Valley of the Kings: Tombs and Treasures of Egypt's Greatest Pharaohs* (Cairo: The American University in Cairo Press, 2002), 94.

28. Arthur Weigall, "The Mummy of Akhenaton," *Journal of Egyptian Archaeology* 8 (1922): 193.

29. Quoted in Joyce Tyldesley, *Tutankhamen's Curse: The Developing History of an Egyptian King* (London: Profile, 2012), 38–39.

30. John Baines and Jaromir Málek, *Atlas of Ancient Egypt* (New York: Facts on File, 1980), 29.

31. Fagan, *The Rape of the Nile*, 249.

## CHAPTER 4: CONTROVERSIES AND SCANDALS IN EGYPTOLOGY

1. Nicholas Reeves and Richard H. Wilkinson, *The Complete Valley of the Kings: Tombs and Treasures of Egypt's Greatest Pharaohs* (Cairo: The American University in Cairo Press, 2002), 78.

2. These distinctive coffins or anthropoid cases are either decorated with huge pairs of wings or covered all over with rows of feathers, symbolizing the protection offered by the goddesses Isis and Nephthys. The *rishi* coffin from KV55 has since been restored to something approaching its former glory, but the gold face mask is gone forever, probably long since melted down.

3. Quoted in Joyce Tyldesley, *Tutankhamen's Curse: The Developing History of an Egyptian King* (London: Profile, 2012), 51–52.

4. Joyce Tyldesley, "The Mysterious Mummy in Tomb 55," in *Written in Bones*, edited by Paul Bahn (London: David & Charles, 2002), 173.

5. These were placed in tombs to protect the deceased from evil forces in the afterlife.

6. Cyril Aldred and A. T. Sandison, "The Tomb of Akhenaten at Thebes," *Journal of Egyptian Archaeology* 47 (1961): 53.

7. Like the false beard, the *uraeus* (the cobra goddess) was a standard symbol of Egyptian kingship and most royal crowns or headdresses featured a small cobra figurine that protruded from the forehead.

8. Tyldesley, "The Mysterious Mummy in Tomb 55," 173.

9. Tyldesley, "The Mysterious Mummy in Tomb 55," 173.

10. Ian Shaw and Paul Nicholson, *The British Museum Dictionary of Ancient Egypt* (London: British Museum Press, 2008), 307.

11. Joyce Tyldesley, *Nefertiti: Egypt's Sun Queen* (London: Penguin, 1999), 93.

12. Tyldesley, *Nefertiti*, 93.

13. Jacobus Van Dijk, "The Amarna Period and the Later New Kingdom," in the *Oxford History of Ancient Egypt*, edited by Ian Shaw (Oxford: Oxford University Press, 2000), 281.

14. Charlotte Booth, *The Curse of the Mummy: And Other Mysteries of Ancient Egypt* (Oxford: Oneworld, 2009), 121.

15. Irwin M. Braverman, Donald B. Redford, and Phillip A. Mackowlak, "Akhenaten and the Strange Physiques of Egypt's 18th Dynasty," *Annals of Internal Medicine* 150 (2009): 560.

16. Barry Kemp, *Ancient Egypt: Anatomy of a Civilization* (London: Routledge, 1989), 265.

17. Zahi Hawass, Yehia Z. Gad, and Somaia Ismail, "Ancestry and Pathology in King Tutankhamen's Family," *Journal of the American Medical Association* 303 (2010): 644.

18. Interestingly, Hawass and his colleagues did identify the mummy from KV55 as Tutankhamen's probable father, Akhenaten.

19. Quoted in Marianne Luban, "Do We Have the Mummy of Nefertiti?" 1999, www.Geocities.com.

20. Her exciting but debatable theory was proposed in the above web article.

21. According to a *Washington Post* article, "Nefertiti Puts a Jolt in Discovery's Ratings" (Wednesday, 20 August 2003), a documentary aired on the Discovery Channel—*Nefertiti Resurrected*—that first broke the news of Fletcher's "discovery" attracted 5.5 million viewers, making it one of the channel's top ten programs of all time.

22. The Younger Lady has what appears to be a gaping wound in the left side of her face that may have been caused by an axe blow, and a possible stab wound just below her left breast.

23. Joann Fletcher, *The Search for Nefertiti* (London: Hodder & Stoughton, 2004), 379.

24. Fletcher, *The Search for Nefertiti*, 355.

25. Joyce Tyldesley, e-mail to author, 29 July 2013.

26. Quoted in Joyce Tyldesley, *Judgement of the Pharaoh: Crime and Punishment in Ancient Egypt* (London: Weidenfeld & Nicolson, 2000), 103.

27. Quoted in Tyldesley, *Tutankhamen's Curse*, 158–159.

28. Bob Brier, *The Murder of Tutankhamen: A 3000-Year-Old Murder Mystery* (London: Phoenix, 1998), 172–173.

29. Richard S. Boyer, Ernst A. Rodin, Todd C. Grey, and R. C. Connolly, "The Skull and Cervical Spine Radiographs of Tutankhamen: A Critical Appraisal," *American Journal of Neuroradiology* 24 (2003): 1145.

30. Boyer et al., "The Skull and Cervical Spine Radiographs of Tutankhamen," 1145.

31. For more on the fascinating letters sent by Ankhesenamen to Suppiluliuma and more on the life and death of Tutankhamen see Bob Brier's *The Murder of Tutankhamen*.

32. Joyce Tyldesley, *The Mummy's Curse: The Developing History of an Egyptian King* (London: Profile, 2012), 158.

33. Christopher Frayling, *The Face of Tutankhamen* (London: Faber and Faber, 1992), 291.

34. Tutankhamen's head was rather brutally cut from his body during the autopsy, along with his legs, arms, hands, and feet.

35. Hawass et al., "Ancestry and Pathology in King Tutankhamen's Family."

36. Tyldesley, *The Mummy's Curse*, 161.

37. W. Benson Harer Jr., "Was Tutankhamen Killed by a Hippo?" *Ancient Egypt* 12 (2012): 50–54.

38. P. Sheldrick, "Was Tutankhamen Killed by a Hippo? The Sequel!" *Ancient Egypt* 13 (2012): 46–49.

39. Garry J. Shaw, "The Death of King Seqenenre Tao," *Journal of the American Research Center in Egypt* 45 (2009): 173.

40. Harer Jr., "Was Tutankhamen Killed by a Hippo?" 54.

41. Janine Bourriau, "The Second Intermediate Period," in the *Oxford History of Ancient Egypt*, edited by Ian Shaw (Oxford: Oxford University Press, 2000), 211.

42. Quoted in Lauren Bearden, "Repatriating the Bust of Nefertiti: A Critical Perspective on Cultural Ownership," *Kennesaw Journal of Undergraduate Research* 2 (2012): 5, http://digitalcommons.kennessaw.edu/kjur/vol2/iss1/2.

43. Just a few of the many fine forgeries attributable to the "Garden Shed Gang" are a bust of Thomas Jefferson by Horatio Greenough (a well-known nineteenth-century American sculptor), which was sold at Sotheby's for £48,000, and a ceramic sculpture of a faun by the famous French artist Paul Gauguin, which ended up being bought by the Art Institute of Chicago for $125,000.

44. Angela P. Thomas, "The Amarna Princess," NEMES Egyptology Society, http://www.nemes.co.uk/briefnotes6.htm.

45. Further proof of the fine workmanship and research that went into the production of the Amarna Princess is provided by its inclusion in Joann Fletchers' *The Search for Nefertiti* as a genuine artifact of the Amarna Period and Manchester Museum's unveiling of it as a genuine piece shortly after its "discovery."

## CHAPTER 5: HARMING EGYPT'S PAST

1. Catherine Sease, "Conservation and the Antiquities Trade," *Journal of the American Institute for Conservation* 36 (1997): 50.

2. Sease, "Conservation and the Antiquities Trade," 51.

3. Peter Cannon-Brookes, "Antiquities in the Market-Place: Placing a Price on Documentation," *Antiquity* 68 (1994): 350.

4. House of Commons Culture, Media and Sport Committee, Minutes of Evidence, memorandum submitted by the UK Museums Association, March 2004: 4, http://www.parliament.the-stationery-office.co.uk/pa/cm199900/cmselect/cmc umeds/371/0032305.htm.

5. Nikos Passas and Blythe Bowman Proulx, "Overview of Crimes and Antiquities," in *Crime in the Art and Antiquities World: Illegal Trafficking in Cultural Property*, edited by Stefano Manacorda and Duncan Chappell (New York: Springer, 2011), 61, doi: 10.1007/978-1-4419-7946-9_3.

6. Neil Brodie and Colin Renfrew, "Looting and the World's Archaeological Heritage: The Inadequate Response," *Annual Review of Anthropology* 34 (2005): 346, doi: 10.1146/annurev.anthro.34.081804.120551.

7. Brodie and Renfrew, "Looting and the World's Archaeological Heritage," 347.

8. David W. J. Gill and Christopher Chippindale, "Material and Intellectual Consequences of the Esteem of Cycladic Figures," *American Journal of Archaeology* 97 (1993): 625.

9. David Gill and Christopher Chippindale, "The Trade in Looted Antiquities and the Return of Cultural Property," *International Journal of Cultural Property* 11 (2002): 52.

10. Charles Palmer and Catherine Beech, quoted in Jason McElroy, "The War against the Illegal Antiquities Trade: Rules of Engagement for Source Nations," *Hastings Communications and Entertainment Law Journal* 547 (2004–2005): 549–566.

11. Simon R. M. Mackenzie, "Dig a Bit Deeper: Law, Regulation and the Illicit Antiquities Market," *British Journal of Criminology* 45 (2005): 251, doi: 10.1093/bjc/azh099.

12. Mackenzie, "Dig a Bit Deeper," 252.

13. Jeanette Greenfield, *The Return of Cultural Treasures* (Cambridge: Cambridge University Press, 1995), 204.

14. Geraldine Norman, quoted in James Chesterman, "A Collector/Dealer's View of Antiquities," *Antiquity* 65 (1991): 538.

15. Lisa J. Borodkin, "The Economics of Antiquities Looting and a Proposed Legal Alternative," *Columbia Law Review* 95 (1995): 377.

16. Patty Gerstenblith, "Controlling the International Market in Antiquities: Reducing the Harm, Preserving the Past," *Chicago Journal of International Law* 8 (2007): 172.

17. Gerstenblith, "Controlling the International Market in Antiquities," 172.

18. See Gill and Chippindale, "Material and Intellectual Consequences of the Esteem of Cycladic Figures," 615–622.

19. Asif Efrat, "Preventing Plunder: International Cooperation against the Illicit Trade in Antiquities," *Oxford Scholarship Online* (2012): 34, doi: 1093/acprof: oso/9780199976305.001.0001.

20. Anonymous New York antiquities dealer, quoted in Mackenzie, "Dig a Bit Deeper," 255.

21. Anonymous London dealer, quoted in Mackenzie, "Dig a Bit Deeper," 256.

22. Folarin Shyllon, "Looting and Illicit Traffic in Antiquities in Africa," in *Crime in the Art and Antiquities World: Illegal Trafficking in Cultural Property*, edited by Stefano Manacorda and Duncan Chappell (New York: Springer, 2011), 136, doi: 10.1007/978-1-4419-7946-9_3.

23. In fact, after his one and only visit to Egypt with a Franco-Italian expedition in 1828–1829, the famous Jean-François Champollion wrote to the caliph urging him to do more to stop the serious looting of the country's past and this letter was influential in the subsequent passing of this act.

24. Quoted in Salima Ikram, "Collecting and Repatriating Egypt's Past: Toward a New Nationalism," in *Contested Cultural Heritage: Religion, Nationalism, Erasure, and Exclusion in a Global World*, edited by Helaine Silverman (New York: Springer, 2011), 143–144.

25. United Nations Educational, Scientific and Cultural Organization.

26. Hawass was the leading figure in a campaign that sought the return to Egypt of famous "illegal" antiquities such as the Rosetta Stone, the Nefertiti bust, and the obelisk from Luxor Temple, which now stands in the Place de la Concorde, Paris.

27. Vivian Davis, quoted in Gill and Chippindale, "The Trade in Looted Antiquities and the Return of Cultural Property," 53. A particularly notable example of the serious damage being done by looters in Egypt is the serious pillaging of the so-called Pyramid Belt in the desert near Cairo, where gangs have used mechanical diggers to plunder archaeological sites. The hundreds of holes left by the diggers can be seen in satellite pictures.

28. Cynthia Ericson, "United States of America v. Frederick Schultz. The National Stolen Property Act Revives the Curse of the Pharaohs," *Tulane Journal of International and Comparative Law* 12 (2004): 509–523.

29. Brodie and Renfrew, "Looting and the World's Archaeological Heritage," 356.

30. As well as being home to the famous "Bent," "Red," and Djoser's famous Step Pyramid, there are further pyramids, numerous tombs, and other ancient remains at Dashur and Saqqara.

31. René Teijgeler, "Politics and Heritage in Egypt. One and a Half Years after the Lotus Revolution," *Archaeologies: Journal of the World Archaeological Congress* (2013): 1–2.

32. Stefano Manacorda and Duncan Chappell, "From Cairo to Vienna and Beyond: Contemporary Perspectives on the Dialogue about Protecting Cultural Artefacts from Plunder," in *Crime in the Art and Antiquities World: Illegal Trafficking in Cultural Property*, edited by Stefano Manacorda and Duncan Chappell (New York: Springer, 2011), 136, doi: 10.1007/978-1-4419-7946-9_3.

33. A freestanding, rectangular shrine made from wood or stone that was kept in the innermost part of a temple, and which contained various ritual objects such as statues of the god and mummified animal remains.

34. Barry Meir, "Antiquities Gallery Will Return Two Limestone Monuments to Egypt," *New York Times*, 2 April 2004, http//www.nytimes.com/2004/04/02/movies/antiquities-gallery-will-return-two-limestone-monuments-to-egypt.html.

## CHAPTER 6: CONTRIBUTIONS TO KNOWLEDGE OF THE PAST

1. Ian Shaw and Paul Nicholson, *The British Museum Dictionary of Ancient Egypt* (London: British Museum Press, 2008), 248.

2. Kathryn A. Bard, *An Introduction to the Archaeology of Ancient Egypt* (Oxford: Blackwell, 2008), 15.

3. Bard, *An Introduction to the Archaeology of Ancient Egypt*, 15.

4. David L. Browman and Douglas R. Givens, "Stratigraphic Excavation: The First New Archaeology," *American Anthropologist* 98 (1996): 83.

5. A large settlement that is associated with Kamose (last king of the Seventeenth Dynasty) and Ahmose I (first king of the Eighteenth Dynasty), the two kings who drove the Hyksos from Egypt.

6. W. F. Allbright, quoted in Stephen B. Luce, *American Journal of Archaeology (News and Discussions)* 46 (1942): 410–411.

7. Browman and Givens, "Stratigraphic Excavation," 86.

8. Sarah Parcak, "What Is Space Archaeology?," http://www.sarahparcak.com/index2.php#/multi-text_5/1/.

9. CNN, "This Week on the 'Next List': A Space Archaeologist," *What's Next*, 22 May 2012, http://whatsnext.blogs.cnn.com/2012/05/22/this-week-on-the-next-list-a-space-archaeologist/.

10. Rudi Goosens et al., "Satellite Imagery and Archaeology: The Example of CORONA in the Altai Mountains," *Journal of Archaeological Science* 33 (2006): 745–755.

11. Sarah Parcak, "The Skeptical Remote Senser: Google Earth and Egyptian Archaeology," in *Beyond the Horizon: Studies in Egyptian Art, Archaeology and History in Honour of Barry J. Kemp*, edited by Salima Ikram and Aidan Dodson (Cairo: Supreme Council of Antiquities, 2009), 365.

12. Parcak, "The Skeptical Remote Senser," 364.

13. See, e.g., Heather Pringle, "Satellite Imagery Uncovers up to 17 Lost Egyptian Pyramids," 2011, http://news.sciencemag.org/2011/05/satellite-imagery-uncovers-17-lost-Egyptian-Pyramids.

14. John Ray, *The Rosetta Stone and the Rebirth of Ancient Egypt* (London: Profile, 2007), 122.

15. Ray, *The Rosetta Stone*, 123.

16. It is not clear exactly what a "wiwi" was.

17. Ray, *The Rosetta Stone*, 129.

18. Steven Snape, "Sennedjem: Building and Buying at Deir el-Medina," in *Ancient Egyptian Tombs: The Culture of Life and Death* (Wiley-Blackwell, 2011), 234, http://onlinelibrary.wiley.com/doi/10.002/9781444/393743.ch16/.

19. For those readers wishing to look in greater detail at the fascinating and evocative Deir el-Medina texts see John Romer's *Ancient Lives: The Story of the Pharaohs' Tombmakers* and A. G. McDowell's *Village Life in Ancient Egypt* (see bibliography for full reference).

20. Lynn Meskell, "An Archaeology of Social Relations in an Egyptian Village," *Journal of Archaeological Method and Theory* 5 (1998): 237.

21. A. G. McDowell, *Village Life in Ancient Egypt: Laundry Lists and Love Songs* (Oxford: Oxford University Press, 1999), 55–56.

22. The royal funerary temples and tombs on the west bank at Thebes.

23. John Romer, *Ancient Lives: The Story of the Pharaohs' Tombmakers* (London: Phoenix, 2003), 23.

24. Benedict Davies, "Misdemeanours at Deir el-Medina," *Ancient Egypt* 11 (2011): 32.

25. Jaroslav Černý, "Papyrus Salt 124 (Brit. Mus. 10055)," *Journal of Egyptian Archaeology* 15 (1929): 245.

26. Unsurprisingly, the most serious crime in ancient Egypt was the robbery of the king's tomb, and in Paneb's time, impalement on a stake often awaited the perpetrators of this crime if they were caught. Those guilty of less serious crimes were rewarded with a range of punishments that included expulsion from the community, forced labor, beatings, and mutilation.

27. McDowell, *Village Life in Ancient Egypt*, 238.

28. Raymond Cohen, "On Diplomacy in the Ancient Near East: The Amarna Letters," *Diplomacy and Statecraft* 7 (1996): 245, doi: 10.1080/09592299608406003.

29. For those readers who want an in-depth look at the Amarna Letters see *The Amarna Letters*, edited and translated by William L. Moran (Baltimore: Johns Hopkins University Press, 1992).

30. Cohen, "On Diplomacy in the Ancient Near East," 253.

31. Steven Snape, "The Amarna Letters," in *Wonderful Things*, edited by Paul Bahn (London: Seven Dials, 2000), 29.

32. Snape, "The Amarna Letters," 29.

33. Cohen, "On Diplomacy in the Ancient Near East," 249.

34. Y. Lynn Holmes, "The Messengers of the Amarna Letters," *Journal of the American Oriental Society* 95 (1975): 377.

35. Cohen, "On Diplomacy in the Ancient Near East," 247.

36. Rosalie David, *The Two Brothers: Death and the Afterlife in the Middle Kingdom* (Bolton: Rutherford Press, 2007) 115.

37. E. Tapp, "The Unwrapping of a Mummy," in *Manchester Museum Mummy Project: Multidisciplinary Research on Ancient Egyptian Mummified Remains*, edited by Rosalie David (Manchester: Manchester Museum, 1979), 89.

38. Quoted in David, *The Two Brothers*, 108.

39. R. A. H. Neave, "The Reconstruction of the Heads and Faces of Three Ancient Egyptian Mummies," in *Manchester Museum Mummy Project: Multidisciplinary Research on Ancient Egyptian Mummified Remains*, edited by Rosalie David (Manchester: Manchester Museum, 1979), 154–155.

40. Neave, "The Reconstruction of the Heads and Faces of Three Ancient Egyptian Mummies," 156.

41. Rosalie David, "Learning from Mummies," *Current World Archaeology* 61 (2013): 27.

## CHAPTER 7: CURRENT DIGS

1. Mark Lehner, "The Pyramid Age Settlement of the Southern Mount at Giza," *Journal of the American Research Center in Egypt* 39 (2002): 27.

2. These large halls were an essential component of Egyptian temples and feature decorated columns symbolizing the papyrus plants that grew in the reed swamps fringing the Primeval Mound, which the Egyptians believed rose out of the primeval waters during the act of creation.

3. This escarpment also contains many finely decorated rock-cut tombs intended for high officials, but these were left unfinished, as Amarna was abandoned after the death of Akhenaten in year seventeen of his reign.

4. Akhenaten's eldest daughter.

5. Abydos was a major sacred center and was in use from the Predynastic Period to early Christian times (c.4000 BC–AD 61). The site is extremely rich in archaeological remains, and includes cemeteries containing the impressive tombs of Predynastic and Early Dynastic rulers, from which many significant artifacts have been recovered. There are also temples belonging to Middle and New Kingdom pharaohs (e.g., Senusret III and Ramesses II), the subterranean Osireion building, and a large Middle Kingdom settlement.

6. Some of the finds from Malqata can be seen today in the Met's Egyptian galleries.

7. Angus Graham et al., "Reconstructing Landscapes and Waterscapes in Thebes, Egypt," *eTopoi. Journal for Ancient Studies* 3 (2012): 135, http://journal.topoi .org/index.php/etopoi/article/viewfile/98/128.

8. This woman was buried with four complete pots by her head and a basket containing various objects (e.g., an ivory comb, fine flint blades, and chunks of galena and ochre), including a small leather bag that amongst other things contained small mud cones, chunks of resin, seeds, tubers, and chips of imported cedar and juniper. This curious and unparalleled collection of objects may indicate that the woman held a special role in life and was perhaps a healer or shaman-like figure.

9. These two ancient Nubian cultures were semi-nomadic cattle herders, who, although sharing some cultural affinities, seem to have been physically distinct

populations. Nubians were often employed as mercenaries in the Egyptian army or in the Medjay (a type of ancient Egyptian police force).

10. Steven Snape, "Neb-Re and the Heart of Darkness: The Latest Discoveries from Zawiyet Umm el-Rakham (Egypt)," *Antiquity* 75 (2001): 20.

11. Steven Snape, "Interesting Times for Neb-Re," *Ancient Egypt* 2 (2001): 16.

12. The expedition is led by Dr. Mark Collier and Dr. Glenn Godenho.

13. Ankhtifi's tomb was first surveyed and recorded by a French expedition in the 1930s, after it was discovered by local quarrymen in 1928.

14. Many other tombs of the First Intermediate Period have been cut into the hill, including that of the provincial governor Sobekhotep, and it is suspected that some of the other tombs near Ankhtifi's are those of members of his family or his high officials.

15. As we have already seen in chapter one, these texts record a possible famine during the time of Ankhtifi and also give an account of his wars with his great enemy, the Thebes-based Eleventh Dynasty.

16. The tomb also features carved and painted decoration on its walls, with the latter including lively and almost cartoon-like depictions of such things as servants bringing food offerings, a squad of archers accompanied by greyhound-like hunting dogs, and Ankhtifi himself, who is seen overseeing his estates and also spearing fish, presumably while fishing in the nearby Nile.

17. The project is co-directed by Dr. Ian Shaw (University of Liverpool) and Dr. Fredrik Hagen (University of Copenhagen).

18. Thutmose III established a harem palace at Gurob that was incorrectly identified by Flinders Petrie as a temple. It was the German archaeologist Ludwig Borchardt who first suggested that it was a building connected with royal women when he carried out excavations at Gurob in 1905, although many harem buildings in ancient Egypt probably had more to do with administration than with the sensual pleasures of the king.

19. *Wedjat* eye amulets are commonly found on Egyptian sites and were believed to provide protection and healing. They symbolize the eye of the god Horus, who is said to have lost his eye in a violent struggle with his uncle, Seth, the god of chaos and confusion, although the goddess Hathor later restored his sight.

20. Elkab is located on the east bank of the Nile some fifty miles south of Luxor. The town was founded in the Early Dynastic Period, although the discovery of prehistoric campsites at the site, dating to around 6200 BC, reveal that people had long seen this location as a favorable area to live.

21. Dirk Huyge, "Death and Life in Old Kingdom Elkab," *Ancient Egypt* 13 (2013): 36.

22. Ross I. Thomas and Alexandra Villing, "Naukratis Revisited 2012: Integrating New Fieldwork and Old Research," in *British Museum Studies in Ancient Egypt and Sudan* 20 (2013): 82, http://www.britishmuseum.org/research_online journals/bmsaes/issue_20/thomas&villing.aspx.

23. Nehmes-Bastet was just one of many priestess/musicians who would have performed religious duties in the temple at Karnak, yet the fact that she was accorded the privilege of a burial close to the royal tombs in the Valley of the Kings indicates that she was a lady of some status.

# BIBLIOGRAPHY

Aldred, Cyril. *Akhenaten: King of Egypt*. London: Thames & Hudson, 1999.

Aldred, Cyril, and A. T. Sandison. "The Tomb of Akhenaten at Thebes." *Journal of Egyptian Archaeology* 47 (1961): 41–65.

Ares, N. "The First Tombs of Ancient Egypt." *Ancient Egypt* 12 (2011): 28–33.

Baines, John. "Communication and Display: The Integration of Early Egyptian Art and Writing." *Antiquity* 63 (1989): 471–482.

Baines, John, and Jaromir Málek. *Atlas of Ancient Egypt*. New York: Facts on File, 1980.

Bard, K. A. "The Egyptian Predynastic: A Review of the Evidence." *Journal of Field Archaeology* 21 (1994): 265–288.

Bard, K. A. "The Emergence of the Egyptian State." In *The Oxford History of Ancient Egypt*, edited by Ian Shaw, 61–88. Oxford: Oxford University Press, 2000.

Bard, K. A. *An Introduction to the Archaeology of Ancient Egypt*. Oxford: Blackwell, 2008.

Bearden, Lauren. "Repatriating the Bust of Nefertiti: A Critical Perspective on Cultural Ownership." *Kennesaw Journal of Undergraduate Research* 2 (2012): 1–16. http://digitalcommons.kennesaw.edu/kjur/vol2/iss1/2.

Betz, Raymond. "The Belgian Excavations in Elkab." *Ancient Egypt* 13 (2013): 22–27.

Bickel, Susanne, Elina Paulin-Grothe, and Nicolas Sartori. *Preliminary Reports on the Work Carried Out during Seasons 2009–2013 by the University of Basel Kings' Valley Project*. http://aegyptologie.unibas.ch/forschung/projekte/university -of-basel-kings-valley-project/report-2009/2010/2011/2012/2013.

Binder, Michaela, Neal Spencer, and Marie Millet. "Cemetery D at Amara West: The Ramesside Period and Its Aftermath." *British Museum Studies in Ancient Egypt and Sudan* 16 (2011): 47–99.

Borodkin, Lisa J. "The Economics of Antiquities Looting and a Proposed Legal Alternative." *Columbia Law Review* 95 (1995): 377–417.

Boyer, Richard S., Ernst A. Rodin, Todd C. Grey, and R. C. Connolly. "The Skull and Cervical Spine Radiographs of Tutankhamen: A Critical Appraisal." *American Journal of Neuroradiology* 24 (2003): 1142–1147.

Braverman, Irwin M., Donald B. Redford, and Phillip A. Mackowlak. "Akhenaten and the Strange Physiques of Egypt's 18th Dynasty." *Annals of Internal Medicine* 50 (2009): 556–560.

Breasted, Charles. *Pioneer to the Past: The Story of James Henry Breasted, Archaeologist*. Chicago: The Oriental Institute, 2009.

Breger, Claudia. "Imperialist Fantasy and Displaced Memory: Twentieth-Century German Egyptologies." *New German Critique* 96 (2005): 135–169.

Brewer, Douglas J., and Emily Teeter. *Egypt and the Egyptians*. Cambridge: Cambridge University Press, 1999.

Brier, Bob. *The Murder of Tutankhamen: A 3000-Year-Old Murder Mystery*. London: Phoenix, 1998.

Brier, Bob. "Treasures of Tanis." *Archaeology* 58 (2005): 18–25.

Brodie, Neil, and Colin Renfrew. "Looting and the World's Archaeological Heritage." *Annual Review of Anthropology* 34 (2005): 343–428.

Buchwald, Jed Z. "Egyptian Stars under Paris Skies." *Engineering and Science* 4 (2003): 21–31.

Cannon-Brookes, Peter. "Antiquities in the Market-Place: Placing a Price on Documentation." *Antiquity* 68 (1994): 349–350.

Carter, Howard. "A Tomb Prepared for Queen Hatshepsut and Other Recent Discoveries at Thebes." *Journal of Egyptian Archaeology* 4 (1917): 107–118.

Carter, Howard. *The Tomb of Tutankhamun*. London: Century, 1983.

Carter, Howard, and Alan H. Gardiner. "The Tomb of Ramesses IV and the Turin Plan of a Royal Tomb." *Journal of Egyptian Archaeology* 4 (1917): 130–158.

Carter, Howard, and A. C. Mace. *The Discovery of the Tomb of Tutankhamen*. New York: Dover, 1977.

Case, Humphrey, and Joan Crowfoot Payne. "Tomb 100: The Decorated Tomb at Hierakonpolis." *Journal of Egyptian Archaeology* 48 (1962): 5–18.

Černý, Jaroslav. "Papyrus Salt 124 (Brit. Mus. 10055)." *Journal of Egyptian Archaeology* 15 (1929): 243–258.

Černý, Jaroslav. "A Note on the Recently Discovered Boat of Cheops." *Journal of Egyptian Archaeology* 41 (1955): 75–79.

Chesterman, James. "A Collector/Dealer's View of Antiquities." *Antiquity* 65 (1991): 538–539.

Clayton, Peter A. *Chronicle of the Pharaohs*. London: Thames & Hudson, 1994.

Close, A. E. "Living on the Edge: Neolithic Herders in the Eastern Sahara." *Antiquity* 64 (1990): 79–96.

Coggins, Clemency. "Archaeology and the Art Market." *Science* 175 (1972): 263–266. http://dx.doi.org/10.1080/09592299608406003.

Cohen, Raymond. "On Diplomacy in the Ancient Near East: The Amarna Letters." *Diplomacy and Statecraft* 7 (1996): 245–270. doi:10.1080/09592299608406003.

Collier, Mark, Bill Manley, and Ian Shaw. "Mo'alla: The Tomb of the Warlord, Ankhtyfy." *Current World Archaeology* 5 (2004): 25–31.

Cronin, Frances. "Egyptian Pyramids Found by Infrared Satellite Images," 24 May 2011. http://www.bbc.co.uk/news/world-13522957.

Crowfoot, J. W. "George Reisner: An Impression." *Antiquity* 17 (1943): 122–128.

Curtis, John. "Letter from Baghdad." *Current World Archaeology* 1 (2003): 5–9.

Dannenfeldt, Karl H. "Egypt and Egyptian Antiquities in the Renaissance." *Studies in the Renaissance* 6 (1959): 7–27.

David, Rosalie. *Manchester Museum Mummy Project: Multidisciplinary Research on Ancient Egyptian Mummified Remains.* Manchester: Manchester Museum, 1979.

David, Rosalie. *The Two Brothers: Death and the Afterlife in Middle Kingdom Egypt.* Bolton: Rutherford Press, 2007.

David, Rosalie. "Learning from Mummies." *Current World Archaeology* 61 (2013): 27.

Davies, Benedict. "Misdemeanours at Deir el-Medina." *Ancient Egypt* 11 (2011): 30–35.

Davies, Vivian, and Renée Friedman. *Egypt.* London: British Museum Press, 1998.

Davies, W. Vivian, and Elizabeth R. O'Connell. "The British Museum Expedition to Elkab and Hagr Edfu, 2009." *British Museum Studies in Ancient Egypt and Sudan* 14 (2009): 51–72.

Davies, W. Vivian, and Elizabeth R. O'Connell. "The British Museum Expedition to Elkab and Hagr Edfu, 2010." *British Museum Studies in Ancient Egypt and Sudan* 16 (2010): 101–132.

Davies, W. Vivian, and Elizabeth R. O'Connell. "The British Museum Expedition to Elkab and Hagr Edfu, 2011." *British Museum Studies in Ancient Egypt and Sudan* 17 (2011): 1–29.

Davies, W. Vivian, and Elizabeth R. O'Connell. "The British Museum Expedition to Elkab and Hagr Edfu, 2012." *British Museum Studies in Ancient Egypt and Sudan* 17 (2012): 51–85.

De Garis-Davies, N. "Mural Paintings in the City of Akhetaten." *Journal of Egyptian Archaeology* 7 (1921): 1–7.

Der Manuelian, Peter. "The Giza Archives Project." *Egyptian Archaeology* 28 (2006): 31–33.

Derricourt, Robin. "Typologies of Egypt: A Typological Review." *Cambridge Archaeological Journal* 22 (2012): 353–363. doi: 10.1017/S0959774312000443.

De Sélincourt, Aubrey, trans. *Herodotus: The Histories.* London: Penguin, 1996.

Desroches-Noblecourt, Christiane. *Tutankhamen.* London: Penguin, 1965.

Dodson, Aidan. "Egypt's First Antiquarians?" *Antiquity* 62 (1988): 513–517.

Drower, Margaret S. *Flinders Petrie: A Life in Archaeology.* Madison: University of Wisconsin Press, 1985.

Edgerton, William F. "The Strikes in Ramses III's Twenty-Ninth Year." *Journal of Near Eastern Studies* 10 (1951): 137–145.

Ericson, Cynthia. "United States of America v. Frederick Schultz. The National Stolen Property Act Revives the Curse of the Pharaohs." *Tulane Journal of International and Comparative Law* 12 (2004): 509–523.

Eyre, C. J. "Crime and Adultery in Ancient Egypt." *Journal of Egyptian Archaeology* 70 (1984): 92–105.

Fletcher, Joann. *The Search for Nefertiti*. London: Hodder & Stoughton, 2004.

Flinders Petrie, W. M., and J. E. Quibell. *Naqada and Ballas 1895*. London: Bernard Quaritch, 1896.

Fortenberry, Diane, ed. *Who Travels Sees More: Artists, Architects and Archaeologists Discover Egypt and the Near East*. Oxford: Oxbow Books, 2007.

Frayling, Christopher. *The Face of Tutankhamun*. London: Faber and Faber, 1992.

Furness, Hannah. "Revealed: The Secrets of a 5,500-year-old Mummy Murder Mystery," 2012. http://www.telegraph.co.uk/newstopics.howaboutthat/9682654/Revealed-the-secrets-of-of-a-5500-year-old-mummy-murder-mystery-html.

Gaimster, David. "Measures against the Illicit Trade in Cultural Objects: The Emerging Strategy in Britain." *Antiquity* 78 (2004): 699–707.

Gerstenblith, Patty. "Controlling the International Market in Antiquities: Reducing the Harm, Preserving the Past." *Chicago Journal of International Law* 8 (2007): 169–195.

Goosens, Rudi, Alain De Wulf, Jean Bourgeois, Wouter Gheyle, and Tom Willems. "Satellite Imagery and Archaeology: The Example of CORONA in the Altai Mountains." *Journal of Archaeological Science* 33 (2006): 745–755. doi: 10.1016/j.jas.2005.10.010.

Gordon, John B. "The UNESCO Convention on the Illicit Movement of Art Treasures." *Harvard Journal of International Law* 12 (1971): 537–556.

Goudsmit, Jaap, and Douglas Brandon-Jones. "Mummies of Olive Baboons and Barbary Macaques in the Baboon Catacomb of the Sacred Animal Necropolis at North Saqqara." *Journal of Egyptian Archaeology* 85 (1999): 45–53.

Graham, Angus, Kristian D. Strutt, Morag Hunter, Sarah Jones, Aurélia Mason, Marie Millet, and Benjamin Pennington. "Reconstructing Landscapes and Waterscapes in Thebes, Egypt." *eTopoi. Journal for Ancient Studies* 3 (2012): 135–142. http://journal.topoi.org/index.php/etopoi/article/viewfile/98/128.

Greenfield, Jeanette. *The Return of Cultural Treasures*. Cambridge: Cambridge University Press, 1996.

Harer Jr., W. Benson. "Was Tutankhamun Killed by a Hippo?" *Ancient Egypt* 12 (2012): 50–54.

Harer Jr., W. Benson. "Was Tutankhamun Killed by a Hippo? The Sequel!" *Ancient Egypt* 13 (2012): 46–49.

Harrison, R. G. "An Anatomical Examination of the Pharaonic Remains Purported to Be Akhenaton." *Journal of Egyptian Archaeology* 52 (1966): 95–119.

Harrison, R. G., and A. B. Abdalla. "The Remains of Tutankhamun." *Antiquity* 46 (1972): 8–14.

Hassan, F. A. "The Predynastic of Egypt." *Journal of World Prehistory* 2 (1988): 135–185.

Hassan, F. A. "The Dynamics of a Riverine Civilization: A Geoarchaeological Perspective of the Nile Valley, Egypt." *World Archaeology* 29 (1997): 51–74.

Hassan, F. A. "The Gift of the Nile." In *Ancient Egypt*, edited by D. P. Silverman, 12–13. London: Duncan Baird, 2003.

Hawass, Zahi. *Valley of the Golden Mummies*. New York: Harry N. Abrams, 2000.

Hawass, Zahi. *Tutankhamun and the Golden Age of the Pharaohs*. Washington: National Geographic Society, 2005.

Hawass, Zahi. "Who Killed Ramesses III?" *British Medical Journal* 345 (2012): 39–40.

Hawass, Zahi, Yehia Z. Gad, and Somaia Ismail. "Ancestry and Pathology in King Tutankhamen's Family." *Journal of the American Medical Association* 303 (2010): 638–647.

Hawass, Zahi, Somaia Ismail, Ashraf Selim, Sahar N. Saleem, Sally Wasef, Ahmed Z. Gad, Rama Saad, Suzan Fares, Hany Amer, Paul Gostner, Yehia Z. Gad, Carsten M. Pusch, and Albert R. Zink. "Revisiting the Harem Conspiracy and Death of Ramesses III: Anthropological, Forensic, Radiological, and Genetic Study." *British Medical Journal* 345 (2012): 1–9.

Hellier, C. A., and R. C. Connolly. "A Re-assessment of the Fetus Found in Tutankhamen's Tomb." *Antiquity* 83 (2009): 165–173.

Hikade, T. "Expeditions to the Wadi Hammamat during the New Kingdom." *Journal of Egyptian Archaeology* 92 (2006): 153–168.

Holmes, Y. Lynn. "The Messengers of the Amarna Letters." *Journal of the American Oriental Society* 95 (1975): 376–381.

*Horizon: The Amarna Project and Amarna Trust Newsletter*, vols. 1–13 (2006–2013). http://www.amarnaproject.com/downloadable_resources.shtml.

House of Commons Culture, Media and Sport Committee. Minutes of Evidence. Memorandum submitted by the UK Museums Association, March 2000. http://www.parliament.the–stationery-office.co.uk/pa/cm199900/cmselect/cmcumeds/371/0032305.htm.

Hughes, Donald J. "Sustainable Agriculture in Ancient Egypt." *Agricultural History* 2 (1992): 12–22.

Humber, Chris. "Auguste Mariette, 1821–1881." *Egyptian Archaeology* 11 (2011): 16–19.

Huyge, Dirk. "Late Palaeolithic and Epipalaeolithic Rock Art in Egypt: Qurta and El-Hosh." *Archéo-Nil* 19 (2009).

Huyge, Dirk. "Death and Life in Old Kingdom Elkab." *Ancient Egypt* 13 (2013): 28–36.

Huyge, Dirk. "'Ice Age' Art at Qurta." *Ancient Egypt* 13 (2013): 32–41.

Huyge, Dirk, and Per Storemyr. "Unique Geometric Rock Art at el-Hosh." *Ancient Egypt* 13 (2013): 24–30.

Huyge, Dirk, Dimitri A. G. Vandenberghe, Morgan De Dapper, Florias Mees, Wouter Claes, and John C. Darnell. "First Evidence of Pleistocene Rock Art in North Africa: Securing the Date of the Qurta Petroglyphs (Egypt) through OSL Dating." *Antiquity* 85 (2011): 1184–1193.

Ikram, Salima. "Domestic Shrines and the Cult of the Royal Family at el-Amarna." *Journal of Egyptian Archaeology* 75 (1982): 89–101.

Ikram, Salima. "Collecting and Repatriating Egypt's Past: Toward a New Nationalism." In *Contested Cultural Heritage: Religion, Nationalism, Erasure, and Exclusion in a Global World*, edited by Helaine Silverman, 141–154. New York: Springer, 2011. doi: 10.1007/978-1-4419-7305-4_1.

Isler-Kerényi, Cornelia. "Are Collectors the Real Looters?" *Antiquity* 68 (1994): 350–352.

Jastrow Jr., Morris. "Sir Gaston Maspero." *Proceedings of the American Philosophical Society* 55 (1916): 3–13.

Johnson, W. Raymond. "Warrior Tut." *Archaeology* 63 (2010).

Jórdeczka, M., H. Królik, M. Masojć, and R. Schild. "Early Holocene Pottery in the Western Desert of Egypt: New Data from Nabta Playa." *Antiquity* 85 (2011): 99–115.

Kadry, Ahmed. "The Solar Boat of Cheops." *International Journal of Nautical Archaeology and Underwater Exploration* 15 (1986): 123–131.

Kemp, Barry. "The City of El-Amarna as a Source for the Study of Urban Society in Egypt." *World Archaeology* 9 (1977): 123–139.

Kemp, Barry. *Ancient Egypt: Anatomy of a Civilization*. London: Routledge, 1989.

Kemp, Barry. "News from Amarna." *Ancient Egypt* 13 (2013): 6.

Kemp, Barry, Anna Stevens, Gretchen R. Dabbs, Melissa Zabecki, and Jerome C. Rose. "Life, Death and Beyond in Akhenaten's Egypt: Excavating the South Tombs Cemetery at Amarna." *Antiquity* 87 (2013): 64–78.

Key, Bill. "Why Belzoni Went to Egypt." *Ancient Egypt* 11 (2011): 28–31.

Klemm, D. D., and R. Klemm. "The Building Stones of Ancient Egypt—A Gift of Its Geology." *African Earth Sciences* 33 (2001): 631–642.

Klemm, D., R. Klemm, and A. Murr. "Gold of the Pharaohs—6000 Years of Gold Mining in Egypt and Nubia." *African Earth Sciences* 33 (2001): 643–659.

Knoblauch, Ann-Marie. "Archaeology as the History of Cultural Property." *The Classical World* 97 (2004): 179–193.

Lambert-Zazulak, Patricia I. Rutherford, and Rosalie A. David. "The International Ancient Egyptian Mummy Tissue Bank at the Manchester Museum as a Resource for the Palaeoepidemiological Study of Schistosomiasis." *World Archaeology* 35 (2003): 223–240.

Lasaponara, R., and N. Masini. "Satellite Remote Sensing in Archaeology: Past, Present, and Future Perspectives." *Journal of Archaeological Science* 38 (2011): 1995–2002. doi: 10.1016/j.jas.2011.02.002.

Lehner, Mark. "The Pyramid Age Settlement of the Southern Mount at Giza." *Journal of the American Research Center in Egypt* 39 (2002): 27–74.

Lehner, Mark. "Giza Plateau Mapping Project: The Oriental Institute 2002–2003 Annual Report." http://oi.uchicago/edu/O1/AR//02-03/02-03_AR_TOC.html.

Lehner, Mark. "Giza Plateau Mapping Project: The Oriental Institute 2007–2008 Annual Report," 49–75. http://oi.uchicago/edu/O1/AR//07-08/07-08_AR_TOC.html.

Lehner, Mark, "Giza Plateau Mapping Project: The Oriental Institute 2007–2010 Annual Report," 40–64. http://oi.uchicago/edu/O1/AR//09-10/09-10_AR_TOC.html.

Limme, Luc. "Elkab, 1937–2007: Seventy Years of Belgian Archaeological Research." *British Museum Studies in Ancient Egypt and Sudan* 9 (2008): 15–50.

Mackenzie, Simon R. M. "Dig a Bit Deeper: Law, Regulation and the Illicit Antiquities Market." *British Journal of Criminology* 45 (2005): 249–268.

Macy Roth, Ann, and Catharine H. Roehrig. "Magical Bricks and the Bricks of Birth." *Journal of Egyptian Archaeology* 88 (2002): 121–139.

Magli, Giulio. "From Abydos to the Valley of the Kings: The Conception of Royal Funerary Landscapes in the New Kingdom." *Mediterranean Archaeology and Archaeometry* 11 (2011): 23–356.

Malek, J. "The Old Kingdom." In *The Oxford History of Ancient Egypt*, edited by Ian Shaw, 89–117. Oxford: Oxford University Press, 2000.

Manacorda, Stefano, and Duncan Chappell. "From Cairo to Vienna and Beyond: Contemporary Perspectives on the Dialogue about Protecting Cultural Artefacts from Plunder." In *Crime in the Art and Antiquities World: Illegal Trafficking in Cultural Property*, edited by Stefano Manacorda and Duncan Chappell, 1–15. New York: Springer, 2011. doi: 10.1007/978-1-4419-7946_1, © Springer Science+Business Media LCC 2011.

Mandel, R. D., and R. D. Simmons. "Quaternary Landscapes Near Kharga Oasis, Western Desert of Egypt." *Geoarchaeology: An International Journal* 16 (2001): 95–117.

McDonald, Mary M. A. "Early African Pastoralism: View from Dakhleh Oasis (South Central Egypt)." *Journal of Anthropological Archaeology* 17 (1998): 124–142.

McDowell, A. G. *Village Life in Ancient Egypt: Laundry Lists and Love Songs.* Oxford: Oxford University Press, 1999.

McElroy, Jason. "The War against the Illegal Antiquities Trade: Rules of Engagement for Source Nations." *Hastings Communications and Entertainment Law Journal* 27 (2004–2005): 547–566.

Menu, Bernadette. *Ramesses the Great: Warrior and Builder.* London: Thames & Hudson, 1999.

Merkel, Howard. "King Tutankhamun, Modern Medical Science, and the Expanding Boundaries of Historical Inquiry." *Journal of the American Medical Association* 303 (2010): 667–668.

Meskell, Lynn. "An Archaeology of Social Relations in an Egyptian Village." *Journal of Archaeological Method and Theory* 5 (1998): 209–243.

Meskell, Lynn. "Intimate Archaeologies: The Case of Kha and Merit." *World Archaeology* 29 (2010): 363–379. http://dx.doi.org/10.1080/00438243.1998.9980385.

Midant-Reynes, B. "The Naqada Period (c.4000–3200 BC)." In *The Oxford History of Ancient Egypt*, edited by Ian Shaw, 44–60. Oxford: Oxford University Press, 2000.

Montserrat, Dominic. "The Representation of Young Males in the 'Fayum Portraits.'" *Journal of Egyptian Archaeology* 79 (1993): 215–225.

Montserrat, Dominic. *Akhenaten: History, Fantasy and Ancient Egypt*. London: Routledge, 2000.

Mumford, Gregory, and Sarah Parcak. "Satellite Image Analysis and Archaeological Fieldwork in El-Markha (South Sinai)." *Antiquity* 76 (2002): 953–954.

Mumford, Gregory, and Sarah Parcak. "Pharaonic Ventures into South Sinai: El-Markha Plain Site 346." *Journal of Egyptian Archaeology* 89 (2003): 83–116.

Murray, M. A. "Burial Customs and Beliefs in the Hereafter in Predynastic Egypt." *Journal of Egyptian Archaeology* 42 (1956): 86–96.

Nicholson, Paul T. "Preliminary Report on Work at the Sacred Animal Necropolis, North Saqqara." *Journal of Egyptian Archaeology* 80 (1994): 1–10.

Nicholson, P. T., and I. Shaw. *Ancient Egyptian Materials and Technology*. Cambridge: Cambridge University Press, 2000.

O'Keefe, Patrick J. *Trade in Antiquities: Reducing Destruction and Theft*. London: Archetype Publications/United Nations, 1997.

Osman, Dalia N. "Occupiers' Title to Cultural Property: Nineteenth-Century Removal of Egyptian Artifacts." *Columbia Journal of Transnational Law* 37 (1998–1999): 969–1002.

Parcak, Sarah. "The Skeptical Remote Senser: Google Earth and Egyptian Archaeology." In *Beyond the Horizon: Studies in Egyptian Art, Archaeology, and History in Honour of Barry J. Kemp*, edited by Salima Ikram and Aidan Dodson, 361–382. Cairo: The Supreme Council of Antiquities, 2009.

Partridge, Robert. "KV-63 Update: The Final Stage." *Ancient Egypt* 7 (2006): 26–30.

Passas, Nikos, and Blythe Bowman Proulx. "Overview of Crimes and Antiquities." In *Crime in the Art and Antiquities World: Illegal Trafficking in Cultural Property*, edited by Stefano Manacorda and Duncan Chappell, 51–67. New York: Springer, 2011. doi: 10.1007/978-1-4419-7946_1, © Springer Science+Business Media LCC 2011.

Peet, T. Eric. "The Great Tomb Robberies of the Ramesside Age. Papyri Mayer A and B." *Journal of Egyptian Archaeology* 2 (1915): 173–177.

Petr, Mark J. "Trading Places: Illicit Antiquities, Foreign Cultural Patrimony Laws, and the U.S. National Stolen Property Act after United States v. Schultz." *Hastings International and Comparative Law Review* 28 (2004–2005): 503–518.

Petrie, W. M. *Seventy Years in Archaeology*. London: Kegan Paul, 2003.

Pouls Wegner, Mary-Ann. "Gateway to the Netherworld." *Archaeology* 66 (2013): 50–53.

Prag, A. J. N. W. "Proportion and Personality in the Fayum Portraits." *British Museum Studies in Ancient Egypt and Sudan* 3 (2002): 56–63. http:www.the britishmuseum.ac.uk/egyptian/bmsaes/issue3/prag.html.

Price, Campbell. *Scotland at Saqqara: The Work of the Saqqara Geophysical Survey Project, 1990–Present*. http://www.scribd.com.doc/126886080/Price-Friends -of-Saqqara- Newsletter-2012.

Price, Campbell. "Under the Scanner: Revealing the Secrets of Egypt's Ancient Dead." *Current World Archaeology* 61 (2013): 42–43.

Pringle, Heather. "Satellite Imagery Uncovers up to 17 Lost Egyptian Pyramids," 2011. http://news.sciencemag.org/2011/05/satellite-imagery-uncovers-17-lost -Egyptian-Pyramids.

Ray, John. *The Rosetta Stone and the Rebirth of Ancient Egypt*. London: Profile, 2007.

Reeves, Nicholas. *The Complete Tutankhamun*. London: Thames & Hudson, 1990.

Reeves, Nicholas. *Ancient Egypt: The Great Discoveries*. London: Thames & Hudson, 2000.

Reeves, Nicholas. *Akhenaten: Egypt's False Prophet*. London: Thames & Hudson, 2001.

Reeves, Nicholas, and Richard H. Wilkinson. *The Complete Valley of the Kings: Tombs and Treasures of Egypt's Greatest Pharaohs*. Cairo: The American University in Cairo Press, 2002.

Risse, Guenter B. "Pharaoh Akhenaton of Ancient Egypt: Controversies among Egyptologists and Physicians Regarding His Postulated Illness." *Journal of the History of Medicine* (January 1971): 3–17.

Romer, John. *Ancient Lives: The Story of the Pharaohs' Tombmakers*. London: Phoenix, 2003.

Rowland, Joanne. "The Delta Survey: Minufiyeh Province." *Journal of Egyptian Archaeology* 93 (2007): 65–77.

Rowland, Joanne, Penelope Wilson, David Jeffreys, Paul T. Nicolson, Barry Kemp, Sarah Parcak, and Pamela Rose. "Fieldwork 2005–2006." *Journal of Egyptian Archaeology* 92 (2006): 1–73.

Savage, S. H. "Descent Group Competition and Economic Strategies in Predynastic Egypt." *Journal of Anthropological Archaeology* 16 (1997): 226–268.

Schild, Romuald, and Fred Wendorf. "Forty Years of the Combined Prehistoric Expedition." *Archaeologia Polona* 40 (2002): 5–22.

Sease, Catherine. "Conservation and the Antiquities Trade." *Journal of the American Institute for Conservation* 36 (1997): 49–58.

Seidlmayer, S. "The First Intermediate Period." In *The Oxford History of Ancient Egypt*, edited by Ian Shaw, 118–147. Oxford: Oxford University Press, 2000.

Silverman, D. P., ed. *Ancient Egypt*. London: Duncan Baird, 1997.

Shaw, I. "Pharaonic Quarrying and Mining: Settlement and Procurement in Egypt's Marginal Regions." *Antiquity* 68 (1994): 108–119.

Shaw, I. *Gurob Harem Palace Project Field Reports*, 2005–2012. http.gurob.org .uk/seasons.php.

Shaw, I., and P. Nicholson. *The British Museum Dictionary of Ancient Egypt*. London: British Museum Press, 2008.

Shaw, Jonathan. "Who Built the Pyramids?" *Harvard Magazine* 99 (2003): 43–50.

Sheldrick, P. "Was Tutankhamun Killed by a Hippo? The Sequel!" *Ancient Egypt* 13 (2012): 46–49.

Shyllon, Folarin. "Looting and Illicit Traffic in Antiquities in Africa." In *Crime in the Art and Antiquities World: Illegal Trafficking in Cultural Property*, edited by Stefano Manacorda and Duncan Chappell, 135–142. New York: Springer, 2011. doi: 10.1007/978-1-4419-7946-9_8, © Springer Science+Business Media LCC 2011.

Sławomir, Rzepka, Anna Wodzińska, Josef Hudec, and Tomasz Herbich. "Tell El-Retaba 2007–2008." *Egypt and the Levant* 19 (2009): 241–280.

Snape, Steven. *Egyptian Temples*. Princes Risborough: Shire, 1996.

Snape, Steven. "The 'Main Deposit' at Hierakonpolis." In *Wonderful Things*, edited by Paul Bahn, 19. London: Seven Dials, 2000.

Snape, Steven. "Making Mummies." In *Tombs, Graves and Mummies*, edited by Paul Bahn, 182. London: Orion, 2000.

Snape, Steven. "Interesting Times for Neb Re." *Ancient Egypt* 2 (2001): 12–16.

Snape, Steven. "Neb-Re and the Heart of Darkness: The Latest Discoveries from Zawiyet Umm el-Rakham (Egypt)." *Antiquity* 75 (2001): 19–20.

Snape, Steven. "Ankhtify: A Time of Change." In *Ancient Egyptian Tombs: The Culture of Life and Death*. Wiley-Blackwell, 2011. http://onlinelbray.wiley.com/doi/10.002/9781444/393743.ch7/.

Snape, Steven. "Sennedjem: Building and Buying at Deir el-Medina." In *Ancient Egyptian Tombs: The Culture of Life and Death*. Wiley-Blackwell, 2011. http://onlinelibrary.wiley.com/doi/10.002/9781444/393743.ch16/.

Spencer, A. J. *Death in Ancient Egypt*. London: Penguin, 1982.

Spencer, Richard. "Tutankhamun's Sister Goes Missing," 2013. hhttp://www.tele graph.co.uk/news/wordnews/africaandindianocean/Egypt/10449689/Tutank hamuns-sister-goes-missing-html.

Sweeney, Deborah. "Friendship and Frustration: A Study in Papyri Deir el-Medina IV–VI." *Journal of Egyptian Archaeology* 84 (1998): 101–122.

Taylor, John H. *Egyptian Coffins*. Princes Risborough: Shire, 1989.

Teijgeler, René. "Politics and Heritage in Egypt. One and a Half Years after the Lotus Revolution." *Archaeologies: Journal of the World Archaeological Congress* (2013): 1–14.

Thoma, A. "Morphology and Affinities of the Nazlet Khater Man." *Journal of Human Evolution* 13 (1984): 287–296.

Thomas, Angela P. *Akhenaten's Egypt*. Princes Risborough: Shire, 1988.

Thomas, Ross I., and Alexandra Villing. "Naukratis Revisited 2012: Integrating New Fieldwork and Old Research." *British Museum Studies in Ancient Egypt and Sudan* 20 (2013): 81–125. http://www.britishmuseum.org/research_onlinejournals/bmsaes/issue_20/thomas&villing. aspx.

Tijhuis, A. J. G. "The Trafficking Problem: A Criminological Perspective." In *Crime in the Art and Antiquities World: Illegal Trafficking in Cultural Property*, edited by Stefano Manacorda and Duncan Chappell, 87–97. New York: Springer, 2011. doi: 10.1007/978-1-4419-7946-9_5, © Springer Science+Business Media LCC 2011.

Trigger, Bruce G. *A History of Archaeological Thought*. New York: Cambridge University Press, 1996.

Tyldesley, Joyce. *Nefertiti: Egypt's Sun Queen*. London: Penguin, 1999.

Tyldesley, Joyce. *Judgement of the Pharaoh: Crime and Punishment in Ancient Egypt*. London: Weidenfeld & Nicolson, 2000.

Tyldesley, Joyce. "Restoring the Royal Mummies." In *Written in Bones*, edited by Paul Bahn, 178. Devon: David & Charles, 2002.

Tyldesley, Joyce. *Egypt: How a Lost Civilization Was Rediscovered*. London: BBC Books, 2005.

Tyldesley, Joyce. *Tutankhamen's Curse: The Developing History of an Egyptian King*. London: Profile, 2012.

Vance Haynes Jr., C., T. A. Maxwell, A. El Hawary, K. A. Nicoll, and S. Stokes. "An Acheulian Site Near Bir Kiseiba in the Darb el Arba'in Desert, Egypt." *Geoarchaeology: An International Journal* 12 (1997): 819–832.

Vermeersch, P. M., E. Paulissen, and P. Van Peer. "Palaeolithic Chert Mining in Egypt." *Archaeologia Polona* 33 (1995): 11–30.

Vermeersch, P. M., E. Paulissen, S. Stokes, C. Charlier, P. Van Peer, C. Stringer, and W. Lindsay. "A Middle Paleolithic Burial of a Modern Human at Taramsa Hill, Egypt." *Antiquity* 72 (1998): 475–484.

Vogel, Carola. "Fallen Heroes? Winlock's 'Slain Soldiers' Reconsidered." *Journal of Egyptian Archaeology* 89 (2003): 239–245.

Walker, Roxanne. "KV-63 Update: Into the Tomb." *Ancient Egypt* 6 (2006): 38–42.

Ward, C. "Boat-Building and Its Social Context in Early Egypt: Interpretations from the First Dynasty Boat-Grave Cemetery at Abydos." *Antiquity* 80 (2006): 118–129.

Watson, Philip. *Egyptian Pyramids and Mastaba Tomb*. Princes Risborough: Shire, 1987.

Weatherhead, Fran. "Painted Pavements in the Great Palace at Amarna." *Journal of Egyptian Archaeology* 78 (1992): 179–194.

Weatherhead, Fran. "Wall-Paintings from the King's House at Amarna." *Journal of Egyptian Archaeology* 81 (1995): 95–113.

Weeks, K. R. *The Lost Tomb: The Greatest Discovery at the Valley of the Kings since Tutankhamen*. London: Weidenfeld & Nicolson, 1998.

Weeks, K. R., ed. *KV 5: A Preliminary Report on the Excavation of the Tomb of the Sons of Rameses II in the Valley of the Kings*. Cairo: The American University Press in Cairo, 2006.

Weeks, K. R., ed. *Valley of the Kings: The Tombs and Temples of Thebes West*. Italy: White Star, 2011.

Weigall, Arthur. "The Mummy of Akhenaton." *Journal of Egyptian Archaeology* 8 (1922): 193–200.

Wendorf, F. "Nabta Playa and Its Role in Northeastern African Prehistory." *Journal of Anthropological Archaeology* 17 (1998): 97–123.

Wendorf, F., A. E. Close, and R. Schild. "Recent Work on the Middle Paleolithic of the Eastern Sahara." *African Archaeological Review* 5 (1987): 49–63.

Wengrow, David. "Rethinking 'Cattle Cults' in Early Egypt: Towards a Prehistoric Perspective of the Narmer Palette." *Cambridge Archaeological Journal* 11 (2001): 91–104.

Wilkinson, Toby A. H. *Early Dynastic Egypt*. London: Routledge, 1999.

Wilkinson, Toby A. H. "What a King Is This: Narmer and the Concept of the Ruler." *Journal of Egyptian Archaeology* 86 (2000): 23–32.

Wilson, P. "Prehistoric Settlement in the Western Delta: A Regional and Local View from Sais (Sa El-Hagar)." *Journal of Egyptian Archaeology* 92 (2006): 75–126.

Winlock, H. E. "The Egyptian Expedition 1925–1927: The Museum's Excavations at Thebes." *The Metropolitan Museum of Art Bulletin* 23, part 2 (1928): 3–58.

Woolley, C. Leonard. "Excavations at Tell el-Amarna." *Journal of Egyptian Archaeology* 8 (1922): 48–82.

# INDEX

# ABOUT THE AUTHOR

**Julian Heath** is an author and freelance archaeological illustrator based in Liverpool. He has a BA and an MA in Archaeology from Liverpool University, where he has lectured on archaeological illustration and the prehistoric world. His publications include *Ancient Echoes* (2006), *Warfare in Prehistoric Britain* (2009), *Sacred Circles* (2011), *Life in Copper Age Britain* (2011), and *Before Farming* (2013), and he has provided the illustrations for Joyce Tyldesley's popular children's book *Stories from Ancient Egypt* and the updated version of the British Museum's *Dictionary of Ancient Egypt*. His main areas of interest are prehistoric Europe and ancient Egypt.